301633
Forrest Olivier
03/09

元と (George
Wilson)
09/40

NATHAN
Strickland
9/7/10

音楽

初級日本語
〔げんき〕

AN INTEGRATED COURSE IN
ELEMENTARY JAPANESE

GENKI

I

Eri Banno 坂野永理
Yutaka Ohno 大野裕
Yoko Sakane 坂根庸子
Chikako Shinagawa 品川恭子

The Japan Times

First edition: May 1999
45th printing: July 2007

Editorial assistance: guild
Illustrations: Noriko Udagawa and Reiko Maruyama
Cover art and Editorial design: Nakayama Design Office
Gin-o Nakayama, Mutsumi Satoh, and Masataka Muramatsu
Published by The Japan Times, Ltd.
5-4, Shibaura 4-chome, Minato-ku, Tokyo 108-0023, Japan
Phone: 03-3453-2013
http://bookclub.japantimes.co.jp/
http://genki.japantimes.co.jp/

ISBN4-7890-0963-7

Printed in Japan

はじめに

　本書は学生へのニーズ調査に始まり、実際にくり返し使用し、学生の反応や意見、感想を受けて、細部にわたる改訂を重ねて作成しました。本書をこのような形で出版するまでに4年余りという時間を要しましたが、そのかいがあり理想の教材に近づくことができたと感じています。この教材によって、学習者は絵やゲームなどを通して楽しく、無理なく日本語の力をつけることができると確信しています。

　本書が完成したのは多くの方々のおかげです。特に出版にあたり、ジャパンタイムズ出版部の関戸千明さんには大変お世話になりました。また、11課以降の作成に加わってくださった渡嘉敷恭子さん、本書を試用し助言をくれた関西外国語大学留学生別科の同僚、実習生、試用版のイラスト担当の田嶋香織さん、翻訳面でご協力いただいた大川ジュディさん、今まで私たちをご指導してくださった先生方に心からお礼を申し上げます。そして、最後に本書作成の出発点であり、原動力でもあった関西外国語大学の留学生に感謝の意を表したいと思います。

Preface

Producing the materials for this textbook involved a long process of surveying students' needs, writing up the results, making detailed revisions to the material based on the surveys, and responding to the reactions and comments of students who used a trial version of this text. It has taken more than four years to complete this project. Our labor has been rewarded, however, because this book is based on our original plan to produce the ideal textbook—one that will enable students to learn Japanese smoothly, while also enjoying lively games and helpful illustrations.

We have an extensive list of people to thank for the completion of this textbook. First, our sincere thanks to Chiaki Sekido of the Publications Department of The Japan Times for seeing this book through the publishing process. Particular acknowledgment goes to Kyoko Tokashiki who helped in the production of Lesson 11 and following, to our colleagues and trainees in the Asian Studies Program of Kansai Gaidai University who attempted the trial version and made invaluable suggestions, to Kaori Tajima for her illustrations in the trial version, to Judy Okawa for translating, and to the teachers whose heartfelt guidance encouraged us throughout the process. Finally, we would also like to express our gratitude to the foreign students at Kansai Gaidai University for providing us with the opportunity to write this book.

初級日本語 [げんき] I

もくじ

▶ 会話•文法編
かい　わ　ぶん　ぽう　へん

▶読み書き編
<ruby>読<rt>よ</rt></ruby>み<ruby>書<rt>か</rt></ruby>き<ruby>編<rt>へん</rt></ruby>

▶巻末
<ruby>巻<rt>かん</rt></ruby><ruby>末<rt>まつ</rt></ruby>

本書について

Ⅰ　対象とねらい

　『初級日本語　げんき』は初めて日本語を学ぶ人のための教材です。第Ⅰ巻・第Ⅱ巻の２冊、全23課で初級日本語の学習を修了します。大学生はもとより、高校生や社会人、日本語を独習しようとしている人も、効果的に日本語が習得できます。文法の説明などは英語で書いてあるので、英語がある程度わかることを前提としています。

　『初級日本語　げんき』は総合教材として、日本語の四技能（聞く・話す・読む・書く）を伸ばし、総合的な日本語の能力を高めていくことを目標としています。正確に文を作ることができても流暢さがなかったり、流暢ではあっても簡単なことしか言えないということがないように、言語の習得の目標とすべき「正確さ」「流暢さ」「複雑さ」がバランスよく高められるように配慮してあります。

Ⅱ　テキストの構成

　テキストは大きく「会話・文法編」「読み書き編」「巻末」から構成されています。以下、順番に説明します。

A ▶会話・文法編

　「会話・文法編」では、基本的な文法を学び、語彙を増やしながら、「話すこと」「聞くこと」について学習します。「会話・文法編」の各課は以下の部分から構成されています。

●会話

　「会話」は、日本に来た留学生とその友人・家族を中心に展開し、学習者が日常生活で経験しそうなさまざまな場面から成っています。会話文を通して、学習者は「あいづち」などを含めた自然なやりとりに触れ、会話の中で文と文がどのようにつながっていくか、どのような部分が省略されたりするかなどを学ぶことができます。「会話」には、その課で学ぶ新しい学習項目が多く含まれているため、課の初めに学習者がこれを読むと非常に難しいと感じるかもしれません。これらの項目は練習を通して定着が図られるので、初めは難しくてもあまり心配しないようにしてください。

　また、「会話」は別売の CD に録音されています。学習者にはこの CD を聞いて、発音やイントネーションなどに気をつけながら、くり返して言う練習をすることを勧めます。

●単語

　「単語」には、その課の「会話」と「練習」に出てくる新しい単語がまとめてあります。この中で、「会話」に出てくる単語には＊印が付けてあります。第 1 課と第 2 課では機能別に単語を提示し、第 3 課からは品詞別に提示してあります。また、巻末には全課の単語を収録した「さくいん」があります。

　「単語」の中の言葉はその後の課でもくり返し出てきますから、学習者は毎日少しずつ覚えるようにしたほうがいいでしょう。第 3 課から、常用漢字で書ける単語にはすべて漢字を併記してありますが、この漢字は覚える必要はありません。

　なお、このテキストでは語のアクセント（拍の高低）を示していません。日本語のアクセントは地域差や個人差（世代間の差など）が激しい上に、語形変化や単語の連結などによる変化も複雑です。ですから、アクセントにはあまり神経質にならず、文のイントネーションなども含め、できるだけ CD の音声を模倣するように心掛けてください。

●文法

　文法説明は、かなり詳しく書いてありますので、独習している人も容易に理解できます。また、教室で学んでいる学習者はあらかじめ文法説明を読んでから授業に臨んでください。

　後の「練習」で取りあげられている項目はすべて「文法」の中で説明してあります。練習はしないが説明が必要な文法や語彙については、「文法」の最後の「表現ノート」に随時まとめてあります。

●練習

　「練習」は、各学習項目に関して基本練習から応用練習へと段階的に配列してあり、学習者がこれらの練習を順番にこなしていくことによって、無理なく日本語が習得できるように配慮してあります。

　答えが一つに決められるような基本練習は CD に録音されており、 ◀» の印がついています。CD には解答も録音されていますから、学習者は各自で自習することが可能です。

　また、「練習」の最後には「まとめの練習」があります。これは複数の学習項目を組み合わせた練習や「会話」を応用して別の会話を作る練習など、その課の学習の仕上げとなる練習です。

●コラム

　課の最後に必要に応じてコラムを設けてあります。このコラムには、第 1 課の「じかん・とし」のようにその課のトピックに関連した表現や、第10課の「駅で」のように場面ごとに使わ

れる表現がまとめてあります。これらの単語も、巻末の「さくいん」に載せてあります。

B ▶ 読み書き編

「読み書き編」では、日本語の文字を学び、文章を読んだり書いたりすることによって、読解力と書く力を伸ばします。第1課でひらがな、第2課でカタカナを学習した後、第3課以降で漢字を学習します。第3課以降の各課は、以下のような構成です。

● 漢字表

漢字表には、その課で学ぶ新出漢字が掲載されています。各課で約15の漢字を学びますが、一度に覚えるのには無理があるので、毎日少しずつ覚えていくようにしてください。漢字表は以下のようになっています。

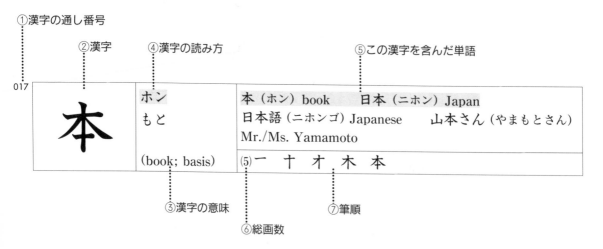

①漢字の通し番号
②漢字
④漢字の読み方
⑤この漢字を含んだ単語
③漢字の意味
⑥総画数
⑦筆順

④と⑤に示された漢字や単語の読み方で、ひらがなで書かれたものは「訓読み」、つまり日本語古来の読みです。カタカナで書かれたものは「音読み」、つまり昔の中国語の発音を輸入したものです。訓読みも音読みも、単語の中で使われた時、音が変化する場合があります。(たとえば、「学」という漢字は「ガク」と読みますが、「学校」という単語の中では「ガッ」と読みます。)そのような派生的な読み方もこの部分に表記されています。

なお、漢字の中には多くの読み方を持っているものもありますが、漢字表には、初級レベルにふさわしい読みが挙げられています。

④と⑤で　　　の中に入っている読み方や単語は、その課で覚えるべきものです。一方、　　　以外のものは参考として挙げたもので、覚えなくてもかまいません。

それぞれの漢字は、ワークブックの読み書き編の中に練習シートがありますので、テキストの漢字表に示された筆順を見ながら何度も練習してください。

●練習

　『げんきⅠ』には、漢字の練習、読解本文と内容についての質問、そして書く練習が載せてあります。漢字の練習は、漢字を分解してできる部品から漢字を再構築する問題や漢字から単語を作る問題など、さまざまな形式の練習を通じて漢字に慣れていくことを目標としています。読解本文は、短く、親しみやすいものを中心に構成しています。それまでに「会話・文法編」で学んだ文法や単語の知識が前提とされており、新出単語はその都度、単語表を掲載しています。練習の最後には、書く練習として作文トピックが提示されています。

　『げんきⅡ』には、読解本文と内容についての質問、そして書く練習が載せてあります。読解本文は、手紙、物語、エッセイ、広告など、さまざまな分野の日本語を取り上げています。その課までに学んだ単語や文法、漢字の知識が前提とされており、課を追うごとに、長さや難易度などが増していきます。新出単語も本文での提出順に掲載されています。練習の最後には、作文トピックが提示されています。

C ▶ 巻末

　第Ⅰ巻・第Ⅱ巻それぞれの巻末に「さくいん」を準備しました。一つは和英さくいんで、各課の単語表やコラムに掲載されている単語を五十音順に再録しました。単語に付された数字は、その単語が導入された課の番号を示しています。英和さくいんでは、各課の単語が訳語のアルファベット順に再録されています。

　その他に、動詞の活用表と助数詞の音の変化をまとめた表を掲載しました。

Ⅲ　表記と書体について

　本文は基本的に、漢字仮名交じりで表記しています。漢字表記は、基本的に常用漢字表に従いましたが、常用漢字に含まれている漢字でも、初級の学習者には無縁であるようなものは、ひらがな表記にしてあります。

　また、「会話・文法編」のみを学習することも可能なように、「会話・文法編」では漢字にはすべてふりがなが振ってあります。

　ただし、「会話・文法編」冒頭の「あいさつ」と第1課、第2課は、学習者の負担を軽減し自習を容易にするため、ひらがな・カタカナ表記とし、ローマ字を併記しました。このローマ字併記はあくまでも補助的なものですから、最初から頼りすぎないように心掛けてください。ひらがなは「読み書き編」の第1課で、カタカナは第2課で、それぞれ学習します。

　なお、「読み書き編」では、漢字を第3課以降に学習していきますが、学習の定着が図れるよう、既習の漢字にはふりがなが振ってありません。

　本文の日本語は、ほとんどが「教科書体」の書体で組まれています。教科書体は手書き文字に近い書体ですから、学習者は自分が書く文字のモデルとすることができます。ただし、実際に印刷された日本語文では、さまざまな書体を見ることがあります。文字によっては、書体によってかなり形が異なります。特に、離れた二つの線が筆づかいによって一つにつながる場合があるので、注意が必要です。

例：	教科書体	明朝体	ゴシック体	手書き文字
	さ	さ	さ	さ
	き	き	き	き
	り	り	り	り
	ら	ら	ら	ら
	こ	こ	こ	こ
	や	や	や	や

Introduction

I Aim and purpose

GENKI: An Integrated Course in Elementary Japanese is a textbook for beginners in the study of the Japanese language. Students can complete the elementary-level study of Japanese in the 23 lessons of this text, which is divided into two volumes. The book is designed mainly for use in university and college courses, but it is also effective for high school students and adults who are beginning to learn Japanese either at school or on their own. Hopefully, students will have at least a basic knowledge of English, because grammar explanations are given in English.

GENKI: An Integrated Course in Elementary Japanese is a comprehensive approach to developing the four basic language skills (listening, speaking, reading, and writing) in order to cultivate overall Japanese-language ability. Much emphasis has been placed on balancing accuracy, fluency, and complexity so that students using the material would not end up speaking accurately yet in a stilted manner, nor fluently yet employing only simple grammatical structures.

II Structure of the textbook

This textbook basically consists of three sections: Dialogue and Grammar, Reading and Writing, and the Appendix. A detailed explanation of each part follows.

A ▶ Dialogue and Grammar

The Dialogue and Grammar section aims at improving students' speaking and listening abilities by learning basic grammar and increasing vocabulary. The Dialogue and Grammar section of each lesson is comprised of the following components:

● Dialogue

The dialogues revolve around the lives of foreign students living in Japan, their friends, and their families, presenting various scenes that students are likely to face in their daily lives. By practicing natural expressions and *aizuchi* (responses that make conversations go smoothly), students are able to understand how sentences are connected and how some phrases are shortened in daily conversation. Because the Dialogue section of each lesson covers a lot of new grammar and vocabulary, students may feel it is too difficult to understand at first. Don't be overly concerned, however, because the grammar and vocabulary will gradually take root with practice.

Dialogues are recorded on the accompanying CD. Students are encouraged to practice regularly by listening to the CD and carefully noting pronunciation and intonation.

●Vocabulary

The Vocabulary section presents all the new words encountered in both the Dialogue and Practice sections of each lesson. Words that appear in the Dialogue are marked with an asterisk (*). Words are listed according to their function in Lessons 1 and 2, and by parts of speech in Lesson 3 and following. In addition, all words presented in the text are also found in the Index at the end of each volume.

Words found in the Vocabulary section of each lesson appear frequently in subsequent lessons, thus students are encouraged to learn them little by little each day. After Lesson 2, commonly used kanji equivalents of some words (Joyo Kanji) are also listed, but students are not required to memorize them.

This textbook does not indicate a word's accents. The accent of a Japanese word varies considerably, depending on the region, the speaker's age (including the generation gap between speakers), the word's paradigmatic form, and its connection with other words. Therefore, don't be overly concerned about the accent, but try to imitate as closely as possible the intonation heard on the accompanying CD.

●Grammar

Grammar explanations are detailed, so that students can easily study them on their own. Students at school are expected to read the grammar explanations before each class.

This section also fully explains the items found in the Practice section that follows. Necessary explanations for the grammar and vocabulary that are not found in the Practice section can be found in the Expression Notes at the end of each Grammar section.

●Practice

This section includes questions related to what was taught in each section of the lesson, providing students with both basic practice and application. By answering the questions sequentially, students can naturally build up their Japanese-language ability. The exercises with only one answer are marked with 🔊 and recorded on the CD, allowing students the opportunity to practice on their own.

The last part of the Practice section contains Review Exercises, which incorporate aspects of the lesson as a whole. For example, some questions combine various topics covered in the lesson, and some call for the creation of new phrases based on what was learned in the Dialogue section.

●**Supplement**

Finally, some lessons include additional or supplementary information. This includes expressions related to the topic of the lesson, as in "Time and age" in Lesson 1, or expressions suitable at certain times or places, as in "At the station" in Lesson 10. Words introduced in the Supplement section are found in the Index of each volume.

B▶Reading and Writing

The Reading and Writing section aims to foster comprehension and writing ability by learning Japanese characters and by providing opportunities to practice both reading and writing. *Hiragana* is introduced in Lesson 1, followed by *katakana* in Lesson 2, and kanji in Lesson 3 and following. From Lesson 3, each lesson contains the following components:

●**Kanji list**

Each new kanji introduced in a lesson is contained in a list, each with about 15 kanji. This makes it easy to memorize a few each day, rather than be overwhelmed with so many at once.

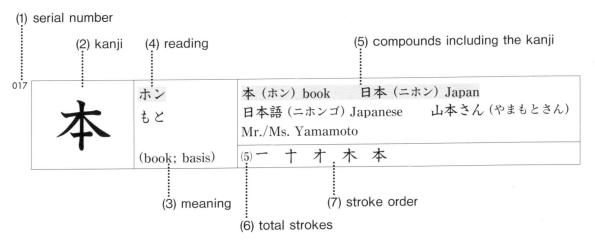

Among the readings shown in (4) and (5), *hiragana* indicates the *kun'yomi*, or Japanese readings for a kanji, while *katakana* indicates the *on'yomi*, or Chinese reading. Both *kun'yomi* and *on'yomi* are sometimes altered in compounds of two or more kanji. For example, the ordinary pronunciation of 学 is "*gaku*," which becomes "*ga(k)*" when the kanji is used in the word 学校. Such derivative readings are also included in (4) and (5).

Although some kanji have many readings, only those readings that are useful at an elementary level are included.

Shaded readings and words in each lesson should be memorized. The others are for reference, so students don't need to memorize them. A practice sheet for each kanji is provided in the Reading and Writing section of the Workbook. Students should practice writing the kanji repeatedly, according to the stroke order shown on the kanji list in the textbook.

●Practice

GENKI I consists of kanji practice, readings for comprehension, questions about the content of the readings, and writing practice. Kanji practice includes various types of questions, such as having students reconstruct a kanji from its various parts or make new words by combining kanji. By tackling these problems, students will realize the goal of practice—to become more proficient in their use of kanji. Basically, the readings are short and deal with subjects familiar to the students. They are easy to understand if the student has learned the vocabulary and grammar taught previously in the Dialogue and Grammar section. When readings include new words, a corresponding word list is provided. Finally, composition topics are given for writing practice.

GENKI II contains readings for comprehension, questions about the content of the readings, and writing practice. The readings employ various styles of Japanese, ranging from letters and fables to essays and advertisements. With a knowledge of the previously learned vocabulary, grammar, and kanji, the readings are easy to understand but grow longer and more difficult in later lessons. Word lists are provided for newly introduced vocabulary. Finally, composition topics are introduced.

C▶Appendix

Volumes 1 and 2 both contain an Index. The Japanese-English Index, in *hiragana* order, lists words found in the Vocabulary and Supplement section of each lesson. The number next to a word indicates the lesson in which the word was introduced. In the English-Japanese Index, English equivalents to Japanese words are arranged in alphabetical order.

Also included in the Appendix are tables of verb conjugations as well as sound inflections of the expressions related to numbers.

Ⅲ Orthography and font

The basic text is written in kanji and *hiragana*. Kanji is used for the most commonly used characters, those that appear in the official list of Joyo Kanji. *Hiragana* is used instead, however, when the Joyo Kanji equivalent would not be necessary for beginning students of Japanese.

So that students can easily study the Dialogue and Grammar section, the pronunciation of every kanji is indicated in *hiragana*. However, to lessen the burden on the students and allow them to study on their own, Greetings and Lessons 1 and 2 are represented in *hiragana* and *katakana*, as well as by romanized forms. It is best not to rely too much on the romanizations, but use them only as a learning aid. Students study *hiragana* and *katakana* in Lessons 1 and 2, respectively, of the Reading and Writing section.

Students study kanji from Lesson 3 in the Reading and Writing section, where pronunciations of the kanji already presented are not indicated in *hiragana*, in order to promote the students' increasing acquisition of kanji.

The Japanese in the basic text is set mainly in the Textbook font, which resembles handwriting and serves as a good model for students. Students will encounter a variety of fonts used for Japanese materials, however, and should be aware that the shape of some characters differ considerably, depending on the font used. Note especially that with some characters, we find two separate strokes in one style are merged into a single stroke.

Example:	Textbook font	Mincho font	Gothic font ·	Handwriting
	さ	さ	さ	さ
	き	き	き	き
	り	り	り	り
	ら	ら	ら	ら
	こ	こ	こ	こ
	や	や	や	や

Japanese Writing System

There are three kinds of characters in Japanese: *hiragana*, *katakana*, and kanji.[1] All three characters can be seen in a single sentence.

テレビを見ます。

<u>*katakana*</u>　kanji　<u>*hiragana*</u>

I watch television.

Hiragana and *katakana*, like the alphabet, represent sounds. As you can see in the above example, *hiragana* has a roundish shape and is used for conjugation endings, function words, and native Japanese words not covered by kanji. *Katakana*, which has rather straight lines, is normally used for writing loanwords and foreign names. For example, the Japanese word for "television" is written in *katakana* as テレビ (*terebi*). Kanji, or Chinese characters, represent not just sounds but also meanings. Mostly, kanji are used for nouns and the stems of verbs and adjectives.

① Hiragana

1. Basic Hiragana Syllables

There are forty-six basic *hiragana* syllables, which are listed below. Once you memorize this chart, you will have the skill to transcribe all of the Japanese sounds.

あ *a*	い *i*	う *u*	え *e*	お *o*
か *ka*	き *ki*	く *ku*	け *ke*	こ *ko*
さ *sa*	し **shi*	す *su*	せ *se*	そ *so*
た *ta*	ち **chi*	つ **tsu*	て *te*	と *to*
な *na*	に *ni*	ぬ *nu*	ね *ne*	の *no*
は *ha*	ひ *hi*	ふ *fu*	へ *he*	ほ *ho*

---

[1] There is another writing system called *rōmaji* (Roman letters) which is used for station names, signs, and so on.

ま *ma*	み *mi*	む *mu*	め *me*	も *mo*
や *ya*		ゆ *yu*		よ *yo*
ら *ra*	り *ri*	る *ru*	れ *re*	ろ *ro*
わ *wa*				を **o*
ん *n*				

*The syllables し, ち, and つ are romanized as *shi*, *chi*, and *tsu*, respectively, which is closer to the English pronunciation.

**を is also pronounced as "*wo*."

The romanization is given for general pronunciation reference.

2. Hiragana with Diacritical Marks

You can transcribe 23 additional sounds by adding diacritical marks. With a pair of short diagonal strokes (ﾞ), the unvoiced consonants *k*, *s*, *t*, and *h* become voiced consonants *g*, *z*, *d*, and *b*, respectively. The consonant *h* changes to *p* with the addition of a small circle (ﾟ).

が *ga*	ぎ *gi*	ぐ *gu*	げ *ge*	ご *go*
ざ *za*	じ *ji*	ず *zu*	ぜ *ze*	ぞ *zo*
だ *da*	*ぢ *ji*	*づ *zu*	で *de*	ど *do*
ば *ba*	び *bi*	ぶ *bu*	べ *be*	ぼ *bo*
ぱ *pa*	ぴ *pi*	ぷ *pu*	ぺ *pe*	ぽ *po*

*ぢ (*ji*) and づ (*zu*) are pronounced the same as じ (*ji*) and ず (*zu*), respectively, and have limited use.

3. Transcribing Contracted Sounds

Small や, ゆ, and よ follow after letters in the second column (*i*-vowel *hiragana*, except い) and are used to transcribe contracted sounds. The contracted sound represents a single syllable.

きゃ *kya*	きゅ *kyu*	きょ *kyo*
しゃ *sha*	しゅ *shu*	しょ *sho*
ちゃ *cha*	ちゅ *chu*	ちょ *cho*
にゃ *nya*	にゅ *nyu*	にょ *nyo*
ひゃ *hya*	ひゅ *hyu*	ひょ *hyo*
みゃ *mya*	みゅ *myu*	みょ *myo*
りゃ *rya*	りゅ *ryu*	りょ *ryo*

ぎゃ *gya*	ぎゅ *gyu*	ぎょ *gyo*
じゃ *ja*	じゅ *ju*	じょ *jo*

びゃ *bya*	びゅ *byu*	びょ *byo*
ぴゃ *pya*	ぴゅ *pyu*	ぴょ *pyo*

4. Transcribing Double Consonants

There is another small letter っ, which is used when transcribing double consonants such as *tt* and *pp*.

Examples: かった *katta* (won) cf. かた *kata* (shoulder)

さっか *sakka* (writer)

はっぱ *happa* (leaf)

ざっし *zasshi* (magazine)

Note that double consonant *n*'s, as in *sannen* (3 years), are written with ん + a *hiragana* with an initial *n* sound (な, に, ぬ, ね, or の).

Examples: さんねん *sannen* (3 years)

あんない *annai* (guide)

5. Other Issues Relating to Transcription and Pronunciation

A. Long Vowels

When the same vowel is placed one right after the other, the pronunciation of the vowel becomes about twice as long as the single vowel. Be sure to hold the sound long enough, because the length of the vowel can change one word to another.

aa	おばあさん	*ob<u>aa</u>san*	(grandmother)	cf. おばさん	*obasan*	(aunt)
ii	おじいさん	*oj<u>ii</u>san*	(grandfather)	cf. おじさん	*ojisan*	(uncle)
uu	すうじ	*s<u>uu</u>ji*	(number)			

ee The long *ee* sound is usually transcribed by adding an い to an *e*-vowel *hiragana*. There are a few words, however, in which え is used instead of い.

えいが	*<u>ee</u>ga*	(movie)
おねえさん	*on<u>ee</u>san*	(big sister)

oo The long *oo* sound is in most cases transcribed by adding an う to an *o*-vowel *hiragana*. There are, however, words in which the long vowel is transcribed with an お, for historical reasons.

ほうりつ	*h<u>oo</u>ritsu*	(law)
とお	*t<u>oo</u>*	(ten)

B. Pronunciation of ん

ん "*n*" is treated like a full syllable, in terms of length. Its pronunciation varies, however, depending on the sound that follows it. Japanese speakers are normally not aware of the different sound values of ん. Therefore, you do not need to worry too much about its pronunciation.[2]

C. Vowels to Be Dropped

The vowels *i* and *u* are sometimes dropped when placed between voiceless consonants (*k*, *s*, *t*, *p*, and *h*), or at the end of an utterance preceded by voiceless consonants.

  Example: すきです *s(u)kides(u)* (I like it.)

---

[2]One variety of the ん pronunciation merits discussing here. When it is followed by a vowel or at the end of an utterance, ん indicates that the preceding vowel is long and nasalized. (Nasalized vowels are shown here with a tilde above vowel letters. You hear nasalized vowels in French words such as "bon," or the English interjection "uh-uh," as in "no.")

  れんあい *rẽai* (romance)
  ほん *hõ* (book)
Followed by *n*, *t*, *d*, *s*, and *z* sounds, ん is pronounced as "n."
  おんな *onna* (woman)
Followed by *m*, *p*, and *b* sounds, ん is pronounced as "m."
  さんぽ *sampo* (stroll)
Followed by *k* and *g* sounds, ん is pronounced as "ng" as in "song."
  まんが *maŋga* (comics)

D. Accent in the Japanese Language

Japanese has a pitch accent: all syllables are pronounced basically either in high or low pitch. Unlike the English stress accent in which stressed syllables tend to be pronounced longer and louder, in Japanese each syllable is pronounced approximately in equal length and stress. The pitch patterns in Japanese vary greatly, depending on the region of the country.

Examples:　あさ　　a_{sa}　　　　(morning)

　　　　　　なまえ　na^{ma_e}　　　(name)

　　　　　　たかい　ta^{ka}_i　　　(high)

ⓘ K a t a k a n a

ア *a*	イ *i*	ウ *u*	エ *e*	オ *o*
カ *ka*	キ *ki*	ク *ku*	ケ *ke*	コ *ko*
サ *sa*	シ **shi*	ス *su*	セ *se*	ソ *so*
タ *ta*	チ **chi*	ツ **tsu*	テ *te*	ト *to*
ナ *na*	ニ *ni*	ヌ *nu*	ネ *ne*	ノ *no*
ハ *ha*	ヒ *hi*	フ *fu*	ヘ *he*	ホ *ho*
マ *ma*	ミ *mi*	ム *mu*	メ *me*	モ *mo*
ヤ *ya*		ユ *yu*		ヨ *yo*
ラ *ra*	リ *ri*	ル *ru*	レ *re*	ロ *ro*
ワ *wa*				ヲ *o*
ン *n*				

*The syllables シ, チ, and ツ are romanized as *shi*, *chi*, and *tsu*, respectively, to give a closer English pronunciation.

ガ *ga*	ギ *gi*	グ *gu*	ゲ *ge*	ゴ *go*
ザ *za*	ジ *ji*	ズ *zu*	ゼ *ze*	ゾ *zo*
ダ *da*	*ヂ *ji*	*ヅ *zu*	デ *de*	ド *do*
バ *ba*	ビ *bi*	ブ *bu*	ベ *be*	ボ *bo*

パ *pa*	ピ *pi*	プ *pu*	ペ *pe*	ポ *po*

*ヂ (*ji*) and ヅ (*zu*) are pronounced the same as ジ (*ji*) and ズ (*zu*), respectively, and have limited use.

キャ *kya*	キュ *kyu*	キョ *kyo*
シャ *sha*	シュ *shu*	ショ *sho*
チャ *cha*	チュ *chu*	チョ *cho*
ニャ *nya*	ニュ *nyu*	ニョ *nyo*
ヒャ *hya*	ヒュ *hyu*	ヒョ *hyo*
ミャ *mya*	ミュ *myu*	ミョ *myo*
リャ *rya*	リュ *ryu*	リョ *ryo*

ギャ *gya*	ギュ *gyu*	ギョ *gyo*
ジャ *ja*	ジュ *ju*	ジョ *jo*

ビャ *bya*	ビュ *byu*	ビョ *byo*
ピャ *pya*	ピュ *pyu*	ピョ *pyo*

The pronunciation of *katakana* and its combinations are the same as those of *hiragana*, except for the following points.

(1) The long vowels are written with ー.

Examples:　カー　　　*kaa*　　(car)

スキー　　*sukii*　　(ski)

スーツ　　*suutsu*　　(suit)

ケーキ　　*keeki*　　(cake)

ボール　　*booru*　　(ball)

When you write vertically, the — mark needs to be written vertically also.

Example:

ボール→　ボ
　　　　｜
　　　　ル

(2) Additional combinations with small vowel letters are used to transcribe foreign sounds that originally did not exist in Japanese.

Examples:

ウィ	ハロウィーン	*harowiin*	(Halloween)
ウェ	ハイウェイ	*haiwee*	(highway)
ウォ	ミネラルウォーター	*mineraruwootaa*	(mineral water)
シェ	シェリー	*sherii*	(sherry)
ジェ	ジェームス	*jeemusu*	(James)
チェ	チェック	*chekku*	(check)
ファ	ファッション	*fasshon*	(fashion)
フィ	フィリピン	*firipin*	(Philippine)
フェ	カフェ	*kafe*	(cafe)
フォ	カリフォルニア	*kariforunia*	(California)
ティ	パーティー	*paatii*	(party)
ディ	ディスコ	*disuko*	(disco)
デュ	デューク	*dyuuku*	(Duke)

(3) The sound "v" is sometimes written with ヴ. For example, the word "Venus" is sometimes written as ビーナス or ヴィーナス.

会話・文法編
かいわ ぶんぽう へん

会話・文法編●もくじ
かいわ　ぶんぽうへん

あいさつ

Greetings

おはよう。	Ohayoo.	Good morning.
おはよう ございます。	Ohayoo gozaimasu.	Good morning. (polite)
こんにちは。	Konnichiwa.	Good afternoon.
こんばんは。	Konbanwa.	Good evening.
さようなら。	Sayoonara.	Good-bye.
おやすみなさい。	Oyasuminasai.	Good night.
ありがとう。	Arigatoo.	Thank you.
ありがとう ございます。	Arigatoo gozaimasu.	Thank you. (polite)
すみません。	Sumimasen.	Excuse me.; I'm sorry.
いいえ。	Iie.	No.; Not at all.
いってきます。	Ittekimasu.	I'll go and come back.
いってらっしゃい。	Itterasshai.	Please go and come back.
ただいま。	Tadaima.	I'm home.
おかえりなさい。	Okaerinasai.	Welcome home.
いただきます。	Itadakimasu.	Thank you for the meal. (before eating)
ごちそうさま。	Gochisoosama.	Thank you for the meal. (after eating)
はじめまして。	Hajimemashite.	How do you do?
どうぞ よろしく。	Doozo yoroshiku.	Nice to meet you.

表現ノート
ひょうげん

おはよう/ありがとう ▶ *Ohayoo* is used between friends and family members, while *ohayoo gozaimasu* is used between less intimate acquaintances, similarly with *arigatoo* and *arigatoo gozaimasu*. The rule of thumb is: if you are on a first-name basis with someone, go for the shorter versions. If you would address someone as Mr. or Ms., use the longer versions. To give a concrete example, the social expectation is such that students are to use the longer variants when they speak with a professor.

さようなら ▶ There are several good-bye expressions in Japanese, the choice among which depends on the degree of separation. *Sayoonara* indicates that the speaker does not expect to see the person spoken to before she "turns a page in her life"; not until a new day arrives, or until fate brings the two together again, or until they meet again in the other world.

> じゃあ、また。　Jaa, mata.
> (between friends, expecting to see each other again fairly soon)
>
> しつれいします。　Shitsureeshimasu.
> (taking leave from a professor's office, for example)
>
> いってきます。　Ittekimasu.
> (leaving home)

すみません ▶ *Sumimasen* means (1) "Excuse me," to get another person's attention, (2) "I'm sorry," to apologize for the trouble you have caused, or (3) "Thank you," to show appreciation for what someone has done for you.

いいえ ▶ *Iie* is primarily "No," a negative reply to a question. In the dialogue, it is used to express the English phrase "Don't mention it," or "You're welcome," with which you point out that one is not required to feel obliged for what you have done for them.

いってらっしゃい/いってきます/ただいま/おかえりなさい ▶ *Ittekimasu* and *itterasshai* is a common exchange used at home when a family member leaves. The person who leaves says *ittekimasu*, which literally means "I will go and come back." And the family members respond with *itterasshai*, which means "Please go and come back."

    Tadaima and *okaeri* are used when a person comes home. The person who arrives home says *tadaima* (I am home right now) to the family members, and they respond with *okaerinasai* (Welcome home).

れんしゅう Ｐ ｒ ａ ｃ ｔ ｉ ｃ ｅ

Act out the following situations with your classmates.

1. You meet your host family for the first time. Greet them.
2. It is one o'clock in the afternoon. You see your neighbor Mr. Yamada.
3. You come to class in the morning. Greet your teacher. Greet your friends.
4. On a crowded train, you stepped on someone's foot.
5. You dropped your book. Someone picked it up for you.
6. It is eight o'clock at night. You happen to meet your teacher at the convenience store.
7. You are watching TV with your host family. It is time to go to sleep.
8. You are leaving home.
9. You have come back home.
10. You are going to start eating.
11. You have finished eating.

第1課 LESSON ⋯⋯⋯1
だい いっ か

あたらしいともだち New Friends

かいわ Dialogue

Mary, an international student who just arrived in Japan, talks to a Japanese student.

Ⓘ

1 メアリー： すみません。いま なんじですか。
　めありい
　Mearii　　Sumimasen.　Ima　nanji desu ka.

2 たけし： じゅうにじはんです。
　Takeshi　Juuniji han desu.

3 メアリー： ありがとう ございます。
　めありい
　Mearii　　Arigatoo　　gozaimasu.

4 たけし： いいえ。
　Takeshi　Iie.

Ⅱ

1 たけし：　　　　あの、りゅうがくせいですか。
Takeshi　　　　Ano,　ryuugakusee desu ka.

2 メアリー：　　ええ。アリゾナだいがくの がくせいです。
Mearii　　　　Ee.　Arizona daigaku no　gakusee desu.

3 たけし：　　　　そうですか。せんもんは なんですか。
Takeshi　　　　Soo desu ka.　Senmon wa　nan desu ka.

4 メアリー：　　にほんごです。いま にねんせいです。
Mearii　　　　Nihongo desu.　Ima　ninensee desu.

Ⅰ

Mary: Excuse me. What time is it now?

Takeshi: It's half past twelve.

Mary: Thank you.

Takeshi: You're welcome.

Ⅱ

Takeshi: Um . . . are you an international student?

Mary: Yes. I am a student at the University of Arizona.

Takeshi: I see. What is your major?

Mary: Japanese. I am a sophomore now.

たんご

V o c a b u l a r y

* あの	ano	um . . .
* いま	ima	now
えいご	eego	English (language)
* ええ	ee	yes
* がくせい	gakusee	student
* 〜ご	. . . go	language ex. にほんご (*nihon-go*) Japanese language
こうこう	kookoo	high school
ごご	gogo	P.M.
ごぜん	gozen	A.M.
〜さい	. . . sai	. . . years old
〜さん	. . . san	Mr./Ms. . . .
* 〜じ	. . . ji	o'clock ex. いちじ (*ichiji*) one o'clock
〜じん	. . . jin	people ex. にほんじん (*nihon-jin*) Japanese people
せんせい	sensee	teacher; Professor . . .
* せんもん	senmon	major
* そうです	soo desu	That's right.
* だいがく	daigaku	college; university
でんわ	denwa	telephone
ともだち	tomodachi	friend
なまえ	namae	name
* なん/なに	nan/nani	what
* にほん	Nihon	Japan
* 〜ねんせい	. . . nensee	. . . year student ex. いちねんせい (*ichinensee*) first-year student
はい	hai	yes
* はん	han	half ex. にじはん (*nijihan*) half past two
ばんごう	bangoo	number
* りゅうがくせい	ryuugakusee	international student
わたし	watashi	I

* Words that appear in the dialogue

ADDITIONAL VOCABULARY

Countries

アメリカ	Amerika	U.S.A.
イギリス	Igirisu	Britain
オーストラリア	Oosutoraria	Australia
かんこく	Kankoku	Korea
スウェーデン	Sueeden	Sweden
ちゅうごく	Chuugoku	China

Majors

かがく	kagaku	science
アジアけんきゅう	ajiakenkyuu	Asian studies
けいざい	keezai	economics
こくさいかんけい	kokusaikankee	international relations
コンピューター	konpyuutaa	computer
じんるいがく	jinruigaku	anthropology
せいじ	seeji	politics
ビジネス	bijinesu	business
ぶんがく	bungaku	literature
れきし	rekishi	history

Occupations

しごと	shigoto	job; work; occupation
いしゃ	isha	doctor
かいしゃいん	kaishain	office worker
こうこうせい	kookoosee	high school student
しゅふ	shufu	housewife
だいがくいんせい	daigakuinsee	graduate student
だいがくせい	daigakusee	college student
べんごし	bengoshi	lawyer

Family

おかあさん	okaasan	mother
おとうさん	otoosan	father
おねえさん	oneesan	older sister
おにいさん	oniisan	older brother
いもうと	imooto	younger sister
おとうと	otooto	younger brother

ぶんぽう Grammar

1 X は Y です

"It is 12:30." "I am a student." "My major is the Japanese language." These sentences will all be translated into Japanese using an appropriate noun and the word *desu*.

〜です。　　*It is . . .*

じゅうにじはんです。　　*(It) is half past twelve.*
Juuniji han desu.

がくせいです。　　*(I) am a student.*
Gakusee desu.

にほんごです。　　*(My major) is the Japanese language.*
Nihongo desu.

Note that none of these sentences has a "subject," like the "it," "I," and "my major" found in their English counterparts. Sentences without subjects are very common in Japanese; Japanese speakers actually tend to omit subjects whenever they think it is clear to the listener what or who they are referring to.

What are we to do, then, when it is not clear what is being talked about? To make explicit what we are talking about, we can say:

_____ は にほんごです。　　_____ *is the Japanese language.*
　　　　wa　nihongo desu.

Where _____ stands for the thing that is talked about, or the "topic," which is later in the sentence identified as *nihongo*. For example,

せんもんは にほんごです。　　*(My) major is the Japanese language.*
Senmon wa　nihongo desu.

Similarly, one can use the pattern *X wa Y desu* to identify a person or a thing X as item Y.

X は Y です。　　*X is Y. As for X, it is Y.*

わたしは スー・キムです。　　*I am Sue Kim.*
Watashi wa　Suu Kimu desu.

やましたさんは　せんせいです。　　　*Mr. Yamashita is a teacher.*
Yamashita san wa　　sensee desu.

メアリーさんは　アメリカじんです。　　*Mary is an American.*
Mearii san wa　　amerikajin desu.

Wa is a member of the class of words called "particles." So is the word *no*, which we will turn to later in this lesson. Particles attach themselves to phrases and indicate how the phrases relate to the rest of the sentence.

Note also that nouns like *gakusee* and *sensee* in the above examples stand alone, unlike their English translations "student" and "teacher," which are preceded by "a." In Japanese, there is no item that corresponds to "a," nor is there any item that corresponds to the plural "-s" at the end of a noun. Without background situations, a sentence like *gakusee desu* is therefore ambiguous between the singular and the plural interpretations; it may mean "We are/you are/they are students," as well as "I am/you are/she is a student."

2　Question Sentences

It is very easy to form questions in Japanese. Basically, all you need to do is add *ka* at the end of a statement.

りゅうがくせいです。
Ryuugakusee desu.
(I am) an international student.

りゅうがくせいですか。[1]
Ryuugakusee desu ka.
(Are you) an international student?

The above sentence, *Ryuugakusee desu ka*, is a "yes/no" question. Question sentences may also contain a "question word" like *nan*[2] (what). In this lesson, we learn how to ask, and answer, questions using the following question words: *nanji* (what time), *nansai* (how old), *nannensee* (what year in school). Note carefully that the order of words in a sentence may be quite different from what you find in your language.

せんもんは　なんですか。
Senmon wa　nan desu ka.
What is your major?

（せんもんは）えいごです。
(Senmon wa)　eego desu.
(My major) is English.

---

[1]It is not customary to write a question mark at the end of a question sentence in Japanese.

[2]The Japanese question word for "what" has two pronunciations: *nan* and *nani*. *Nan* is used immediately before *desu* or before a "counter" like *ji* (o'clock). The other form, *nani*, is used before a particle. *Nani* is also used in the combination *nanijin* (person of what nationality).

いま　なんじですか。
Ima　nanji desu ka.
What time is it now?

（いま）　くじです。
(Ima)　kuji desu.
It is nine o'clock.

メアリーさんは　なんさいですか。
Mearii san wa　nansai desu ka.
How old are you, Mary?

じゅうきゅうさいです。
Juukyuusai desu.
I'm nineteen years old.

なんねんせいですか。
Nannensee desu ka.
What year are you in college?

にねんせいです。
Ninensee desu.
I'm a sophomore.

でんわばんごうは　なんですか。
Denwa bangoo wa　nan desu ka.
What is your telephone number?

186の7343です。
Ichi hachi roku no nana san yon san desu.
It is 186-7343.

3　noun₁の noun₂

No is a particle that connects two nouns. The phrase *Toozai daigaku no gakusee* means "(a) student at Tozai University." The second noun *gakusee* provides the main idea[3] (being a student) and the first one *Toozai daigaku* makes it more specific (not a high school, but a college student). *No* is very versatile. In the first example below, it acts like the possessive ("x's") in English, but that is not the only role *no* can play. See how it connects two nouns in the following examples.

たけしさんの　でんわばんごう
Takeshi san no　denwa bangoo
Takeshi's phone number

だいがくの　せんせい
daigaku no　sensee
a *college* professor

にほんごの　がくせい
nihongo no　gakusee
a student *of the Japanese language*

にほんの　だいがく
nihon no　daigaku
a college *in Japan*

Observe that in the first two examples, the English and Japanese words are arranged in the same order, while in the last two, they are in the opposite order. Japanese seems to be more consistent in arranging ideas here; the main idea always comes at the end, with any further description placed before it.

---

[3]Here is what we mean by the "main idea." In the phrase *Takeshi san no denwa bangoo* (Takeshi's phone number), the noun *denwa bangoo* (phone number) is the main idea, in the sense that if something is Takeshi's phone number, it is a phone number. The other noun *Takeshi san* is not the main idea, because Takeshi's phone number is not Takeshi.

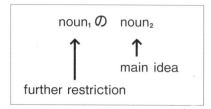

A phrase of the form "noun₁ *no* noun₂" acts more or less like one big noun. You can put it wherever you can put a noun, as in the following example:

たけしさんの おかあさん は こうこうの せんせい です。
Takeshi san no   okaasan wa   kookoo no   sensee desu.
Takeshi's mother is a high school teacher.

表現ノート
ひょうげん

Expression Notes ②

あの▶ *Ano* indicates that you have some reservations about saying what you are going to say next. You may be worried about interrupting something someone is currently doing, or sounding rude and impolite for asking personal questions, for example.

はい/ええ▶ Both *hai* and *ee* mean "yes" in response to yes-no questions. Compared to *hai*, *ee* is more conversational and relaxed. In more informal situations, *un* is used.

   Hai is also used to respond to a knock at the door or to the calling of one's name, meaning "Here," as follows. (*Ee* cannot be replaced in this case.)

Teacher: スミスさん？   *Mr. Smith?*
         Sumisu san?

Student: はい。   *Here.*
         Hai

そうですか▶ *Soo desu ka* acknowledges that you have understood what was just said. "Is that so?" or "I see."

Pronunciation of は▶ The particle は is pronounced "*wa*," not "*ha*." It should be written with は. All other instances of "*wa*" are written with わ.

わたしの でんわばんごうは 37-8667です。
Watashi no denwa bangoo wa san nana no hachi roku roku nana desu.
My telephone number is 37-8667.

There are a few exceptions, such as *konnichiwa* (good afternoon) and *konbanwa* (good evening). They are usually written with こんにちは and こんばんは.

Numbers ▶ Many number words have more than one pronunciation. Refer to the table at the end of this book for a general picture.

0　ゼロ and れい are both commonly used.

1　いち, but pronounced as いっ in いっぷん (one minute) and いっさい (one-year old).

2　に all the time. When you are reading out each digit separately, as when you give your phone number, it may be pronounced with a long vowel, as にい.

3　さん all the time. The part that follows it may change shape, as in さんぷん, instead of さんふん.

4　よん is the most basic, but fourth-year student is よねんせい and four o'clock is よじ. In some combinations that we will later learn, it is read as し (as in しがつ, April). The part that follows this number may change shape too, as in よんぷん.

5　ご all the time. When read out separately, it may be pronounced with a long vowel, as ごう.

6　ろく, but pronounced as ろっ in ろっぷん.

7　なな is the most basic, but seven o'clock is しちじ.

8　はち, but usually pronounced as はっ in はっぷん and はっさい.

9　きゅう is the most basic, but nine o'clock is くじ.

10　じゅう, but pronounced as じゅっ in じゅっぷん and じゅっさい.

Giving one's telephone number ▶ The particle *no* is usually placed in between the local exchange code and the last four digits. Therefore, the number 012-345-6789 is *zero ichi ni, san yon go no, roku nana hachi kyuu.*

せんせい▶ The word *sensee* is usually reserved for describing somebody else's occupation. *Watashi wa sensee desu* makes sense, but may sound slightly arrogant, because the word *sensee* actually means an "honorable master." If you (or a member of your family) are a teacher, and if you want to be really modest, you can use the word *kyooshi* instead.

さん▶ *San* is placed after a name as a generic title. It goes both with a given name and a family name. Children are referred to as *chan* (and boys in particular as *kun*), rather than as *san*. Professors and doctors are usually referred to with the title *sensee*. *San* and other title words are never used in reference to oneself.

Referring to the person you are talking to ▶ The word for "you," *anata*, is not very commonly used in Japanese. Instead, we use the name and a title like *san* and *sensee* to refer to the person you are talking to. Therefore, a sentence like "Ms. Hart, are you Swedish?" should be:

ハートさんは スウェーデンじんですか。
Haato san wa sueedenjin desu ka.

instead of ハートさん、あなたは スウェーデンじんですか。
Haato san,   anata wa   sueedenjin desu ka.

Japanese names ▶ When Japanese give their name, they say their family name first and given name last. Usually, they don't have middle names. When they introduce themselves, they often say only their family name. Here are some typical Japanese names.

Family name	Given name	
	Men	Women
さとう Satoo	ひろし Hiroshi	ゆうこ Yuuko
すずき Suzuki	いちろう Ichiroo	めぐみ Megumi
たかはし Takahashi	けんじ Kenji	くみこ Kumiko
たなか Tanaka	ゆうき Yuuki	なおみ Naomi
いとう Itoo	まさひろ Masahiro	きょうこ Kyooko

れんしゅう　Ｐｒａｃｔｉｃｅ

(I) すうじ　(Numbers)

0	ゼロ／れい zero　ree				
1	いち ichi	11	じゅういち juuichi	30	さんじゅう sanjuu
2	に ni	12	じゅうに juuni	40	よんじゅう yonjuu
3	さん san	13	じゅうさん juusan	50	ごじゅう gojuu
4	よん／し／(よ) yon　shi　(yo)	14	じゅうよん／じゅうし juuyon　juushi	60	ろくじゅう rokujuu
5	ご go	15	じゅうご juugo	70	ななじゅう nanajuu
6	ろく roku	16	じゅうろく juuroku	80	はちじゅう hachijuu
7	なな／しち nana　shichi	17	じゅうなな／じゅうしち juunana　juushichi	90	きゅうじゅう kyuujuu
8	はち hachi	18	じゅうはち juuhachi	100	ひゃく hyaku
9	きゅう／く kyuu　ku	19	じゅうきゅう／じゅうく juukyuu　juuku		
10	じゅう juu	20	にじゅう nijuu		

A. Read the following numbers.

(a) 5　　(b) 9　　(c) 7　　(d) 1　　(e) 10

(f) 8　　(g) 2　　(h) 6　　(i) 4　　(j) 3

B. Read the following numbers.

(a) 45　　(b) 83　　(c) 19　　(d) 76　　(e) 52

(f) 100　　(g) 38　　(h) 61　　(i) 24　　(j) 97

C. What are the answers?

(a) 5＋3　(b) 9＋1　(c) 3＋4　(d) 6－6　(e) 10＋9　(f) 8－7　(g) 40－25

ⓘ じかん （Time）

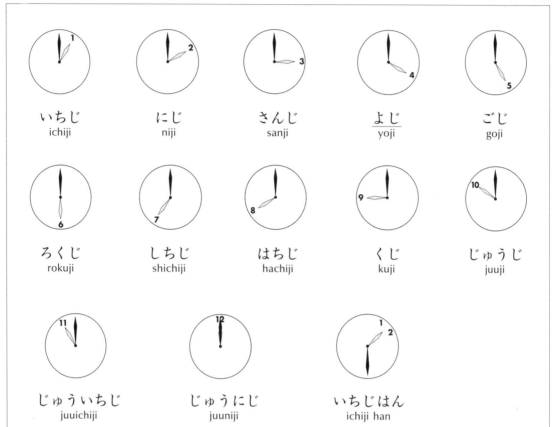

いちじ
ichiji

にじ
niji

さんじ
sanji

よじ
yoji

ごじ
goji

ろくじ
rokuji

しちじ
shichiji

はちじ
hachiji

くじ
kuji

じゅうじ
juuji

じゅういちじ
juuichiji

じゅうにじ
juuniji

いちじはん
ichiji han

A. Look at the following pictures and answer the questions.

Example: Q：いま なんじ ですか。
Ima　nanji desu ka.

A：いちじはんです。
Ichiji han desu.

Ex.

(1)

(2)

(3)

(4)

(5)

(6)

B. Answer the questions. 🔊

Example: Q：とうきょうは いま なんじですか。
Tookyoo wa　　ima　　nanji desu ka.

A：ごぜん さんじです。
Gozen　　sanji desu.

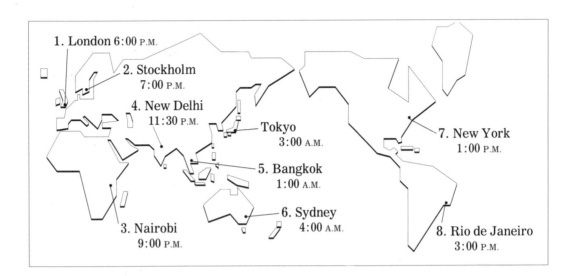

1. London 6:00 P.M.
2. Stockholm 7:00 P.M.
4. New Delhi 11:30 P.M.
Tokyo 3:00 A.M.
7. New York 1:00 P.M.
5. Bangkok 1:00 A.M.
3. Nairobi 9:00 P.M.
6. Sydney 4:00 A.M.
8. Rio de Janeiro 3:00 P.M.

Ⅲ でんわばんごう (Telephone Numbers)

A. Read the following people's telephone numbers. 🔊

Example: やました 283-9547 → にはちさんの きゅうごよんなな
Yamashita　　　　　　　ni hachi san no　kyuu go yon nana

1. メアリー　　　951-0326
Mearii

2. たけし　　　362-4519
Takeshi

3. スー　　　691-4236
Suu

4. ロバート　　　852-1032
Robaato

B. Pair Work—Read the dialogue below with your partner. 🔊

A：でんわばんごうは なんですか。
Denwa bangoo wa　　nan desu ka.

B：283-9547です。
Ni hachi san no kyuu go yon nana desu.

A：283-9547ですね。
   Ni hachi san no kyuu go yon nana desu ne.

B：はい、 そうです。
   Hai,   soo desu.

C. Group Work—Use the dialogue above and ask three classmates their telephone numbers.

name	telephone number
(　　　　　　　　)	(　　　　　　　　　　　)
(　　　　　　　　)	(　　　　　　　　　　　)
(　　　　　　　　)	(　　　　　　　　　　　)

Ⅳ にほんごの がくせい

Translate the following phrases into Japanese using の (no).

Example: student of the Japanese language → にほんごの がくせい
    nihongo no   gakusee

1. my teacher
2. my telephone number
3. my name
4. Takeshi's major
5. Mary's friend
6. student of the University of London
7. teacher of the Japanese language
8. high school teacher

Ⅴ メアリーさんは アメリカじんです

A. Look at the chart on the next page and describe each person using the cues in (a) through (e).

1. たけしさん　2. スーさん　3. ロバートさん　4. やましたせんせい
  Takeshi san   Suu san   Robaato san   Yamashita sensee

(a) nationality

Example: メアリーさん → メアリーさんは アメリカじんです。
   Mearii san   Mearii san wa   amerikajin desu.

(b) year in school

Example: メアリーさん → メアリーさんは にねんせいです。
   Mearii san   Mearii san wa   ninensee desu.

(c) age

Example: メアリーさん   →   メアリーさんは　じゅうきゅうさいです。
　　　　　　Mearii san　　　　　　Mearii san wa　　　juukyuu sai desu.

(d) school

Example: メアリーさん   →   メアリーさんは　アリゾナだいがくの
　　　　　　Mearii san　　　　　　Mearii san wa　　　Arizona daigaku no

がくせいです。
gakusee desu.

(e) major

Example: メアリーさん   →   メアリーさんの　せんもんは　にほんごです。
　　　　　　Mearii san　　　　　　Mearii san no　　　senmon wa　　nihongo desu.

	Hart, Mary	きむらたけし Kimura Takeshi	Kim, Sue	Smith, Robert	やましたせんせい Yamashita sensee
Nationality	American	Japanese	Korean (かんこくじん) kankokujin	British (イギリスじん) igirisujin	Japanese
Year	2nd year	4th year	3rd year	4th year	
Age	19	22	20	22	47
School	U. of Arizona	Tozai Univ.	Seoul Univ.	U. of London	Tozai Univ.
Major	Japanese	history (れきし) rekishi	computer (コンピューター) konpyuutaa	business (ビジネス) bijinesu	(Japanese teacher)

B. Pair Work—Ask and answer questions using the given cues.

Example 1: メアリーさん／アメリカじん
　　　　　　Mearii san　　　amerikajin

Q：メアリーさんは　アメリカじんですか。
　　Mearii san wa　　　amerikajin desu ka.

A：ええ、そうです。
　　Ee,　　soo desu.

Example 2: メアリーさん／さんねんせい
Mearii san　　　　sannensee

　　　　Q：メアリーさんは　さんねんせいですか。
　　　　　Mearii san wa　　　　sannensee desu ka.

　　　　A：いいえ、にねんせいです。
　　　　　Iie,　　ninensee desu.

1. メアリーさん／アリゾナだいがくの　がくせい
Mearii san　　　　Arizona daigaku no　　　gakusee

2. メアリーさん／いちねんせい
Mearii san　　　　ichinensee

3. たけしさん／にほんじん
Takeshi san　　nihonjin

4. たけしさん／にほんだいがくの　がくせい
Takeshi san　　　Nihon daigaku no　　　gakusee

5. たけしさん／じゅうきゅうさい
Takeshi san　　　juukyuusai

6. スーさん／スウェーデンじん
Suu san　　　　sueedenjin

7. スーさんの　せんもん／けいざい (economics)
Suu san no　　　senmon　　　keezai

8. ロバートさんの　せんもん／ビジネス
Robaato san no　　　senmon　　　bijinesu

9. ロバートさん／よねんせい
Robaato san　　　　yonensee

10. ロバートさん／にじゅういっさい
Robaato san　　　　nijuuissai

11. やましたせんせい／にほんじん
Yamashita sensee　　　nihonjin

12. やましたせんせい／ハワイだいがくの　せんせい
Yamashita sensee　　　Hawai daigaku no　　　sensee

Ⅵ おとうさんは　かいしゃいんです

A. Look at the chart below and describe each person with regard to (a) and (b). 🔊

1. おかあさん
okaasan
2. おにいさん
oniisan
3. いもうと
imooto

(a) occupation/school

Example:　おとうさん　→　メアリーさんの　おとうさんは　かいしゃいんです。
　　　　　otoosan　　　　　Mearii san no　　　　otoosan wa　　　kaishain desu.

(b) age

Example: おとうさん → メアリーさんの おとうさんは よんじゅうはっさいです。
otoosan   Meʳii san no   otoosan wa   yonjuuhassai desu.

Mary's host family

	おとうさん otoosan (father)	おかあさん okaasan (mother)	おにいさん oniisan (elder brother)	いもうと imooto (younger sister)
Occupation/ School	かいしゃいん kaishain (works for a company)	しゅふ shufu (housewife)	だいがくいんせい daigakuinsee (graduate student)	こうこうせい kookoosee (high school student)
Age	48	45	23	16

B. Answer the questions using the chart above.

1. おとうさんは かいしゃいんですか。
   Otoosan wa   kaishain desu ka.

2. おとうさんは なんさいですか。
   Otoosan wa   nansai desu ka.

3. おかあさんは せんせいですか。
   Okaasan wa   sensee desu ka.

4. おかあさんは なんさいですか。
   Okaasan wa   nansai desu ka.

5. おにいさんは かいしゃいんですか。
   Oniisan wa   kaishain desu ka.

6. おにいさんは なんさいですか。
   Oniisan wa   nansai desu ka.

7. いもうとは だいがくせいですか。
   Imooto wa   daigakusee desu ka.

8. いもうとは なんさいですか。
   Imooto wa   nansai desu ka.

Ⅶ まとめの れんしゅう (Review Exercises)

A. Class Activity—Ask five classmates questions and fill in the chart below.

Example questions:

- おなまえは？ (What is your name?)
  Onamae wa?

- どこから きましたか。 (Where do you come from?)
  Doko kara　kimashita ka.

- しごと (occupation) は なんですか。
  Shigoto wa　nan desu ka.

- なんねんせいですか。
  Nannensee desu ka.

- なんさいですか。
  Nansai desu ka.

- せんもんは なんですか。
  Senmon wa　nan desu ka.

Name	Nationality	Occupation/ School	Age	Major, etc.

B. Self-introduction—Introduce yourself to the class.

Example:

はじめまして。メアリー・ハートです。
Hajimemashite.　Mearii Haato desu.

アリゾナだいがくの がくせいです。 いま
Arizona daigaku no　gakusee desu.　Ima

にねんせいです。 せんもんは にほんごです。
ninensee desu.　Senmon wa　nihongo desu.

じゅうきゅうさいです。 どうぞ よろしく。
Juukyuusai desu.　Doozo　yoroshiku.

C. Class Activity—Ask your classmates what their majors are, and find someone who has the following major.

Example:　Q：せんもんは　なんですか。
　　　　　　　　Senmon wa　　　nan desu ka.

　　　　　　A：にほんごです。
　　　　　　　　Nihongo desu.

　　　　　　　　　　　　　　　　　name

1. Japanese　　　　　_____

2. economics　　　　_____

3. English　　　　　_____

4. history　　　　　_____

5. business　　　　_____

じかん・とし
Time / Age

Time

hours		minutes			
1	いちじ ichiji	1	いっぷん ippun	11	じゅういっぷん juuippun
2	にじ niji	2	にふん nifun	12	じゅうにふん juunifun
3	さんじ sanji	3	さんぷん sanpun	13	じゅうさんぷん juusanpun
4	よじ yoji	4	よんぷん yonpun	14	じゅうよんぷん juuyonpun
5	ごじ goji	5	ごふん gofun	15	じゅうごふん juugofun
6	ろくじ rokuji	6	ろっぷん roppun	16	じゅうろっぷん juuroppun
7	しちじ shichiji	7	ななふん nanafun	17	じゅうななふん juunanafun
8	はちじ hachiji	8	はっぷん／はちふん happun　hachifun	18	じゅうはっぷん／ juuhappun
9	くじ kuji	9	きゅうふん kyuufun		じゅうはちふん juuhachifun
10	じゅうじ juuji	10	じゅっぷん juppun	19	じゅうきゅうふん juukyuufun
11	じゅういちじ juuichiji			20	にじゅっぷん nijuppun
12	じゅうにじ juuniji			30	さんじゅっぷん sanjuppun

Age　なんさいですか。／おいくつですか。　(How old are you?)
　　　　Nansai desu ka.　　Oikutsu desu ka.

The counter suffix 〜さい is used to indicate "-years old."

1	いっさい issai	5	ごさい gosai	9	きゅうさい kyuusai
2	にさい nisai	6	ろくさい rokusai	10	じゅっさい jussai
3	さんさい sansai	7	ななさい nanasai	11	じゅういっさい juuissai
4	よんさい yonsai	8	はっさい hassai	20	はたち* hatachi

*For 20 years old, はたち (hatachi) is usually used, although にじゅっさい (nijussai) can be used.

第2課 LESSON……2
だいにか
かいもの Shopping

かいわ Dialogue

Ⅰ Mary goes to a flea market.

1 メアリー： すみません。これは いくらですか。
Mearii Sumimasen. Kore wa ikura desu ka.

2 みせのひと： それは さんぜんえんです。
Mise no hito Sore wa sanzen en desu.

3 メアリー： たかいですね。じゃあ、あのとけいは いくらですか。
Mearii Takai desu ne. Jaa, ano tokee wa ikura desu ka.

4 みせのひと： あれは さんぜんごひゃくえんです。
Mise no hito Are wa sanzengohyaku en desu.

5 メアリー： そうですか。あれも たかいですね。
Mearii Soo desu ka. Are mo takai desu ne.

6 みせのひと： これは せんはっぴゃくえんですよ。
Mise no hito Kore wa senhappyaku en desu yo.

7 メアリー： じゃあ、そのとけいを ください。
Mearii Jaa, sono tokee o kudasai.

* * *

A man finds a wallet on the ground.

8 しらないひと： これは だれの さいふですか。
Shiranai hito Kore wa dare no saifu desu ka.

9 メアリー： わたしの さいふです。
Mearii Watashi no saifu desu.

ありがとうございます。
Arigatoo gozaimasu.

Ⅱ After shopping, Mary goes to a restaurant.

1 ウエートレス：いらっしゃいませ。メニューを どうぞ。
Ueetoresu Irasshaimase. Menyuu o doozo.

2 メアリー：　　　　どうも。　これは　なんですか。
　 Mearii　　　　　　Doomo.　　Kore wa　　nan desu ka.

3 ウエートレス：どれですか。　ああ、　とんかつです。
　 Ueetoresu　　　Dore desu ka.　Aa,　　　tonkatsu desu.

4 メアリー：　　　　とんかつ？　さかなですか。
　 Mearii　　　　　　Tonkatsu?　　Sakana desu ka.

5 ウエートレス：いいえ、さかなじゃありません。にくです。おいしいですよ。
　 Ueetoresu　　　Iie,　　　sakana ja arimasen.　　　Niku desu.　Oishii desu yo.

6 メアリー：　　　　じゃあ、これを　おねがいします。
　 Mearii　　　　　　Jaa,　　kore o　onegaishimasu.

　　　　　　　　　　　　＊　　　　　　　　　＊　　　　　　　　　＊

7 メアリー：　　　　すみません、おてあらいは　どこですか。
　 Mearii　　　　　　Sumimasen,　otearai wa　　doko desu ka.

8 ウエートレス：あそこです。
　 Ueetoresu　　　Asoko desu.

Ⅰ

Mary: Excuse me. How much is this?

Vendor: It is 3,000 yen.

Mary: It's expensive. Well then, how much is that watch?

Vendor: That is 3,500 yen.

Mary: I see. That is expensive, too.

Vendor: This is 1,800 yen.

Mary: Then, I'll take that watch.

　　　　　　　＊　　　　＊　　　　＊

Stranger: Whose wallet is this?

Mary: It's my wallet. Thank you very much.

Ⅱ

Waitress: Welcome. Here's the menu.

Mary: Thank you. What is this?

Waitress: Which one? Oh, it is *tonkatsu* (pork cutlet).

Mary: *Tonkatsu*? Is it fish?

Waitress: No, it is not fish. It is meat. It is delicious.

Mary: Then, I'll have this.

　　　　　　　＊　　　　＊　　　　＊

Mary: Excuse me. Where is the restroom?

Waitress: It is over there.

たんご

Vocabulary

Words That Point

* これ	kore	this one
* それ	sore	that one
* あれ	are	that one (over there)
* どれ	dore	which one
この	kono	this . . .
* その	sono	that . . .
* あの	ano	that . . . (over there)
どの	dono	which . . .
* あそこ	asoko	over there
* どこ	doko	where
* だれ	dare	who

Food

* おいしい	oishii	delicious
* さかな	sakana	fish
* とんかつ	tonkatsu	pork cutlet
* にく	niku	meat
* メニュー	menyuu	menu
やさい	yasai	vegetable

Things

えんぴつ	enpitsu	pencil
かさ	kasa	umbrella
かばん	kaban	bag
くつ	kutsu	shoes
* さいふ	saifu	wallet
ジーンズ	jiinzu	jeans
じしょ	jisho	dictionary
じてんしゃ	jitensha	bicycle
しんぶん	shinbun	newspaper
テープ	teepu	tape
* とけい	tokee	watch; clock
トレーナー	toreenaa	sweat shirt

* Words that appear in the dialogue

ノート	nooto	notebook
ペン	pen	pen
ぼうし	booshi	hat; cap
ほん	hon	book

Places

* おてあらい	otearai	restroom
きっさてん	kissaten	cafe
ぎんこう	ginkoo	bank
としょかん	toshokan	library
ゆうびんきょく	yuubinkyoku	post office

Countries

アメリカ	Amerika	U.S.A.
イギリス	Igirisu	Britain
かんこく	Kankoku	Korea
ちゅうごく	Chuugoku	China

Majors

けいざい	keezai	economics
コンピューター	konpyuutaa	computer
ビジネス	bijinesu	business
れきし	rekishi	history

Family

おかあさん	okaasan	mother
おとうさん	otoosan	father

Money Matters

* いくら	ikura	how much
* ～えん	. . . en	. . . yen
* たかい	takai	expensive

Expressions

* いらっしゃいませ	irasshaimase	Welcome (to our store)
* (～を)おねがいします	(. . . o) onegaishimasu	. . . , please.
* (～を)ください	(. . . o) kudasai	Please give me . . .
* じゃあ	jaa	then . . . ; if that is the case, . . .
* (～を)どうぞ	(. . . o) doozo	Here it is.
* どうも	doomo	Thank you.

ぶんぽう　Ｇｒａｍｍａｒ

1　これ　それ　あれ　どれ

What do we do when we want to talk about things that we do not know the names of? We say "this thing," "that one," and so forth. In Japanese, we use *kore*, *sore*, and *are*.

これは　いくらですか。　　　　　　　　*How much is this?*
Kore wa　ikura desu ka.

それは　さんぜんえんです。　　　　　　*That is 3,000 yen.*
Sore wa　sanzen en desu.

Kore refers to a thing that is close to you, the speaker ("this thing here"). *Sore* is something that is close to the person you are talking to ("that thing in front of you"), and *are* refers to a thing that is neither close to the speaker nor the listener ("that one over there").

あれは　わたしの　ペンです。
Are wa　　watashi no　　pen desu.

これは　わたしの　ペンです。　　　　それは　わたしの　ペンです。
Kore wa　watashi no　pen desu.　　　Sore wa　watashi no　pen desu.

There is also an expression *dore* for "which." Here we will learn to use *dore* in sentences like:

どれですか。　　　　　　　*Which one is it (that you are talking about)?*
Dore desu ka.

In this lesson, we will not explore the full extent to which the word *dore* can be put to use, because there is a slight complication with question words like *dore*. Question words like *dore* and *nani* cannot be followed by the particle *wa*. Instead, you must use the particle *ga* and say:

どれが あなたの ペンですか。 *Which one is your pen?*
Dore ga　anata no　　pen desu ka.

2　この/その/あの/どの ＋ noun

If you want to be slightly more specific than *kore*, *sore*, and *are*, you can use *kono*, *sono*, and *ano* together with a noun. (Note here that the *re* series must always stand alone, while the *no* series must always be followed by a noun.) Thus, if you know that the item in your hand is a watch (*tokee*), instead of:

これは いくらですか。 *How much is this?*
Kore wa　ikura desu ka.

you can say:

このとけいは いくらですか。 *How much is this watch?*
Kono tokee wa　　ikura desu ka.

Similarly, if you are talking about a watch that is held by the person you are talking to, you can say:

そのとけいは さんぜんえんです。 *That watch is 3,000 yen.*
Sono tokee wa　　sanzen en desu.

And if the watch is far from both the speaker and the listener, you can say:

あのとけいは さんぜんごひゃくえんです。 *That watch over there is 3,500 yen.*
Ano tokee wa　　sanzengohyaku en desu.

If you already know that one of several watches is 3,500 yen but do not know which, you can say:

どのとけいが さんぜんごひゃくえんですか。 *Which watch is 3,500 yen?*
Dono tokee ga　　sanzengohyaku en desu ka.

Since *dono* is a question word, just like *dore* discussed above, we cannot use the particle *wa* with it; we must use *ga*.

To summarize:

これ（は〜）	この noun（は〜）	close to the person speaking
それ（は〜）	その noun（は〜）	close to the person listening
あれ（は〜）	あの noun（は〜）	far from both people
どれ（が〜）	どの noun（が〜）	unknown

3　だれの noun

In Lesson 1, we learned how to say things like *Mearii san no denwa bangoo* (Mary's phone number) and *Takeshi san no okaasan* (Takeshi's mother). We now learn how to ask who something belongs to. The question word for "who" is *dare*, and for "whose," we simply add the particle *no*.

これは　だれの　かばんですか。
Kore wa 　dare no　 kaban desu ka.
Whose bag is this?

それは　スーさんの　かばんです。
Sore wa 　Suu san no　 kaban desu.
That is Sue's bag.

4　ここ　そこ　あそこ　どこ

We will learn just one more *ko-so-a-do* set in this lesson: *koko*, *soko*, *asoko*, and *doko* are words for places.

ここ	*here, near me*
そこ	*there, near you*
あそこ	*over there*
どこ	*where*

You can ask for directions by saying:

すみません、ゆうびんきょくは　どこですか。　　*Excuse me, where is the post office?*
Sumimasen,　　yuubinkyoku wa　　doko desu ka.

If you are close by, you can point toword the post office and say:

（ゆうびんきょくは）　あそこです。　　　　*(The post office is) right over there.*
(Yuubinkyoku wa)　　asoko desu.

We will learn how to give more specific directions in Lesson 4.

5　noun も

In Lesson 1, we learned how to say "Item A is this, item B is that." We now learn how to say "Item A is this, and item B is this, too."

たけしさんは　にほんじんです。	*Takeshi is a Japanese person.*
Takeshi san wa　　nihonjin desu.	
みちこさんも　にほんじんです。	*Michiko is Japanese, <u>too</u>.*
Michiko san mo　　nihonjin desu.	

Note that these two sentences are almost identical in shape. This is natural, as they both claim that a certain person is Japanese. The second sentence, however, is different from the first in that we do not find the particle *wa* in it. We have *mo* instead. *Mo* is a particle that indicates that that item, *too*, has the given property. One thing that you should watch out for is exactly where the particle is placed. In English, the word "too" can be placed after the sentence as a whole, as in the example above. Not so in Japanese. In the above example, *mo* must directly follow *Michiko san*.

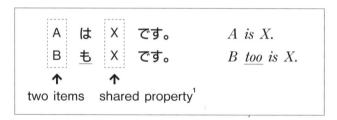

6　noun じゃありません

To negate a statement of the form *X wa Y desu*, where Y is a noun, you replace *desu* with *ja arimasen*.[2]

| やまださんは　がくせいじゃありません。 | *Mr. Yamada is not a student.* |
| Yamada san wa　　gakusee ja arimasen. | |

---

[1] We cannot use *mo* to describe a situation like the following: Our friend, Pat, has dual citizenship; Pat is a Japanese, but at the same time, she is an American. To describe the second half of this situation, we cannot say, *Patto mo amerikajin desu*, because the sentence would mean that Pat, in addition to somebody that has been mentioned, is an American. Neither can we say, *Patto wa amerikajin mo desu*. (Japanese speakers would say, *Patto wa amerikajin demo arimasu*.)

[2] In the dialogues, there are two sentences that end with *desu*, which call for special attention: *Are mo takai desu ne* (That one too is expensive), and *Oishii desu yo* (It is delicious). These sentences cannot be negated by replacing *desu* with *ja arimasen*, because *takai* and *oishii* are not nouns. *Are mo takai ja arimasen* and *oishii ja arimasen* are therefore not grammatical. Instead, one would have to say *takaku arimasen* and *oishiku arimasen*. We will learn about the conjugation pattern of adjectives in Lesson 5.

Ja in *ja arimasen* is a contraction of *dewa*. In written Japanese, the uncontracted form is more common; thus, the above sentence more likely appears in writing as *Yamada san wa gakusee dewa arimasen*.

affirmative:	(X は) Y です。	*X is Y.*
negative:	(X は) Y <u>じゃありません</u>。	*X is not Y.*

7 ～ね/～よ

Statements often end with the tags *ne* or *yo*, depending on the way the speaker views the interaction with the listener. If the speaker is seeking the listener's confirmation or agreement to what has been said, then *ne* ("right?") could be added.

りーさんの　せんもんは　ぶんがくですね。　　*Ms. Lee, your major is literature, right?*
Rii san no　　　senmon wa　　bungaku desu ne.

これは　にくじゃありませんね。　　*This is not meat, is it?*
Kore wa　niku ja arimasen ne.

Another particle, *yo* ("I tell you"), is added to a statement if the speaker wants to assure the listener of what has been said. With *yo* added, a statement becomes an authoritative decree.

とんかつは　さかなじゃありませんよ。
Tonkatsu wa　　　sakana ja arimasen yo.
Let me assure you. "Tonkatsu" is not fish.

スミスさんは　イギリスじんですよ。
Sumisu san wa　　　igirisujin desu yo.
(In case you're wondering,) Mr. Smith is British.

表現ノート
ひょうげん

(〜を)ください▶ *(. . . o) kudasai* is "Please give me X." You can use it to request (concrete) items in general.

(〜を)おねがいします▶ *(. . . o) onegaishimasu* too is a request for item X. When used to ask for a concrete object, *(. . . o) onegaishimasu* sounds slightly more upscale than *(. . . o) kudasai*. It is heard often when ordering food at a restaurant ("I will have . . ."). *(. . . o) onegaishimasu* can also be used to ask for "abstract objects," such as repairs, explanations, and understanding.

(〜を)どうぞ▶ *(. . . o) doozo* is used when an offer is made with respect to item X. In the dialogue, the restaurant attendant uses it when she is about to hand the menu to the customer. It may also be used when a person is waiting for you to come forth with item X; a telephone operator, asking for your name, would probably say *Onamae o doozo*. (*O* is a politeness marker. Therefore *onamae* is "your honorable name.")

On the pronunciation of number words ▶ Note that the words for 300, 600, 800, 3,000 and 8,000 involve sound changes. "Counters" whose first sound is *h*, like *hyaku* (hundred), generally change shape after 3, 6, and 8. Some counters that begin with *s*, like *sen* (thousand), change shape after 3 and 8. Refer to the table at the end of the volume.

Big numbers ▶ In addition to the digit markers for tens (*juu*), hundreds (*hyaku*), and thousands (*sen*), which are found in Western languages as well, Japanese uses the marker for tens of thousands (*man*). Thus 20,000, for example, is *niman* ($=2\times10,000$), rather than *nijuusen* ($=20\times1,000$). While the next unit marker in Western languages is one million, Japanese describes that number as $100\times10,000$, that is, *hyakuman*.

More complicated numbers can be considered the sums of smaller numbers, as in the following examples.

234,567 =	23×10,000	にじゅうさんまん	(nijuusanman)
	4× 1,000	よんせん	(yonsen)
	5× 100	ごひゃく	(gohyaku)
	6× 10	ろくじゅう	(rokujuu)
	7	なな	(nana)

れんしゅう　Ｐ　ｒ　ａ　ｃ　ｔ　ｉ　ｃ　ｅ

Ⅰ すうじ　(Numbers)

100	ひゃく hyaku	1,000	せん sen	10,000	いちまん ichiman
200	にひゃく nihyaku	2,000	にせん nisen	20,000	にまん niman
300	さんびゃく sanbyaku	3,000	さんぜん sanzen	30,000	さんまん sanman
400	よんひゃく yonhyaku	4,000	よんせん yonsen	40,000	よんまん yonman
500	ごひゃく gohyaku	5,000	ごせん gosen	50,000	ごまん goman
600	ろっぴゃく roppyaku	6,000	ろくせん rokusen	60,000	ろくまん rokuman
700	ななひゃく nanahyaku	7,000	ななせん nanasen	70,000	ななまん nanaman
800	はっぴゃく happyaku	8,000	はっせん hassen	80,000	はちまん hachiman
900	きゅうひゃく kyuuhyaku	9,000	きゅうせん kyuusen	90,000	きゅうまん kyuuman

A. Read the following numbers.

(a) 34　　(b) 67　　(c) 83　　(d) 99　　(e) 125

(f) 515　　(g) 603　　(h) 850　　(i) 1,300　　(j) 3,400

(k) 8,900　　(l) 35,000　　(m) 64,500　　(n) 92,340

B. Look at the pictures and answer how much the things are.

Example:　Q：ペンは　いくらですか。
　　　　　　　Pen wa　ikura desu ka.

　　　　　　A：はちじゅうえんです。
　　　　　　　Hachijuu en desu.

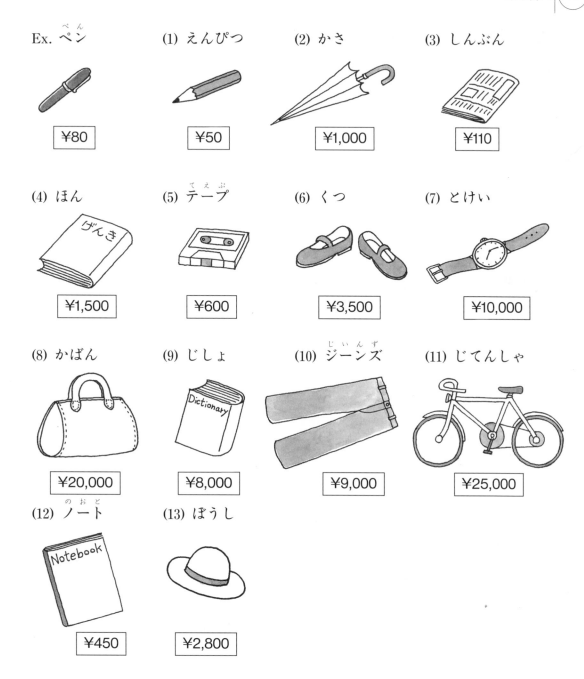

Ex. ペン ￥80

(1) えんぴつ ￥50

(2) かさ ￥1,000

(3) しんぶん ￥110

(4) ほん げんき ￥1,500

(5) テープ ￥600

(6) くつ ￥3,500

(7) とけい ￥10,000

(8) かばん ￥20,000

(9) じしょ Dictionary ￥8,000

(10) ジーンズ ￥9,000

(11) じてんしゃ ￥25,000

(12) ノート Notebook ￥450

(13) ぼうし ￥2,800

C. Pair Work—One of you looks at picture A and the other looks at picture B (p. 50). (Don't look at the other picture.) Find out the price of all items.

Example: A：えんぴつは いくらですか。
Enpitsu wa   ikura desu ka.

B：ひゃくえんです。
Hyaku en desu.

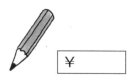

￥ [   ]

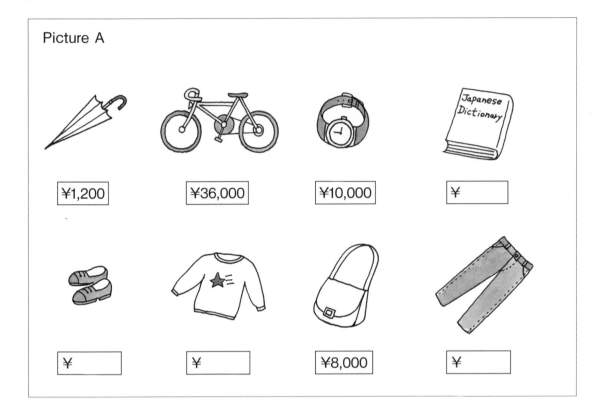

Picture A

¥1,200   ¥36,000   ¥10,000   ¥

¥   ¥   ¥8,000   ¥

Ⅱ これは なんですか

A. Items (1) through (6) are near you, and items (7) through (12) are near your friend. Your friend asks what these things are. Answer the questions. Pay attention to これ (kore) and それ (sore). 🔊

Example 1:   Your friend：それは なんですか。
                           Sore wa   nan desu ka.
                 You：これは ペンです。
                           Kore wa   pen desu.

Example 2:   Your friend：これは なんですか。
                           Kore wa   nan desu ka.
                 You：それは トレーナーです。
                           Sore wa   toreenaa desu.

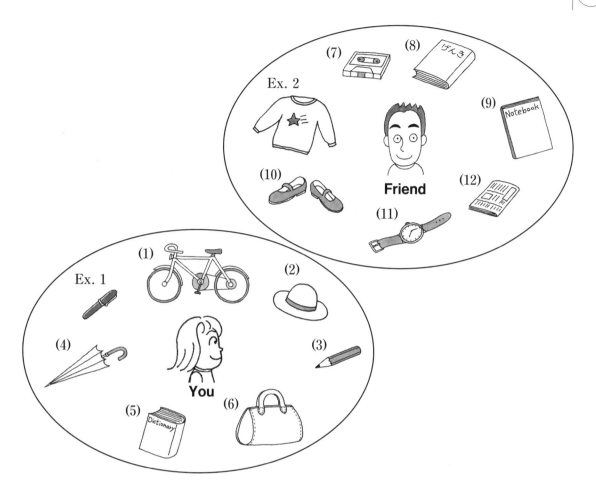

B. Look at the picture and tell what each building is. 🔊

Example: Q：あれは　なんですか。
                    Are wa   nan desu ka.

              A：あれは　としょかんです。
                    Are wa   toshokan desu.

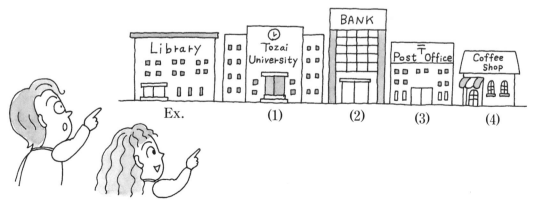

C. Pair Work—Point out five things in the classroom and ask your partner what they are using これ (*kore*), それ (*sore*), or あれ (*are*). Refer to the picture on p. 53 for the vocabulary.

Example 1:

A：あれは なんですか。
　　Are wa　nan desu ka.

B：あれは とけいです。
　　Are wa　tokee desu.

Example 2:

A：それは なんですか。
　　Sore wa　nan desu ka.

B：これは ペンです。
　　Kore wa　pen desu.

D. Pair Work—One of you looks at card A and the other looks at card B (p. 51). Ask and answer questions to find out the price of each item. Use この (*kono*), その (*sono*), or あの (*ano*) appropriately.

Example:　Customer：このほんは いくらですか。
　　　　　　　　　　　　Kono hon wa　ikura desu ka.

　　　　　Store attendant：にせんひゃくえんです。
　　　　　　　　　　　　　　Nisen hyaku en desu.

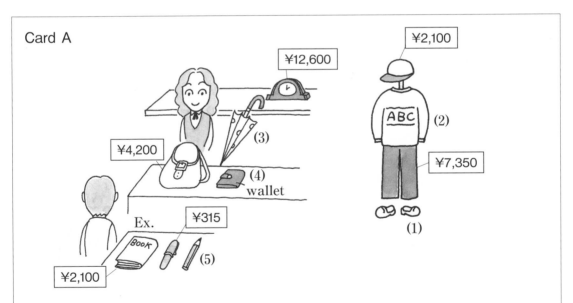

Card A

¥2,100

¥12,600

(2)

¥4,200

(3)

¥7,350

(4)
wallet

Ex.　¥315

(5)

(1)

¥2,100

Part I. You are a store attendant. Tell the customer how much each item is.

Part II. You are a customer. Ask for the prices of items (1)-(5).

Ⅲ これは だれの かさですか

Pair Work—Point at each item below (picture A) and ask whose it is. Your partner will refer to the picture B (p. 52) and tell you who it belongs to.

Example:　A：これは だれの かさですか。
　　　　　　　Kore wa　dare no　kasa desu ka.
　　　　　　B：メアリーさんの かさです。
　　　　　　　Mearii san no　　　　kasa desu.

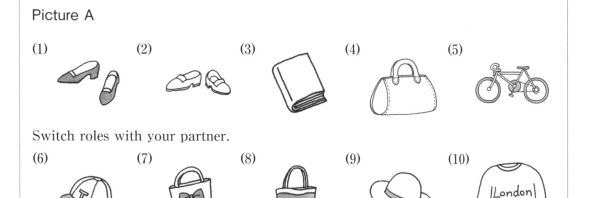

Picture A

(1)　　　　　(2)　　　　　(3)　　　　　(4)　　　　　(5)

Switch roles with your partner.

(6)　　　　　(7)　　　　　(8)　　　　　(9)　　　　　(10)

Ⅳ やまださんも にほんじんです

Look at the pictures below and describe each picture.

Example:

おとうさんは にほんじんです。
Otoosan wa　　　nihonjin desu.

おかあさんも にほんじんです。
Okaasan mo　　　nihonjin desu.

Ex.　Japanese

Father　　　　　　　　　　　Mother

(1) second year

Mary   Tanaka

(2) ¥5,800

(3) 22-years old

Takeshi   Robert

(4) とけい
tokee

(5) vegetable

(6) U. of London students

Robert   Nancy

Ⓥ メアリーさんは にほんじんじゃありません
め あ り い

A. Look at the chart on the next page and answer the questions. 🔊

Example: Q：メアリーさんは にほんじんですか。
め あ り い
Mearii san wa   nihonjin desu ka.

A：いいえ、にほんじんじゃありません。アメリカじんです。
あ め り か
Iie,   nihonjin ja arimasen.   Amerikajin desu.

1. たけしさんは ちゅうごくじんですか。
Takeshi san wa   chuugokujin desu ka.

2. ロバートさんは アメリカじんですか。
ろ ば あ と   あ め り か
Robaato san wa   amerikajin desu ka.

3. やましたせんせいは かんこくじんですか。
Yamashita sensee wa   kankokujin desu ka.

4. ロバートさんの せんもんは にほんごですか。
ろ ば あ と
Robaato san no   senmon wa   nihongo desu ka.

5. スーさんの せんもんは けいざいですか。
す う
Suu san no   senmon wa   keezai desu ka.

6. たけしさんは とうざいだいがくの がくせいですか。
Takeshi san wa   Toozai daigaku no   gakusee desu ka.

7. メアリーさんは ロンドンだいがくの がくせいですか。
   Mearii san wa   Rondon daigaku no   gakusee desu ka.

8. たけしさんは にねんせいですか。
   Takeshi san wa   ninensee desu ka.

9. スーさんは いちねんせいですか。
   Suu san wa   ichinensee desu ka.

10. ロバートさんは よねんせいですか。
    Robaato san wa   yonensee desu ka.

	Hart, Mary	きむらたけし Kimura Takeshi	Kim, Sue	Smith, Robert	やましたせんせい Yamashita sensee
Nationality	American	Japanese	Korean	British	Japanese
School	U. of Arizona	Tozai Univ.	Seoul Univ.	U. of London	Tozai Univ.
Major	Japanese	history	computer	business	(Japanese teacher)
Year	2nd year	4th year	3rd year	4th year	

B. Pair Work—Ask your partner whose belongings items (1) through (7) are. Your partner will refer to the picture on the next page and answer the questions.

Example:　A：これは メアリーさんの さいふですか。　　　　　Ex.
　　　　　　　　Kore wa Mearii san no   saifu desu ka.
　　　　　　B：いいえ、メアリーさんの さいふじゃありません。
　　　　　　　　Iie,   Mearii san no   saifu ja arimasen.
　　　　　　A：これは リーさんの さいふですか。
　　　　　　　　Kore wa Rii san no   saifu desu ka.
　　　　　　B：ええ、リーさんの さいふです。
　　　　　　　　Ee,   Rii san no   saifu desu.

(1)　　　(2)　　　(3)　　　(4)　　　(5)　　　(6)　　　(7)

メアリー
Mearii

リー
Rii

ようこ
Yooko

Ⓥ まとめの れんしゅう (Review Exercises)

A. Role Play—One student is a store attendant. The other is a customer. Use Dialogue I as a model.

B. Role Play—One student is a waiter/waitress. The other student goes to a restaurant. Look at the menu below and order some food or drink, using Dialogue Ⅱ as a model.

メニュー

ていしょく

_{すぱげってぃ}
スパゲッティ

_{かれえ}
カレー

そば

うどん

_{さんどいっち}
サンドイッチ

_{あいすくりいむ}
アイスクリーム

_{らあめん}
ラーメン

_{はんばあがあ}
ハンバーガー

_{こおひい}
コーヒー

_{こおら}
コーラ

_{さらだ}
サラダ

_{じゅうす}
ジュース

_{みるく}
ミルク

こうちゃ

Pair Work Ⅰ C.

Example:　A：えんぴつは　いくらですか。
　　　　　　　　Enpitsu wa　　　ikura desu ka.

　　　　　　B：ひゃくえんです。
　　　　　　　　Hyaku en desu.

¥100

Picture B

¥ 　　　¥ 　　　¥ 　　　¥3,700

¥4,500　　　¥9,000　　　¥ 　　　¥7,000

Pair Work Ⅱ D.

Example: Customer：このほんは　いくらですか。
Kono hon wa　ikura desu ka.

Store attendant：にせんひゃくえんです。
Nisen hyaku en desu.

Card B

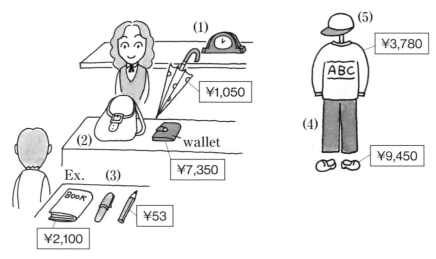

(1)

¥1,050

(2)

wallet

¥7,350

Ex.　(3)

Book

¥2,100

¥53

(5)

¥3,780

ABC

(4)

¥9,450

Part I. You are a customer. Ask for the price of items (1)-(5).

Part II. You are a store attendant. Tell the customer how much each item is.

Pair Work Ⅲ

Example: A：これは だれの かさですか。
Kore wa   dare no   kasa desu ka.
B：メアリーさんの かさです。
Mearii san no   kasa desu.

Picture B

| スー | たけし | メアリー | ロバート | やましたせんせい |
| Suu | Takeshi | Mearii | Robaato | Yamashita sensee |

きょうしつ
In the Classroom

でんき
denki

こくばん
kokuban

テレビ
terebi

カーテン
kaaten

ドア
doa

ビデオ
bideo

まど
mado

じしょ
jisho

ほん
hon

えんぴつ
enpitsu

けしゴム
keshigomu

いす
isu

つくえ
tsukue

ペン
pen

かばん
kaban

Useful Expressions

わかりました。 Wakarimashita.	I understand./I understood.
わかりません。 Wakarimasen.	I don't understand./I don't know.
ゆっくり いってください。 Yukkuri itte kudasai.	Please speak slowly.
もういちど いってください。 Moo ichido itte kudasai.	Please say it again.
ちょっと まってください。 Chotto matte kudasai.	Please wait.

第3課 L E S S O N 3

デートの約束 Making a Date
やく そく

会話 D i a l o g u e
かい わ

(I) Mary and Takeshi are talking.

1 たけし：　　メアリーさん、週末はたいてい何をしますか。
　　　　　　　　　　　　しゅうまつ　　　　　　　なに

2 メアリー：　そうですね。たいていうちで勉強します。でも、ときどき映画を見ま
　　　　　　　　　　　　　　　　　　べんきょう　　　　　　　　　　　　　えい が　　み

3 　　　　　　す。

4 たけし：　　そうですか……じゃあ、土曜日に映画を見ませんか。
　　　　　　　　　　　　　　　　　　ど よう び　　えい が　　み

5 メアリー：　土曜日はちょっと……
　　　　　　　ど よう び

6 たけし：　　じゃあ、日曜日はどうですか。
　　　　　　　　　　　　にちよう び

7 メアリー：　いいですね。

(II) On Sunday morning, at Mary's host family's.

1 メアリー：　おはようございます。

2 お母さん：　おはよう。早いですね。
　　かあ　　　　　　　　　はや

3 メアリー：　ええ、今日は京都に行きます。京都で映画を見ます。
　　　　　　　　　　きょう　きょう と　い　　　　きょう と　えい が　　み

4 お母さん：　いいですね。何時ごろ帰りますか。
　　かあ　　　　　　　　なん じ　　　　かえ

5 メアリー：　九時ごろです。
　　　　　　　く じ

6 お母さん：　晩ごはんは？
　　かあ　　　　ばん

7 メアリー：　食べません。
　　　　　　　た

8 お母さん：　そうですか。じゃあ、いってらっしゃい。
　　かあ

9 メアリー：　いってきます。

I

Takeshi: Mary, what do you usually do on the weekend?

Mary: Let's see. I usually study at home. But I sometimes see movies.

Takeshi: I see . . . then, would you like to see a movie on Saturday?

Mary: Saturday is not a good day. (lit., Saturday is a little bit [inconvenient] . . .)

Takeshi: Then, how about Sunday?

Mary: That's fine.

II

Mary: Good morning.

Host mother: Good morning. You are early, aren't you?

Mary: Yes, I'm going to Kyoto today. I will see a movie in Kyoto.

Host mother: Good. Around what time will you come back?

Mary: Around nine.

Host mother: How about dinner?

Mary: I will not eat.

Host mother: I see. Well, have a nice day.

Mary: Good-bye.

単語
たん　ご

V o c a b u l a r y

N o u n s

Entertainment and Sports

* えいが	映画	movie
おんがく	音楽	music
ざっし	雑誌	magazine
スポーツ		sports
デート		date (romantic, not calendar)
テニス		tennis
テレビ		TV
ビデオ		video tape; VCR

Foods and Drinks

あさごはん	朝御飯	breakfast
おさけ	お酒	sake; alcohol
おちゃ	お茶	green tea
コーヒー		coffee
* ばんごはん	晩御飯	dinner
ハンバーガー		hamburger
ひるごはん	昼御飯	lunch
みず	水	water

Places

いえ	家	home; house
* うち		home; house; my place
LL エルエル		language lab
がっこう	学校	school

Time

あさ	朝	morning
あした		tomorrow
いつ		when
* きょう	今日	today
* ～ごろ		at about
こんばん	今晩	tonight
* しゅうまつ	週末	weekend
* どようび	土曜日	Saturday
* にちようび	日曜日	Sunday

* Words that appear in the dialogue

まいにち	毎日	every day
まいばん	毎晩	every night

U - v e r b s

* いく	行く	to go　(*destination* に/へ)
* かえる	帰る	to go back; to return (*destination* に/へ)
きく	聞く	to listen; to hear　(〜を)
のむ	飲む	to drink　(〜を)
はなす	話す	to speak; to talk (*language* を/で)
よむ	読む	to read　(〜を)

R u - v e r b s

おきる	起きる	to get up
* たべる	食べる	to eat　(〜を)
ねる	寝る	to sleep; to go to sleep
* みる	見る	to see; to look at; to watch (〜を)

I r r e g u l a r　V e r b s

くる	来る	to come　(*destination* に/へ)
* する		to do　(〜を)
* べんきょうする	勉強する	to study　(〜を)

A d j e c t i v e s

* いい		good
* はやい	早い	early

A d v e r b s

あまり＋ negative		not much
ぜんぜん＋ negative	全然	not at all
* たいてい	大抵	usually
* ちょっと		a little
* ときどき	時々	sometimes
よく		often; much

E x p r e s s i o n s

* そうですね		That's right.; Let me see.
* でも		but
* どうですか		How about . . . ?; How is . . . ?

文法 Grammar
ぶん ぽう

1 Verb Conjugation

Verbs in Japanese conjugate, or take various shapes. In this lesson, we learn three forms: (1) the "dictionary forms," (2) the present tense affirmative forms, and (3) the present tense negative forms.[1] There are two kinds of verbs that follow regular conjugation patterns, and an example of each is below.

	ru-verb	u-verb
verb bases	tabe	ik
dictionary forms	食べる (to eat)	行く (to go)
present, affirmative	食べます	行きます
present, negative	食べません	行きません
stems	食べ	行き

食べる belongs to the group of verbs called the "ru-verbs." Ru-verbs are so called, because you add the suffix ru to the verb base (tabe, in the above example) to form the dictionary form. For the two long forms we learn in this lesson, you simply add the suffixes masu and masen, instead of ru, to the bases. We learn four ru-verbs in this lesson:

食べる	寝る	起きる	見る
食べます	寝ます	起きます	見ます

Another major group of verbs is called the "u-verbs." The dictionary form of an u-verb like 行く can be broken down into the base (ik in the above example) and the suffix u. The long forms like 行きます and 行きません, then, are formed with the base plus suffixes imasu and imasen. You may find the u-verb conjugations slightly more difficult than the ru-verb conjugations, because of the extra vowel i. We learn six u-verbs in this lesson:

飲む	読む	話す	聞く	行く	帰る
飲みます	読みます	話します	聞きます	行きます	帰ります

---

[1] The use of the term "dictionary forms" is by no means restricted to listings in a dictionary. They also appear in various constructions in actual sentences. We will learn their uses in later chapters. Don't be misled by the names given to the long forms too; the "present tense" in Japanese can indicate both the "present" and the "future." We will return to this issue in Section 2 below. For the moment, we will concentrate on the forms, not the meaning of these verbs.

In later lessons, we will have many opportunities to refer to the parts like 食べ and 行き, which come before ます and ません in the long forms. For the sake of ease of reference, we will call these parts (same as bases with *ru*-verbs, and bases plus *i* with *u*-verbs) "stems."

In addition to *ru*-verbs and *u*-verbs, there are two "irregular verbs." Note that the vowels in their bases are different in the short (dictionary) forms and the long forms.

	irregular verbs	
dictionary forms	する (to do)	くる (to come)
present, affirmative	します	きます
present, negative	しません	きません
stems	し	き

These two verbs are also used to form compound verbs. In this lesson, we learn the verb 勉強する, which conjugates just like the verb する.

It is important to remember which verb belongs to which conjugation class. It is a good idea, therefore, to memorize each verb as a set: instead of memorizing just the dictionary form, try to memorize the dictionary form *and* the present tense affirmative, like 行く − 行きます. This is especially important with verbs that end with the *hiragana* る, because they may be irregular verbs like する and くる, or *ru*-verbs, or *u*-verbs whose bases just happen to end with the consonant *r*. If you know the verb classes and the rules that apply to them, you know why it is wrong to say ×見ります and ×帰ます.[2]

	見る (= a *ru*-verb)	帰る (= an *u*-verb that ends with る)
verb bases	*mi*	*kaer*
long forms	見ます／見ません	帰ります／帰りません
stems	見	帰り

---

[2]Things are not as bad as you might expect after reading the above paragraph. The key lies in the second from the last syllable in a dictionary form. The irregular verbs set aside, if you see the vowels *a*, *o*, or *u* right before the final る, you can be absolutely sure that they are *u*-verbs. (We have not learned any such verbs yet.) Unfortunately for us, the logic does not follow in the other direction; there are *ru*-verbs and *u*-verbs that have the vowels *i* and *e* before the final る. 寝る has the vowel *e* before る and is a *ru*-verb. 帰る, on the other hand, has the same sound sequence, but is an *u*-verb.

2 Verb Types and the "Present Tense"

In this lesson we learn about a dozen verbs that describe basic human actions. These are often called "action verbs," and the "present tense" of these verbs either means (1) that a person habitually or regularly engages in these activities, or (2) that a person will, or is planning to, perform these activities in the future.

Habitual actions:

私はよくテレビを見ます。　　　　　　　　　*I often watch TV.*

メアリーさんはときどき朝ごはんを食べません。　*Mary sometimes doesn't eat breakfast.*

Future actions:

私はあした京都に行きます。　　　　　*I will go to Kyoto tomorrow.*

スーさんは今日うちに帰りません。　　*Sue will not return home today.*

3 Particles

Nouns used in sentences generally must be followed by particles, which indicate the relations that the nouns bear to the verbs.[3] In this lesson, we learn four particles: で, に, へ, and を.

で　The particle で indicates where the event described by the verb takes place.[4]

図書館で本を読みます。　　　　*I will read books in the library.*

うちでテレビを見ます。　　　　*I will watch TV at home.*

に　The particle に has many meanings, but here we will learn two: (1) the goal toward which things move, and (2) the time at which an event takes place.

(1) goal of movement

私は今日学校に行きません。　　*I will not go to school today.*

私はうちに帰ります。　　　　　*I will return home.*

---

[3]In spoken language, particles are often "dropped." We will learn more about such cases in Lesson 15.
[4]In later lessons, we will be introduced to verbs that require particles other than で to express location.

(2) time

| 日曜日に京都に行きます。
<small>にちよう び ──きょうと ── い</small> | *I will go to Kyoto on Sunday.* |
| 十一時に寝ます。
<small>じゅういち じ ── ね</small> | *I will go to bed at eleven.* |

(Some time words stand alone, without the particle に tagging along, which will be discussed in Section 4 below.)

Approximate time references can be made by substituting ごろ or ごろに for に. Thus,

| 十一時ごろ(に)寝ます。
<small>じゅういち じ ── ね</small> | *I will go to bed at about eleven.* |

へ The particle へ, too, indicates the goal of movement. The sentences in (1) above therefore can be rewritten using へ instead of に. Note that this particle is pronounced "*e*."

| 私は今日学校へ行きません。
<small>わたし きょう がっこう ── い</small> | *I will not go to school today.* |
| 私はうちへ帰ります。
<small>わたし ── かえ</small> | *I will return home.* |

Note that へ may replace the particle に only in the goal-of-movement sense. The particle に for time references and other uses, which we will learn about in later lessons, cannot be so replaced.

を The particle を indicates "direct objects," the kind of things that are directly involved in, or affected by, the event. Note that this particle is pronounced "*o*."

コーヒーを飲みます。 <small>── の</small>	*I drink coffee.*
テープを聞きます。 <small>── き</small>	*I listen to tapes.*
テレビを見ます。 <small>── み</small>	*I watch TV.*

4 Time Reference

You need the particle に with (1) the days of the week like "on Sunday," and (2) numerical time expressions, like "at 10:42," and "in September."

| 日曜日に行きます。
<small>にちよう び ── い</small> | *I will go on Sunday.* |
| 十時四十二分に起きます。
<small>じゅう じ よんじゅう に ふん ── お</small> | *I get up at 10:42.* |

九月に帰ります。　　　　　　*I will go back in September.*
く　がつ　かえ

You do not use the particle に with (1) time expressions defined relative to the present moment, such as "today" and "tomorrow," (2) expressions describing regular intervals, such as "every day," and (3) the word for "when."

あした来ます。　　　　　　*I will come tomorrow.*
き

毎晩テレビを見ます。　　　　*I watch TV every evening.*
まいばん　　　　み

いつ行きますか。　　　　　　*When will you go?*
い

You normally do not use に with (1) the parts of a day, like "in the morning" and "at night," and (2) the word for "weekend." Unlike words like あした and 毎晩 above, how-
まいばん
ever, these words are sometimes followed by に, depending on styles, emphases, and personal preferences.

朝(に)新聞を読みます。　　　*I read the newspaper in the morning.*
あさ　　しんぶん　よ

週末(に)何をしますか。　　　*What will you do on weekends?*
しゅうまつ　　なに

5　〜ませんか

You can use ませんか (= the present tense negative verb, plus the question particle) to extend an invitation. It should be noted that its affirmative counterpart, ますか, *cannot* be so used. Thus a sentence like 昼ごはんを食べますか can only be construed as a question,
ひる　　た
not as an invitation.

昼ごはんを食べませんか。　　*What do you say to having lunch with me?*
ひる　　た
いいですね。　　　　　　　　*Sounds great.*

テニスをしませんか。　　　　*Will you play tennis with me?*
うーん、ちょっと。　　　　　*Um, it's slightly (inconvenient for me at this moment).*

6　Word Order

Japanese sentences are fairly flexible in the arrangement of elements that appear in them. Generally, sentences are made up of several noun-particle sequences followed by a verb or an adjective, which in turn is often followed by a sentence-final particle such as か, ね, or よ. Among the noun-particle sequences, their relative orders are to a large extent free.

A typical sentence, therefore, looks like the following, but several other arrangements of noun-particle sequences are also possible.

私は 今日 図書館で 日本語を 勉強します。
topic time place object verb

I will study Japanese in the library today.

私は よく 七時ごろ うちへ 帰ります。
topic frequency time goal verb

I often go back home at around seven.

7   Frequency Adverbs

You can add a frequency adverb such as 毎日 (everyday), よく (often), and ときどき (sometimes) to a sentence to describe how often you do something.

私はときどき喫茶店に行きます。   *I sometimes go to a coffee shop.*

In this lesson, we also learn two adverbs which describe how *infrequent* an activity or an event is; ぜんぜん (never; not at all) and あまり (not often; not very much). These adverbs anticipate the negative at the end of the sentence. If you use ぜんぜん or あまり, in other words, you need to conclude the sentence with ません.

私はぜんぜんテレビを見ません。   *I do not watch TV at all.*

たけしさんはあまり勉強しません。   *Takeshi does not study much.*

8   The Topic Particle は

As we saw in Lesson 1, the particle は presents the topic of one's utterance ("As for item X, it is such that . . ."). It puts forward the item that you want to talk about and comment on. You may have noted that the topic phrases in sentences such as メアリーさんは三年生です (Mary is a third-year student), and 私の専門は日本語です (My major is Japanese language), are the subjects of those sentences. A topic phrase, however, need not be the subject of a sentence. We see three sentences in the dialogue of this lesson where nonsubject phrases are made topics with the help of the particle は.

メアリーさん、週末はたいてい何をしますか。
Mary, what do you usually do on the weekend?

今日<ruby>今日<rt>きょう</rt></ruby>は京都<ruby>京都<rt>きょうと</rt></ruby>に行<ruby>行<rt>い</rt></ruby>きます。
I'm going to Kyoto today.

In the above two examples, は promotes time expressions as the topic of each sentence. Its effects can be paraphrased like these: "Let's talk about weekends; what do you do on weekends?" "Let me say what I will do today; I will go to Kyoto."

晩<ruby>晩<rt>ばん</rt></ruby>ごはんは？　　　　　食<ruby>食<rt>た</rt></ruby>べません。
How about dinner?　　　　　*I will not eat.*

In this example, は is used in directing the listener's attention and thereby inviting a comment or completion of a sentence. You may also note that the broached topic, 晩<ruby>晩<rt>ばん</rt></ruby>ごはん, does not stand in subject relation to the verb, but is rather its direct object.

表現ノート<ruby>表現ノート<rt>ひょうげん</rt></ruby>　　　　　Expression Notes ④

行<ruby>行<rt>い</rt></ruby>く/来<ruby>来<rt>く</rt></ruby>る▶ When you move to a place where the hearer is, you say "I'm coming." in English. However in the same situation, 私<ruby>私<rt>わたし</rt></ruby>は行<ruby>行<rt>い</rt></ruby>きます is used in Japanese. 来<ruby>来<rt>く</rt></ruby>る is a movement toward the place where the speaker is. 行<ruby>行<rt>い</rt></ruby>く is a movement in a direction away from the speaker.

ちょっと▶ ちょっと literally means "a little," "a bit," "a small amount," as in ちょっとください (Please give me a little) and ちょっと待<ruby>待<rt>ま</rt></ruby>ってください (Please wait for a moment). It is commonly used for a polite refusal. In this case, it means "inconvenient," "impossible," and so on. Japanese people don't normally reject requests, suggestions, or invitations with いいえ (No), because it sounds too direct.

A：土曜日<ruby>土曜日<rt>どようび</rt></ruby>に映画<ruby>映画<rt>えいが</rt></ruby>を見<ruby>見<rt>み</rt></ruby>ませんか。　　*Will you see a movie on Saturday?*
B：土曜日<ruby>土曜日<rt>どようび</rt></ruby>は、ちょっと。　　*Saturday is not convenient.*
　　　　　　　　　　　　　　(lit., Saturday is a little bit.)

練 習 P r a c t i c e
れん しゅう

① 図書館で本を読みます
と しょ かん ほん よ

A. Change the following verbs into 〜ます and 〜ません. 🔊

Example: たべる → たべます

たべる → たべません

1. のむ   2. きく   3. みる   4. する   5. はなす

6. いく   7. くる   8. かえる   9. ねる   10. よむ

11. おきる   12. べんきょうする

B. Look at the pictures below and make sentences using the cues. 🔊

(a) Add the appropriate verbs to the following direct objects.

Example: 雑誌 → 雑誌を読みます。
ざっし   ざっし よ

Ex. 雑誌   (1) テープ   (2) テニス   (3) ハンバーガー
ざっし

library/2:00   L.L./4:30   school/Saturday   McDonald's/5:00

(4) コーヒー   (5) テレビ   (6) 日本語
にほんご

coffee shop/3:00   home/tonight   college/every day

(b) Add the place to the above sentences.

Example: library → 図書館で雑誌を読みます。
とし ょ か ん　ざ っ し　　よ

C. Look at the pictures below and make sentences using the cues.

Example: go to the post office → 郵便局に行きます。
ゆうびんきょく　　い

Ex.　go to the post office　(1) go to the library　(2) come to school

1:00　　　　　　　　　3:00　　　　　8:30

(3) come to the coffee shop　(4) return home　(5) return to the U. S.

　　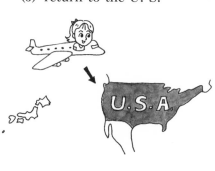

5:30　　　　　　tomorrow

D. Pair Work—Make questions, using verbs we have learned in this lesson.

Example: Ａ：図書館で雑誌を読みますか。
とし ょ か ん　ざ っ し　　よ
Ｂ：ええ、読みます。／いいえ、読みません。
よ　　　　　　　　　　　　　　よ

E. Pair Work—Guessing game

Ask questions and find out the items your partner has chosen.

1. Before you start, both of you will choose one item in each row of the table and mark it.
2. In each row, using the verb and one of the four items, make a yes-or-no-question sentence and find out which item your partner has chosen.
3. You can ask at most two questions with one verb. If you have guessed correctly the item your partner has chosen, you score a point. Your partner will not give away the right answer when you ask a wrong question.
4. When you have asked questions about all the verbs in the table, switch roles with your partner and answer their questions.
5. Tabulate the score. You win the game if you have scored higher than your partner.

Example:　Ａ：学校に行きますか。
　　　　　Ｂ：いいえ、行きません。
　　　　　Ａ：喫茶店へ行きますか。
　　　　　Ｂ：はい、行きます。(A guessed what B marked, therefore A won.)

〜に行きます	post office	school	coffee shop	library
〜を見ます	TV	movie	video	cartoon（まんが）
〜を飲みます	sake	green tea	water	coffee
〜を読みます	book	newspaper	magazine	Japanese book
〜をします	date	study	telephone	tennis

Ⅱ 何時に起きますか
なんじ　お

A. Look at Mary's schedule and answer the following questions. 🔊

Mary's Schedule

7:30 A.M.	get up
8:00	eat breakfast
8:30	go to school
12:00	eat lunch
3:00 P.M.	drink coffee
4:00	play tennis
5:00	go home
6:30	eat dinner
7:00	watch TV
8:00	study
11:30	go to bed

1. メアリーさんは何時に起きますか。
　　　　　　　　なんじ　お
2. メアリーさんは何時に学校に行きますか。
　　　　　　　　なんじ　がっこう　い
3. メアリーさんは何時に昼ごはんを食べますか。
　　　　　　　　なんじ　ひる　　　　た
4. メアリーさんは何時にコーヒーを飲みますか。
　　　　　　　　なんじ　　　　　　　の
5. メアリーさんは何時にうちに帰りますか。
　　　　　　　　なんじ　　　　かえ
6. メアリーさんは何時に勉強しますか。
　　　　　　　　なんじ　べんきょう
7. メアリーさんは何時に寝ますか。
　　　　　　　　なんじ　ね

B. Pair Work—Ask your partner what time they do the following things.

Example:　A：何時に起きますか。
　　　　　　　　なんじ　お
　　　　　　B：八時に起きます。
　　　　　　　　はちじ　お

Your partner's schedule

time	
(　　　　　)	get up
(　　　　　)	eat breakfast
(　　　　　)	go to school
(　　　　　)	eat lunch
(　　　　　)	go home
(　　　　　)	go to bed

C. Look at the pictures in I-B (p. 65) and I-C (p. 66), and add the time expressions to the sentences. 🔊

Example:　2:00　→　二時に図書館で本を読みます。
　　　　　　　　　　　に　じ　としょかん　ほん　よ

Ⅲ コーヒーを飲みませんか

A. Make suggestions using the cues below.

Example: drink coffee → コーヒーを飲みませんか。

1. see a movie
2. come to my house
3. play tennis
4. eat dinner
5. study in the library
6. talk at a coffee shop
7. drink tea at home
8. listen to the music

B. Pair Work—Ask your friend out for the activities in the pictures.

Example: A：映画を見ませんか。
B：いいですね。／ううん、ちょっと……。

Ex. (1) (2) (3)

(4) (5) (6)

Ⅳ 毎日本を読みます
まいにちほん　　よ

How often do you do the following activities? Answer the questions using the expressions below.

Example: Q：本を読みますか。
ほん　よ
A：ええ、よく読みます。／いいえ、あまり読みません。
よ　　　　　　　　　　　　　　　　よ

1. スポーツをしますか。
2. 雑誌を読みますか。
ざっし　よ
3. 図書館に行きますか。
としょかん　い
4. 映画を見ますか。
えいが　み
5. コーヒーを飲みますか。
の
6. 日本の音楽を聞きますか。
にほん　おんがく　き
7. 朝ごはんを食べますか。
あさ　　　　た

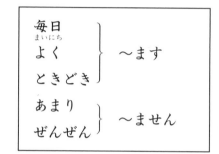

毎日
まいにち
よく
ときどき ｝ ～ます

あまり
ぜんぜん ｝ ～ません

Ⅴ まとめの練習　(Review Exercises)
れんしゅう

A. Answer the following questions.

1. 何時に起きますか。
なんじ　お
2. どこで勉強しますか。
べんきょう
3. いつテレビを見ますか。
み
4. スポーツをしますか。
5. 週末はどこに行きますか。
しゅうまつ　　　　い
6. 朝、何を食べますか。
あさ　なに　た
7. 今晩、何をしますか。
こんばん　なに
8. 毎晩、何時ごろ寝ますか。
まいばん　なんじ　　ね

B. Tell your classmates what your plans are today/tomorrow/on the weekend.

Example: 今日は二時にＬＬに行きます。三時に図書館で日本語を勉強します。
きょう　にじ　エルエル　い　　さんじ　としょかん　にほんご　べんきょう
六時ごろうちに帰ります。
ろくじ　　　　　かえ

C. Class Activity—Find someone who . . .

name

1. gets up at 7 o'clock.   _____

2. eats breakfast every day.   _____

3. speaks French.   _____

4. watches TV at home.   _____

5. listens to Japanese music.   _____

6. plays tennis.   _____

D. Suggest to a classmate that you do something together over the weekend. Use Dialogue Ⅰ as a model.

Example:　Ａ：Ｂさんはテニスをしますか。

　　　　　Ｂ：はい。

　　　　　Ａ：じゃあ、日曜日<small>にちようび</small>にテニスをしませんか。

　　　　　Ｂ：日曜日<small>にちようび</small>はちょっと……。

　　　　　Ａ：そうですか。じゃあ、土曜日<small>どようび</small>はどうですか。

　　　　　Ｂ：ええ、いいですね。

第4課 | L E S S O N ·······4

初めてのデート The First Date
はじ

会話 D i a l o g u e
かい わ

Ⅰ Mary goes downtown.

1 メアリー： すみません。マクドナルドはどこですか。

2 知らない人： あのデパートの前ですよ。
　し　　ひと　　　　　　　　　　まえ

3 メアリー： ありがとうございます。

Ⅱ In the evening, at Mary's host family's house.

1 メアリー： ただいま。

2 お父さん： おかえりなさい。映画はどうでしたか。
　　とう　　　　　　　　　　　　えいが

3 メアリー： 見ませんでした。たけしさんは来ませんでした。
　　　　　み　　　　　　　　　　　　　　　　き

4 お父さん： えっ、どうしてですか。
　　とう

5 メアリー： わかりません。だから、一人で本屋とお寺に行きました。
　　　　　　　　　　　　　　　ひとり　ほんや　　てら　い

6 お父さん： 人がたくさんいましたか。
　　とう　　ひと

7 メアリー： はい。お寺で写真をたくさん撮りました。
　　　　　　　　てら　しゃしん　　　　　と

8 　　　　　 デパートにも行きました。はい、おみやげです。
　　　　　　　　　　　　　い

9 お父さん： ありがとう。
　　とう

10 お母さん： あっ、メアリーさん、
　　 かあ

11 　　　　　 さっき電話がありましたよ。
　　　　　　　　でんわ

Ⅲ On the phone.

1 たけし： はい、木村です。

2 メアリー： もしもし、たけしさんですか。メアリーです。

3 たけしさん、今日来ませんでしたね。

4 たけし： 行きましたよ。ハーゲンダッツの前で一時間待ちました。

5 メアリー： えっ。ハーゲンダッツじゃありませんよ。マクドナルドですよ。

6 たけし： マクドナルド……ごめんなさい！

Ⅰ

Mary: Excuse me. Where is McDonald's?

Stranger: It is in front of that department store.

Mary: Thank you.

Ⅱ

Mary: I'm home.

Host father: Welcome home. How was the movie?

Mary: I didn't see it. Takeshi didn't come.

Host father: Oh, why?

Mary: I don't know. So, I went to a bookstore and a temple alone.

Host father: Were there a lot of people?

Mary: Yes. I took many pictures at the temple. I also went to a department store.
Here's a souvenir for you.

Host father: Thank you.

Host mother: Oh, Mary, you had a phone call a little while ago.

Ⅲ

Takeshi: This is Kimura.

Mary: Hello, is this Takeshi? This is Mary. Takeshi, you didn't come today, did you?

Takeshi: I went there. I waited for one hour in front of the Häagen-Dazs place.

Mary: Not Häagen-Dazs. McDonald's!

Takeshi: McDonald's . . . I'm sorry!

単語
たん ご

Ｖ ｏ ｃ ａ ｂ ｕ ｌ ａ ｒ ｙ

Ｎ ｏ ｕ ｎ ｓ

Activities

アルバイト		part-time job
かいもの	買い物	shopping
クラス		class

People and Things

あなた		you
いぬ	犬	dog
* おみやげ	お土産	souvenir
こども	子供	child
ごはん	御飯	rice; meal
* しゃしん	写真	picture; photograph
つくえ	机	desk
てがみ	手紙	letter
ねこ	猫	cat
パン		bread
* ひと	人	person

Places

* おてら	お寺	temple
こうえん	公園	park
スーパー		supermarket
* デパート		department store
バスてい	バス停	bus stop
びょういん	病院	hospital
ホテル		hotel
* ほんや	本屋	bookstore
まち	町	town; city
レストラン		restaurant

Time

きのう	昨日	yesterday
* さっき		a little while ago
* 〜じかん	〜時間	hour
cf. いちじかん	一時間	one hour

* Words that appear in the dialogue

せんしゅう	先週	last week
とき	時	when . . . ; at the time of . . .
		（〜の）
げつようび	月曜日	Monday
かようび	火曜日	Tuesday
すいようび	水曜日	Wednesday
もくようび	木曜日	Thursday
きんようび	金曜日	Friday

U-verbs

	あう	会う	to meet; to see (a person)
			(*person* に)
*	ある		there is . . .　（〜が）
	かう	買う	to buy　（〜を）
	かく	書く	to write　（*person* に *thing* を）
*	とる	撮る	to take (pictures)　（〜を）
*	まつ	待つ	to wait　（〜を）
*	わかる		to understand　（〜が）

Ru-verb

| * | いる | | (a person) is in . . . ; stays at . . . |
| | | | (*place* に) |

Adverbs and Other Expressions

	〜ぐらい		about (approximate measurement)
*	ごめんなさい		I'm sorry.
*	だから		so; therefore
*	たくさん		many; a lot
	〜と		together with (a person)
*	どうして		why
*	ひとりで	一人で	alone
*	もしもし		Hello? (used on the phone)

Location Words

	みぎ	右	right　（〜の）
	ひだり	左	left　（〜の）
*	まえ	前	front　（〜の）
	うしろ	後ろ	back　（〜の）
	なか	中	inside　（〜の）
	うえ	上	on　（〜の）

した	下	under	（〜の）
そば		near	（〜の）
となり	隣	next	（〜の）
あいだ	間	between	（*A* と *B* の）
そこ		there	
ここ		here	

文法 G r a m m a r
ぶん ぽう

1 Xがあります/います

Xがあります means "there is/are X (nonliving thing)." The particle が introduces, or presents, the item X. You can use あります when you want to say that there is something at a certain location.

あそこにマクドナルドがあります。 *There's a McDonald's over there.*

Note that あります is different from other verbs we have seen so far on the following three counts. One, it calls for the particle に, rather than で, for the place description. Two, the place description usually comes at the beginning of the sentence. Three, the thing description is usually followed by the particle が, rather than は.

You can also use あります to say that you *have* or *own* something.[1]

テレビがありません。 *I don't have a TV.*

時間がありますか。 *Do you have time?*
じ かん

We also use あります when we want to say that *an event will take place*.[2]

火曜日にテストがあります。 *There will be an exam on Tuesday.*
か ようび

あしたは日本語のクラスがありません。 *There will be no Japanese class tomorrow.*
に ほん ご

When you want to present a *person* or some other sentient being, rather than a thing, you need to use the verb います.[3] Thus,

---

[1] Note the difference between:
テレビがありません (I don't have a TV), the negative version of テレビがあります, and
テレビじゃありません (It isn't a TV), the negative version of テレビです.

[2] In a minor detail which we will not discuss any further here, when あります is used in the sense of an event taking place, the place description is followed by the particle で, like normal verbs and unlike the other uses of あります. Note also that some time expressions (such as 日曜日に) come with the particle に, and some others (such as あした) do not (see Lesson 3). The rule applies to the あります sentences as well.

[3] Note that the same verb "is" in English comes out differently in Japanese:
あそこに留学生がいます。 *There is an international student over there.*
りゅうがくせい
メアリーさんは留学生です。 *Mary is an international student.*
りゅうがくせい
います and あります are strictly for descriptions of existence and location, while です is for description of an attribute of a person or a thing.

あそこに留学生がいます。　　　　　*There's an international student over there.*

(place に)	thing が	あります	
	person が	います	*There is/are . . .*

2　Describing Where Things Are

We learned in Lesson 2 that to ask for the location of item X, you can use the word どこ (where) and say X はどこですか.

マクドナルドはどこですか。　　　　*Where's McDonald's?*

In response, one can, of course, point and say:

マクドナルドは {あそこ / そこ / ここ} です。　*McDonald's is* {*over there.* / *right there near you.* / *right here.*}

In this lesson, we will learn to describe locations in more detail. More specifically, we learn to describe the location of an item relative to another item, as in "X is in front of Y." The Japanese version looks like X は Y の前です.

（マクドナルドは）あのデパートの前です。
It's in front of that department store.

Other useful words describing locations are as follows:

location words		
X は Y の {みぎ / ひだり / まえ / うしろ / なか / うえ / した / そば[4] / となり[5]} です。	*X is* {*to the right of* / *to the left of* / *in front of* / *behind* / *inside* / *on/above* / *under/beneath* / *near* / *next to*} *Y.*	
X は Y と Z のあいだです。	*X is between Y and Z.*	

銀行は図書館の<u>となり</u>です。
_{ぎんこう} _{としょかん}
The bank is next to the library.

かさはテーブルの<u>下</u>です。
_{した}
The umbrella is under the table.

レストランはデパートと病院の<u>間</u>です。
_{びょういん} _{あいだ}
The restaurant is between the department store and the hospital.

One can use any of the above location words together with a verb to describe an event that occurs in the place. To use these phrases with verbs such as 食べる and 待つ, one will need the particle で.

私はハーゲンダッツの<u>前で</u>メアリーさんを待ちました。
_{わたし} _{まえ} _ま
I waited for Mary in front of the Häagen-Dazs place.

3 Past Tense

The past tense forms of verbs look like the following, where ～ stands for the stem of a verb.

	affirmative	negative
present tense	～<u>ます</u>	～<u>ません</u>
past tense	～<u>ました</u>	～<u>ませんでした</u>

メアリーさんは九時ごろうちに帰りました。   *Mary returned home at about nine.*
_{く じ} _{かえ}

私はきのう日本語を勉強しませんでした。   *I did not study Japanese yesterday.*
_{わたし} _{に ほん ご} _{べんきょう}

The various details of formation of the long forms that we learned in Lesson 3, like the *ru*-verb/*u*-verb/irregular verb distinctions, all apply to the past tense forms as well.

---

[4]Another word for "near" that is also commonly used is ちかく.
[5]Both XはYのとなりです and XはYのよこです describe situations where two items (X and Y) are found side by side. For a となり sentence to be considered appropriate, items X and Y need to belong to the same category; two people, two buildings, and so forth. In contrast, an item can be よこ in relation to another item even if they are quite distinct.
    ○電話はトイレの<u>よこ</u>です。   *The telephone is by the restroom.*
    _{でん わ}
    ×電話はトイレの<u>となり</u>です。   (odd)
    _{でん わ}

The past tense versions of "X は Y です" sentences look like the following.

	affirmative	negative
present tense	〜です	〜じゃありません
past tense	〜でした	〜じゃありませんでした[6]

山下先生は東西大学の学生でした。
Mr. Yamashita was a student at Tozai University.

あれは日本の映画じゃありませんでした。
That was not a Japanese movie.

4　たくさん

Expressions of quantity in Japanese are rather different from those in English. In Japanese, if you want to add a quantity word like たくさん to the direct object of a sentence, you can either place it before the noun, or after the particle を.

私は京都で { 写真をたくさん / たくさん写真を } 撮りました。　*I took many pictures in Kyoto.*

{ 野菜をたくさん / たくさん野菜を } 食べました。　*I ate a lot of vegetables.*

5　一時間

The duration of an activity is expressed with a bare noun, like 一時間. Such a noun stands alone (that is, not followed by any particle) and usually appears immediately before the verb.

メアリーさんはそこでたけしさんを一時間待ちました。
Mary waited for Takeshi there for an hour.

For an approximate measurement, you can add ぐらい[7] after 〜時間.

---

[6] As was the case with the present tense じゃありません, written language would more likely have ではありませんでした, instead of the contracted form じゃありませんでした.

[7] As we learned in Lesson 3, for "at about a certain time" we have another word ごろ.

私はきのう日本語を三時間ぐらい勉強しました。
I studied Japanese for about three hours yesterday.

6 と

The particle と has two functions. One is to connect two nouns A *and* B.[8]

日本語と英語を話します。   *I speak Japanese <u>and</u> English.*

京都と大阪に行きました。   *I went to Kyoto <u>and</u> Osaka.*

The other meaning of と is "together with"; it describes *with whom* you do something.[9]

メアリーさんはスーさんと韓国に行きます。
Mary will go to Korea <u>with</u> Sue.

7 も

We learned in Lesson 2 that we use the particle も in reference to the second item which shares a common attribute with the first. You can also use も when two or more people perform the same activity.

私はきのう京都に行きました。   *I went to Kyoto yesterday.*

山下先生もきのう京都に行きました。   *Professor Yamashita went to Kyoto yesterday, too.*

Or when someone buys, sees, or eats two or more things.

メアリーさんはくつを買いました。   *Mary bought shoes.*

メアリーさんはかばんも買いました。   *Mary bought a bag, too.*

In both cases, も directly marks an item on the list of things or people that have something in common. Observe that も *replaces* the particles は, が, or を in these sentences.

You can also use も when you go to two places, do something on two different occasions, and so forth.

---

[8] You can use と to connect nouns only. We will learn about connecting verbs and sentences in Lesson 6.

[9] "With" as in "with chopsticks" requires another particle. See Lesson 10.

私は先週京都に行きました。 　　　　　　*I went to Kyoto last week.*

　　大阪にも行きました。 　　　　　　　*I went to Osaka, too.*

ロバートさんは土曜日にパーティーに行きました。

　　　　　　　　　Robert went to a party on Saturday.

　　日曜日にもパーティーに行きました。

　　　　　　　　　He went to a party on Sunday, too.

We put も *after* the particle に in these sentences. More generally, particles other than は, が, and を are used together with も, rather than being replaced by it.

表現ノート　　　　　　　　　　　Expression Notes ⑤

X の前▶ X の前 is often used in the sense of "across (the street) from X" or "opposite X." You may also hear another word that is used in the sense of across, namely, X のむかい.

If something is behind X, or farther away from a street and cannot be directly seen because of the intervening X, in addition to calling it X の後ろ, you can also describe it as being X のうら.

えっ/あっ▶ In the dialogues, we observe Mary's host father saying えっ, and her host mother saying あっ. えっ is like the incredulous "what?" that you use when you have heard something that is hard to believe. あっ is used when you have suddenly noticed or remembered something. The small っ at the end of these little words indicates that these words, when pronounced, are very short.

二時間半▶ 半 (half) appears after the unit word like 時間. Thus, "two hours and a half" is 二時間半, rather than 二半時間.

もしもし▶ もしもし is "hello," which is used only in telephone conversations. Some people use もしもし when they place a call. Some other people use it when they receive a call.

練習 Practice
れん しゅう

① 大学があります
だいがく

A. Look at the picture and tell what you see, using あります or います.

B. Answer the following questions.

1. あなたの町に日本のレストランがありますか。
   まち　にほん

2. あなたの家に猫がいますか。
   いえ　ねこ

3. あなたの学校に何がありますか。
   がっこう　なに

4. あなたの学校に日本人の学生がいますか。
   がっこう　にほんじん　がくせい

5. デパートに何がありますか。
   なに

6. この教室 (classroom) にだれがいますか。
   きょうしつ

7. 動物園 (zoo) に何がいますか。
   どうぶつえん　なに

8. あなたの国 (country) に何がありますか。
   くに　なに

9. あなたの家に何がありますか。
   いえ　なに

C. Look at Takeshi's schedule for the week and answer the following questions. 🔊

	School	After School
Monday	French English Computer	
Tuesday	History	club activity
Wednesday	French English Computer	
Thursday	History	club activity
Friday	English (TEST)	party
Saturday	NO SCHOOL	date
Sunday	NO SCHOOL	part-time job

club activity	クラブ
party	パーティー
test	テスト

Example:　Q：月曜日にフランス語のクラスがありますか。
　　　　　　A：はい、あります。

1. 月曜日に英語のクラスがありますか。
2. 火曜日にコンピューターのクラスがありますか。
3. 木曜日にフランス語のクラスがありますか。
4. 土曜日にクラスがありますか。
5. 水曜日に何がありますか。
6. 金曜日に何がありますか。
7. 日曜日に何がありますか。

D. Pair Work—Write down your next week's schedule and ask each other what plans you have on each day of the week.

Example:　A：月曜日に何がありますか。
　　　　　　B：日本語のクラスがあります。

	Your Schedule	Your Partner's Schedule
月曜日 げつようび		
火曜日 かようび		
水曜日 すいようび		
木曜日 もくようび		
金曜日 きんようび		
土曜日 どようび		
日曜日 にちようび		

Ⅱ 図書館はどこですか
としょかん

A. Look at the picture and tell where the following things are.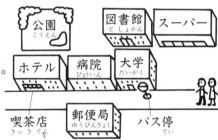

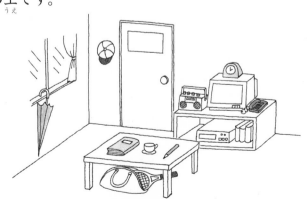

Example: 図書館
としょかん
→ 図書館は大学の後ろです。
としょかん　だいがく　うし
図書館はスーパーのとなりです。
としょかん

1. 郵便局　　　2. 喫茶店　　　3. バス停
ゆうびんきょく　　きっさてん　　　てい

4. 公園　　　　5. スーパー　　　6. 病院
こうえん　　　　　　　　　　　びょういん

B. Look at the picture and tell where the following things are.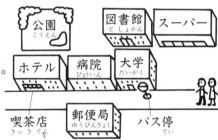

Example: 本　→　本はつくえの上です。
ほん　　　ほん　　　うえ

1. えんぴつ

2. ラケット (racket)

3. 時計
とけい

4. 電話
でんわ

5. かばん

6. ぼうし

C. Pair Work—Ask and answer questions to find where the buildings are.
One student looks at map A. The other student looks at map B (p. 93). Don't
look at the other's map.

Example:　A：公園はどこですか。
　　　　　　　　こうえん
　　　　　　B：公園はホテルのとなりです。
　　　　　　　　こうえん

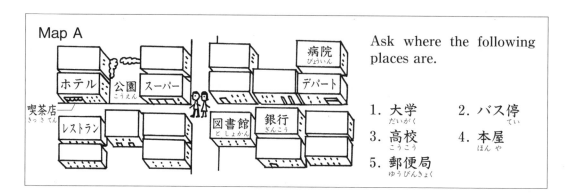

Map A

Ask where the following places are.

1. 大学
　　だいがく
2. バス停
　　　　てい
3. 高校
　　こうこう
4. 本屋
　　ほん や
5. 郵便局
　　ゆうびんきょく

Ⅲ 先生は二十二歳でした
　　　　せんせい　　にじゅうにさい

A. Look at the information about Prof. Yamashita 25 years ago and answer the
questions.

Twenty-five years ago, Prof. Yamashita was
　　　twenty-two years old
　　　senior at a college
　　　good student
　　　his major—Japanese history

Example:

　Q：山下先生は大学生 (college student) でしたか。
　　　やましたせんせい　　だいがくせい
　A：はい、山下先生は大学生でした。
　　　　　　やましたせんせい　　だいがくせい

　Q：山下先生は十九歳でしたか。
　　　やましたせんせい　　じゅうきゅうさい
　A：いいえ、山下先生は十九歳じゃありませんでした。
　　　　　　　　やましたせんせい　　じゅうきゅうさい

1. 山下先生は子供でしたか。
　　やましたせんせい　　こども
2. 山下先生は一年生でしたか。
　　やましたせんせい　　いちねんせい
3. 山下先生はいい学生でしたか。
　　やましたせんせい　　　　がくせい
4. 山下先生の専門は英語でしたか。
　　やましたせんせい　せんもん　えいご
5. 山下先生の専門は歴史でしたか。
　　やましたせんせい　せんもん　れきし

B. Pair Work—Guessing game

Ask questions and find out the prices your partner has chosen.

1. Before you start, both of you will choose one price in each row of the table and mark it.
2. In each row, use the item and one of the four prices, make a yes-or-no-question sentence and find out which price your partner has chosen.
3. You can ask at most two questions with one item. If you have guessed correctly the price your partner has chosen, you score a point. Your partner will not give away the right answer when you ask a wrong question.
4. When you have asked questions about all the items in the table, switch roles with your partner and answer their questions.
5. Tabulate the score. You win the game if you have scored higher than your partner.

Example:　A：そのかばんは二万円でしたか。
　　　　　B：いいえ、二万円じゃありませんでした。
　　　　　A：一万五千円でしたか。
　　　　　B：はい、そうです。

かばん	￥5,000	￥10,000	￥15,000	￥20,000
かさ	￥600	￥1,000	￥1,300	￥2,000
ぼうし	￥1,600	￥2,000	￥2,400	￥3,000
トレーナー	￥3,500	￥4,000	￥6,500	￥8,000
時計	￥3,000	￥10,000	￥17,000	￥25,000

C. Pair Work—Suppose you got one thing as a birthday present and choose it from the items on the next page. Your partner guesses what you got. Answer your partner's questions.

Example:　B：プレゼントはかばんでしたか。
　　　　　A：ええ、かばんでした。
　　　　　　　いいえ、かばんじゃありませんでした。

Ⅳ 月曜日に何をしましたか
<small>げつよう び　　なに</small>

A. Change the following verbs into 〜ました and 〜ませんでした.

Example:　たべる　→　たべました

　　　　　　たべる　→　たべませんでした

1. はなす　2. かう　3. よむ　4. かく　5. くる　6. まつ　7. おきる　8. わかる

9. する　10. とる　11. ある　12. ねる　13. きく　14. かえる　15. のむ

B. The pictures below show what Mary did last week. Tell what she did.

Example:　メアリーさんは月曜日に図書館で勉強しました。
<small>　　　　　　　　　　げつよう び　　　としょかん　　べんきょう</small>

Ex. Monday　　　(1) Tuesday　　　　(2) Wednesday　　　(3) Thursday

in the library　　　at home　　　　at school　　　at a coffee shop

(4) Friday　　　　　(5) Saturday　　　　(6) Sunday

at a friend's house　　　　in Kyoto　　　at a department store

C. Look at the pictures in B and answer the questions. 🔊

Example:　Q：メアリーさんは月曜日に図書館で勉強しましたか。
　　　　　A：はい、勉強しました。
　　　　　Q：メアリーさんは月曜日に映画を見ましたか。
　　　　　A：いいえ、見ませんでした。

1. メアリーさんは火曜日に手紙を書きましたか。
2. メアリーさんは水曜日に喫茶店に行きましたか。
3. メアリーさんは木曜日に日本人の友だちに会いましたか。
4. メアリーさんは金曜日にお寺に行きましたか。
5. メアリーさんは土曜日にテニスをしましたか。
6. メアリーさんは日曜日に買い物をしましたか。

D. Look at the pictures above and answer the questions. 🔊

Example:　Q：メアリーさんは月曜日に何をしましたか。
　　　　　A：図書館で勉強しました。

1. メアリーさんは水曜日に何をしましたか。
2. メアリーさんは火曜日に何をしましたか。
3. メアリーさんはいつ映画を見ましたか。
4. メアリーさんはいつ買い物をしましたか。
5. メアリーさんは金曜日にどこで晩ごはんを食べましたか。
6. メアリーさんは木曜日にどこで友だちに会いましたか。

E. Pair Work—Ask what your partner did on Monday, Tuesday, etc.

Example:　A：月曜日に何をしましたか。
　　　　　B：テニスをしました。

Ⅴ 子供の時よく本を読みましたか

Pair Work—Using the expressions below, ask your partners how often they did the following activities when they were a child or in high school.

Example:　A：子供の時／高校の時 よく本を読みましたか。
　　　　　　B：はい、よく読みました。
　　　　　　　　いいえ、あまり読みませんでした。

1. 勉強する
2. スポーツをする
3. 映画を見る
4. 公園に行く
5. 手紙を書く
6. デートをする

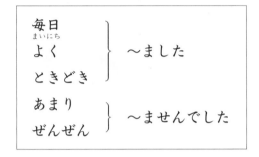

毎日
よく
ときどき ⎫ ～ました
あまり
ぜんぜん ⎫ ～ませんでした

Ⅵ コーヒーも飲みます

A. Compare sentences (a) and (b), and change sentence (b) using も。

Example:　(a) ハンバーガーは二百円です。
　　　　　　(b) コーヒーは二百円です。　→　コーヒーも二百円です。

1. (a) たけしさんは時計を買いました。
   (b) たけしさんはかばんを買いました。
2. (a) ロバートさんは日本語を勉強します。
   (b) メアリーさんは日本語を勉強します。
3. (a) たけしさんは土曜日にアルバイトをします。
   (b) たけしさんは日曜日にアルバイトをします。
4. (a) メアリーさんはうちで日本語を話します。
   (b) メアリーさんは学校で日本語を話します。
5. (a) あした、メアリーさんはたけしさんに会います。
   (b) あした、メアリーさんはスーさんに会います。
6. (a) 先週、LL に行きませんでした。
   (b) きのう、LL に行きませんでした。

B. Describe the pictures using も.

Example:　山本さんは学生です。
　　　　　　やまもと　　　　がくせい
　　　　　　田中さんも学生です。
　　　　　　たなか　　　　　がくせい

Ex.　やまもと　たなか

student

(1)

きむら　やまぐち

go to a party

(2)

ごはん　パン

(3)

コーヒー　おちゃ

(4)

I speak English　Hablo español

(5)

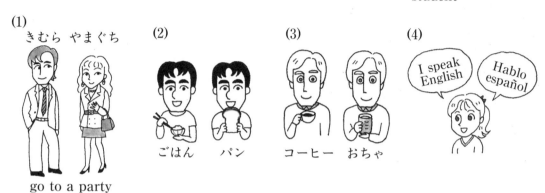

こうえん　　　　おてら

うち　　　　としょかん

(6)

(7)

どようび　　　にちようび

(8)

かようび　もくようび

(9)

とうきょう

ひろしま

Ⅶ まとめの練習 (Review Exercises)

A. Answer the following questions.

1. 毎日、何時に起きますか。
2. たいてい何時間ぐらい寝ますか。
3. 毎日、何時間勉強しますか。
4. よくだれと昼ごはんを食べますか。
5. よく友だちに手紙を書きますか。
6. 先週、スポーツをしましたか。
7. きのう、どこで晩ごはんを食べましたか。
8. 先週、写真をたくさん撮りましたか。

B. Pair Work—A and B want to play basketball together. The following is A's schedule for this week. (B's schedule is on p. 93.) Play the roles of A and B with your partner. Ask each other what the other is doing and decide on what day you will play basketball.

Example:

A：バスケット(basketball)をしま

　　せんか。

B：いいですね。

A：月曜日はどうですか。

B：月曜日は図書館で勉強します。

　　火曜日は？

A's Schedule

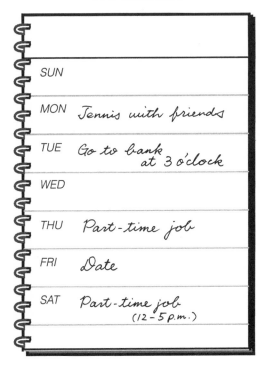

SUN	
MON	Tennis with friends
TUE	Go to bank at 3 o'clock
WED	
THU	Part-time job
FRI	Date
SAT	Part-time job (12 – 5 p.m.)

Pair Work Ⅱ C.

Example: 　A：公園はどこですか。
　　　　　　　こうえん

　　　　　　B：公園はホテルのとなりです。
　　　　　　　　こうえん

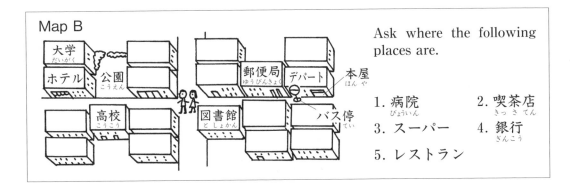

Map B

Ask where the following places are.

1. 病院　　　　2. 喫茶店
　　びょういん　　　　　きっさてん
3. スーパー　　4. 銀行
　　　　　　　　　　　　ぎんこう
5. レストラン

Pair Work Ⅶ B.

Example:

A：バスケット(basketball)をしま
　せんか。

B：いいですね。

A：月曜日はどうですか。
　　げつようび

B：月曜日は図書館で勉強します。
　　げつようび　としょかん　べんきょう
　火曜日は？
　　かようび

B's Schedule

SUN	6 p.m. Jogging
MON	Study in the library
TUE	
WED	Shopping in Osaka
THU	Dinner at friend's house
FRI	
SAT	

位置
（い）（ち）

Locations

つくえの<u>上</u>
（うえ）

つくえの<u>そば</u>

つくえの<u>下</u>
（した）

かばんの<u>中</u>
（なか）

左　　右
（ひだり）（みぎ）

← →
よこはま　とうきょう

やまださんの
<u>となり</u>

やまださんの
<u>後ろ</u>
（うし）

やまださんと
さとうさんの<u>間</u>
（あいだ）

やまださん

さとうさん

やまださんの<u>前</u>
（まえ）

日・週・月・年
ひ・しゅう・つき
Days/Weeks/Months/Years

Days

日曜日 にちようび	月曜日 げつようび	火曜日 かようび	水曜日 すいようび	木曜日 もくようび	金曜日 きんようび	土曜日 どようび
1 ついたち	**2** ふつか	**3** みっか	**4** よっか	**5** いつか	**6** むいか
7 なのか	**8** ようか	**9** ここのか	**10** とおか	**11** じゅういちにち	**12** じゅうににち	**13** じゅうさんにち
14 じゅうよっか	**15** じゅうごにち	**16** じゅうろくにち	**17** じゅうしちにち	**18** じゅうはちにち	**19** じゅうくにち	**20** はつか
21 にじゅういちにち	**22** にじゅうににち	**23** にじゅうさんにち	**24** にじゅうよっか	**25** にじゅうごにち	**26** にじゅうろくにち	**27** にじゅうしちにち
28 にじゅうはちにち	**29** にじゅうくにち	**30** さんじゅうにち	**31** さんじゅういちにち			

Months

いちがつ（一月）	—January	しちがつ（七月）	—July
にがつ（二月）	—February	はちがつ（八月）	—August
さんがつ（三月）	—March	くがつ（九月）	—September
しがつ（四月）	—April	じゅうがつ（十月）	—October
ごがつ（五月）	—May	じゅういちがつ（十一月）	—November
ろくがつ（六月）	—June	じゅうにがつ（十二月）	—December

Time Words

Day	Week	Month	Year
おとといい the day before yesterday	せんせんしゅう （先々週） the week before last	にかげつまえ （二か月前） the month before last	おととし the year before last
きのう（昨日） yesterday	せんしゅう（先週） last week	せんげつ（先月） last month	きょねん（去年） last year
きょう（今日） today	こんしゅう（今週） this week	こんげつ（今月） this month	ことし（今年） this year
あした tomorrow	らいしゅう（来週） next week	らいげつ（来月） next month	らいねん（来年） next year
あさって the day after tomorrow	さらいしゅう （再来週） the week after next	さらいげつ （再来月） the month after next	さらいねん （再来年） the year after next

第5課 LESSON ·····5

沖縄旅行 A Trip to Okinawa
おき なわ りょ こう

会話 Dialogue
かい わ

（Ⅰ）Robert and Ken are vacationing in Okinawa.

1 ロバート： いい天気ですね。
てんき

2 け ん： そうですね。でも、ちょっと暑いですね。
あつ

3 ロバート： わあ、きれいな海！
うみ

4 け ん： 泳ぎましょう。
およ

*　　　　　　*　　　　　　*

5 け ん： ロバートさんはどんなスポーツが好きですか。
す

6 ロバート： サーフィンが好きです。
す

7 　　　　　 あした一緒にやりましょうか。
いっしょ

8 け ん： でも、難しくありませんか。
むずか

9 ロバート： 大丈夫ですよ。
だいじょうぶ

（Ⅱ）At the post office.

1 ロバート： すみません。はがきは、イギリスまでいくらですか。

2 郵便局員： 七十円です。
ゆうびんきょくいん なな じゅうえん

3 ロバート： じゃあ、七十円切手を二枚お願いします。それから、五十円切手を一枚
ななじゅうえんきって にまい ねが ごじゅうえんきって いちまい

4 　　　　　 ください。

Ⅲ On Monday at school.

1 たけし：　　　ロバートさん、はがき、ありがとう。旅行は楽しかったですか。
　　　　　　　　　　　　　　　　　　　　　りょこう　たの

2 ロバート：　　ええ。沖縄の海はとてもきれいでしたよ。
　　　　　　　　　　おきなわ　うみ

3 たけし：　　　よかったですね。ぼくも海が大好きです。飛行機の切符は高かったで
　　　　　　　　　　　　　　　　　　　　うみ　だいす　　　　ひこうき　きっぷ　たか

4 　　　　　　　すか。

5 ロバート：　　いいえ、あまり高くありませんでした。たけしさんのデートはどうで
　　　　　　　　　　　　　　たか

6 　　　　　　　したか。

7 たけし：　　　……

（Ⅰ）

Robert: Nice weather.

Ken: Yes. But it is a little hot.

Robert: Wow, beautiful sea!

Ken: Let's swim.

　　　　　　　　*　　　　　*　　　　　*

Ken: What kind of sports do you like, Robert?

Robert: I like surfing. Shall we do it together tomorrow?

Ken: But isn't it difficult?

Robert: No.

（Ⅱ）

Robert: Excuse me. How much is a postcard to Britain?

Person at the post office: 70 yen.

Robert: Then, two 70-yen stamps, please. And one 50-yen stamp, please.

（Ⅲ）

Takeshi: Robert, thank you for the postcard. Did you enjoy the trip?

Robert: Yes. The sea was very beautiful in Okinawa.

Takeshi: Good. I like the sea very much, too. Was the airline ticket expensive?

Robert: No, it wasn't so expensive. How was your date, Takeshi?

Takeshi: . . .

単語
たん　ご

Vocabulary

Nouns

*	うみ	海	sea
*	きって	切手	postal stamps
*	きっぷ	切符	ticket
*	サーフィン		surfing
	しゅくだい	宿題	homework
	たべもの	食べ物	food
	たんじょうび	誕生日	birthday
	テスト		test
*	てんき	天気	weather
	のみもの	飲み物	drink
*	はがき	葉書	postcard
	バス		bus
*	ひこうき	飛行機	airplane
	へや	部屋	room
*	ぼく	僕	I (used by men)
	やすみ	休み	holiday; day off; absence
*	りょこう	旅行	travel

い-adjectives

	あたらしい	新しい	new
*	あつい	暑い	hot (weather)
	あつい	熱い	hot (objects)
	いそがしい	忙しい	busy (people/days)
	おおきい	大きい	large
	おもしろい	面白い	interesting
	こわい	怖い	frightening
	さむい	寒い	cold (weather—not used for objects)
*	たのしい	楽しい	fun
	ちいさい	小さい	small
	つまらない		boring
	ふるい	古い	old (thing—not used for people)
*	むずかしい	難しい	difficult

* Words that appear in the dialogue

やさしい		easy (problem); kind (person)
やすい	安い	inexpensive; cheap (thing)

な-adjectives

きらい(な)	嫌い	disgusted with; to dislike (〜が)
* きれい(な)		beautiful; clean
げんき(な)	元気	healthy; energetic
しずか(な)	静か	quiet
* すき(な)	好き	fond of; to like (〜が)
だいきらい(な)	大嫌い	to hate
* だいすき(な)	大好き	very fond of; to love
にぎやか(な)		lively
ハンサム(な)		handsome
ひま(な)	暇	not busy; to have a lot of free time

U-verbs

* およぐ	泳ぐ	to swim
きく	聞く	to ask (*person* に)
のる	乗る	to ride; to board (〜に)
* やる		to do; to perform (〜を)

Ru-verb

でかける	出かける	to go out

Adverbs and Other Expressions

* いっしょに	一緒に	together
* それから		and then
* だいじょうぶ	大丈夫	It's okay.; Not to worry.; Everything is under control.
とても		very
どんな		what kind of . . .
* 〜まい	〜枚	[counter for flat objects]
* 〜まで		to (a place); as far as (a place); till (a time)

文法 G r a m m a r
ぶん　ぽう

1　Adjectives

There are two types of adjectives in Japanese. One type is called "い-adjectives," and the other type "な-adjectives." い and な are their last syllables when they modify nouns.

い-adjectives:

<u>おもしろい</u>映画　*an interesting movie*
えい が

きのう、おもしろい映画を見ました。　*I saw an interesting movie yesterday.*
えい が　　み

<u>こわい</u>先生　*a scary teacher*
せんせい

山下先生はこわい先生です。　*Professor Yamashita is a scary teacher.*
やましたせんせい　　　　　せんせい

な-adjectives:

<u>きれいな</u>写真　*a beautiful picture*
しゃしん

京都できれいな写真を撮りました。　*I took a beautiful picture in Kyoto.*
きょうと　　　　　しゃしん　と

<u>元気な</u>先生　*an energetic teacher*
げん き　せんせい

山下先生は元気な先生です。　*Professor Yamashita is an energetic teacher.*
やましたせんせい　げん き　せんせい

Japanese adjectives conjugate for tense (present and past), polarity (affirmative and negative), and so forth, just as verbs do. The two types of adjectives follow different conjugation patterns.

い-adjectives　い-adjectives change shape as follows. You will want to be very careful here, because the pattern is rather complicated.

おもしろい		affirmative	negative
	present	おもしろいです	おもしろくありません
		It is interesting.	*It is not interesting.*
	past	おもしろかったです	おもしろくありませんでした
		It was interesting.	*It was not interesting.*

It is interesting (and confusing) that the idea of past tense is encoded differently in the affirmative and the negative polarities: (おもしろ)かった です is "past＋affirmative," while (おもしろ)くありません でした is "negative＋past.[1]"

Unlike verbs, adjectives conjugate fairly regularly. The only irregularity worth noticing at this stage is the behavior of the adjective いい (good). The first syllable of いい is changed to よ in all forms except the dictionary form and the long present tense affirmative form.[2]

いい (irregular)		affirmative	negative
	present	いいです	よくありません
	past	よかったです	よくありませんでした

な-adjectives   The conjugation pattern of な-adjectives is much more straightforward. It actually is exactly the same as the conjugation table of です which follows a noun, as discussed in Lesson 4.[3]

元気(な) げんき		affirmative	negative
	present	元気です げんき *She is healthy.*	元気じゃありません げんき *She is not healthy.*
	past	元気でした げんき *She was healthy.*	元気じゃありませんでした げんき *She was not healthy.*

The final syllable な is dropped in these long forms of な-adjectives.

---

[1]Some speakers follow a more regular conjugation, where です is inert in both polarities. For these speakers, the chart looks like the following:

	affimative	negative
present	〜いです	〜くないです
past	〜かったです	〜くなかったです

[2]There actually are alternate forms, よい and よいです, but they are much less frequently used than いい and いいです.

[3]As with い-adjectives, some speakers prefer an alternative paradigm, such as the following:

	affirmative	negative
present	〜です	〜じゃないです
past	〜でした	〜じゃなかったです

2　好き(な)/きらい(な)

In this lesson, we learn two な-adjectives that are very important from the grammatical point of view. They are 好き(な) (to be fond of; to like), and きらい(な) (to be disgusted with; to dislike). The meaning of these adjectives is relational, and you need two terms: a person to like or dislike something on the one hand, and a person or a thing on the other hand that is liked or disliked. In sentences, these two terms usually appear with the particles は and が, respectively.[4]

$$
\text{X は Y が} \left\{ \begin{array}{c} \text{好き} \\ \text{きらい} \end{array} \right\} \text{です。} \qquad X \left\{ \begin{array}{c} likes \\ dislikes \end{array} \right\} Y.
$$

ロバートさんは日本語のクラスが好きです。　　*Robert likes his Japanese classes.*

山下先生は魚がきらいです。　　*Professor Yamashita dislikes fish.*

The item that is liked or disliked can also be a person. You may want to be cautious using these words in reference to your preference for a specific person, however, because 好きです is usually taken to be an admission of one's *romantic* interest.[5]

Let us note three more things about 好き(な) and きらい(な) before we go on. One, if you like or dislike something (or somebody) very much, you can use the intensified forms of 好きです and きらいです, namely, 大好きです and 大きらいです. These forms are more common than the combinations of 好き(な) and きらい(な) and the degree modifier とても, to which we will turn shortly.

Two, when Japanese people want to say that they neither like nor dislike something, they usually say:

好きでもきらいでもありません。　　*I neither like nor dislike (it).*

Three, you can use 好きな and きらいな as modifiers of nouns. For example, you can say things like:

---

[4]In contexts where you are contrasting two or more items, the particle は is used instead of が. Thus, 私は野菜は好きですが、肉はきらいです。　　*I like* vegetables, *but I don't like* meat.

[5]In the expression of romantic or familial affection, the complex particle のことが can replace が. Thus, たけしさんはメアリーさんのことが好きです。　＝メアリーさんが好きです。
Takeshi is in love with Mary.

これは私の好きなテレビです。　　　*This is <u>my favorite</u> TV program.*

3　Degree Expressions

If you want to say things like "very hot," and "a little hot," you can add "degree adverbs" like とても (very) and ちょっと (a little; slightly) before adjectives.

沖縄の海はとてもきれいでした。　　　*The sea was very beautiful in Okinawa.*

この部屋はちょっと暑いです。　　　*This room is a little hot.*

Instead of having とても added to them, 好き(な) and きらい(な) have their own intensified forms, 大好き(な) (like very much) and 大きらい(な) (hate).

たけしさんはコーヒーが大好きです。
Takeshi likes coffee a lot.

キムさんはなっとうが大きらいです。
Ms. Kim hates natto (a Japanese fermented soybean delicacy).

4　〜ましょう/〜ましょうか

Take a long form of a verb and replace the ending with ましょう or ましょうか and you will get the Japanese expression for "let's . . . ," which you can use to suggest a plan of action.

一緒に図書館で勉強しましょう。
Let's study in the library together.

喫茶店でコーヒーを飲みましょうか。
Shall we drink coffee at a coffee shop?

5　Counting

There are two important things you should know about counting items in Japanese. One, we use different number words for different kinds of items; the words used for counting people are different from the words used for counting books, for example. Two, number words often come *after*, rather than *before*, the items counted in a sentence.

リーさんは　切手を　三枚　買いました。　　　*Lee bought three stamps.*
　　　　　　 item 　number

The number word, 三枚, is made up of the numeral 三 and the "counter" 枚. This counter is used for sheets of paper and other flat objects. There will be other counters in later lessons—for people, for books, for sticklike objects, and so forth.

表現ノート
ひょうげん

Expression Notes ⑥

忙しい/にぎやか(な) ▶忙しい is used when we describe people and is not
いそが   いそが
used for places. When you want to say that Tokyo is busy, you should use
にぎやか(な).

たけしさんは忙しいです。　　*Takeshi is busy.*
　　　　　　いそが
東京はにぎやかです。　　　　*Tokyo is busy/lively.*
とうきょう

Note that the sentence below is also acceptable, since the subject "I" is omitted in the sentence.

日曜日は忙しいです。　　＝日曜日は(私は)忙しいです。
にちよう び　いそが　　　　にちよう び　わたし　いそが
I am busy on Sunday.

練習 P r a c t i c e
れん　しゅう

① 高いです
たか

A. Change the following adjectives into the affirmatives. 🔊

Example:　たかい　　→　たかいです
　　　　　　げんきな　→　げんきです

　1. やすい　　　2. あつい　3. さむい　　4. おもしろい　5. つまらない
　6. いそがしい　7. いい　　8. しずかな　9. にぎやかな　10. きれいな
　11. ひまな

B. Change the following adjectives into the negatives. 🔊

Example:　やすい　→　やすくありません
　　　　　　ひまな　→　ひまじゃありません

　1. さむい　　2. ふるい　3. こわい　　4. あたらしい　5. むずかしい
　6. ちいさい　7. いい　　8. げんきな　9. しずかな　10. きれいな
　11. ハンサムな

C. Look at the pictures below and make sentences.

Example:　この時計は高いです。
　　　　　　　　と けい　たか
　　　　　　この時計は安くありません。
　　　　　　　　と けい　やす

Ex.　　　　　　　(1)　　　　　　　(2)　　　　　　　(3)

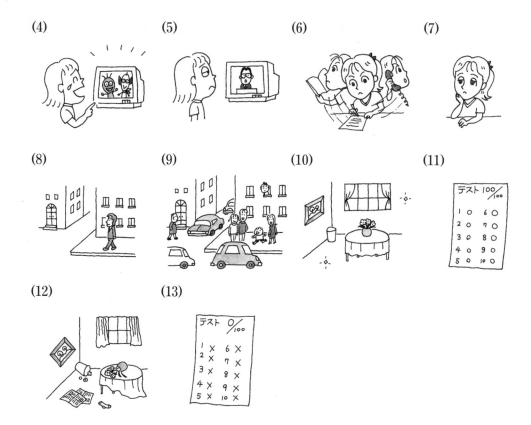

(4)　(5)　(6)　(7)

(8)　(9)　(10)　(11)

(12)　(13)

D.　Answer the following questions.

Example:　Q：日本語のクラスは難しいですか。

　　　　　A：ええ、難しいです。／いいえ、難しくありません。

1. 今日はひまですか。　　　　　2. 先生はやさしいですか。
3. 学校は大きいですか。　　　　4. 部屋はきれいですか。
5. 日本の食べ物はおいしいですか。　6. 日本の食べ物は安いですか。

E.　Pair Work—Make affirmative and negative sentences with your partner.

Example:　きれいな

　　　→　友達の部屋はきれいです。でも、私の部屋はきれいじゃあり
　　　　　ません。

1. おもしろい　　2. いい　　　　3. こわい　　　4. おいしい

5. 高い　　　　　6. ハンサムな　7. 元気な　　　8. ひまな

F. Pair Work—Make your own sentences on the topics below using adjectives, and tell your partner.

Example: テストは難しくありません。やさしいです。
むずか

1. 私は
   わたし
2. 私の町は
   わたし まち
3. 私のとなりの人は
   わたし ひと
4. 私の部屋は
   わたし へや
5. 東京は
   とうきょう
6. ハワイは

Ⅱ 高かったです
   たか

A. Change the following adjectives into the past affirmatives.

Example: たかい → たかかったです
         げんきな → げんきでした

1. やすい   2. あつい   3. さむい   4. おもしろい   5. つまらない

6. いそがしい   7. いい   8. しずかな   9. にぎやかな   10. きれいな

11. ひまな

B. Change the following adjectives into the past negatives.

Example: やすい → やすくありませんでした
         げんきな → げんきじゃありませんでした

1. たかい   2. たのしい   3. やさしい   4. つまらない   5. おおきい

6. いい   7. いそがしい   8. にぎやかな   9. しずかな   10. きれいな

11. ひまな

C. This is what Robert wrote down about the trip to Okinawa. Look at the memo and make sentences.

Example:
沖縄は暑かったです。
おきなわ あつ

| Ex. Okinawa—hot |
| 1. food—not expensive |
| 2. food—delicious |
| 3. hotel—not big |
| 4. hotel—new |
| 5. restaurant—not quiet |
| 6. sea—beautiful |
| 7. surfing—interesting |

D. Pair Work—Use the chart below and practice a dialogue with your partner, substituting the underlined parts. A and B are talking about A's vacation.

Example:　A is Robert.

→　A：休みに沖縄に行きました。
　　　やす　　おきなわ　い
　　B：そうですか。どうでしたか。
　　A：とても暑かったです。
　　　　　　あつ

Ex. Robert	went to Okinawa	very hot
(1) Mary	saw a movie	scary
(2) Takeshi	stayed home（うちにいる）	very boring
(3) Sue	went to a party	not fun
(4) Mr. Yamashita	went to flea market（フリーマーケット）	not cheap
(5) 私 わたし		

Ⅲ 高い時計ですね
たか　と けい

A. Look at the pictures and make comments on them. 🔊

Example:　時計　→　高い時計ですね。
　　　　　と けい　　　たか　と けい

Ex.

(1) ホテル

(2) テレビ

(3) 宿題
しゅくだい

(4) 人
ひと

(5) 人
ひと

(6) 町
まち

(7) 部屋
へや

B. Answer the questions using the given cues.

Example:　Q：メアリーさんはどんな人ですか。

　　　　　A：メアリーさんはやさしい人です。

Ex.　メアリー　　　　(1) スー　　　　　(2) ロバート　　　　(3) たけし

　　　kind　　　　　　beautiful　　　　interesting　　　　energetic

Ⅳ 魚が好きですか

A. Pair Work—Choose the items from the following categories and ask your partners whether they like them.

Example:　A：メアリーさんは肉が好きですか。

　　　　　B：はい、好きです／大好きです。

　　　　　　　いいえ、きらいです／大きらいです。

1. Foods: meat／なっとう (fermented beans)／ice cream（アイスクリーム）

2. Sports: aerobics（エアロビクス）／skiing（スキー）／skating（スケート）

3. Music: hard rock（ハードロック）／jazz（ジャズ）／classical music（クラシック）

4. School Work: test／Japanese class／homework

5. Drinks: sake／green tea／coffee

＊ If you neither like it nor dislike it, you can use 好きでもきらいでもありません。

B. Answer the following questions.

1. どんなスポーツが好きですか。

2. どんな食べ物が好きですか。

3. どんな飲み物が好きですか。

4. どんな映画が好きですか。

5. どんな音楽が好きですか。

Ⓥ 映画を見ましょう
えいが み

A. Change the following into ましょう sentences. 🔊

Example: 日本語を話す　→　日本語を話しましょう。
　　　　　 にほんご はな　　　　　にほんご はな

1. うちに帰る
　　　かえ
2. 先生に聞く
　　 せんせい き
3. 映画を見る
　　 えいが み
4. はがきを買う
　　　　　 か
5. 出かける
　　 で
6. 待つ
　　 ま
7. 泳ぐ
　　 およ
8. 写真を撮る
　　 しゃしん と
9. バスに乗る
　　　　　 の

B. Pair Work—Make follow-up suggestions using ましょうか.

Example: 寒いですね。
　　　　　 さむ
　　→　　A：寒いですね。お茶を飲みましょうか。
　　　　　　 さむ　　　　ちゃ の
　　　　　B：そうしましょう。

1. 暑いですね。
　　 あつ
2. 十二時ですね。
　　 じゅうに じ
3. この宿題は難しいですね。
　　　　 しゅくだい むずか
4. あしたは先生の誕生日ですよ。
　　　　　　 せんせい たんじょうび
5. あのレストランはおいしいですよ。
6. あしたはテストがありますね。

Ⅵ まとめの練習　(Review Exercises)
れんしゅう

A. Pair Work—Ask your partner the following questions.

1. Were you busy last week?
2. Were you fine last week?
3. Was your high school big/old?
4. Was your watch expensive?
5. Is your bag new?
6. Is your room small/clean?
7. Is your teacher kind?

B. Class Activity—Show and tell

Bring pictures you took on a trip. Explain to your class where you went, what you did, how it was, etc. And later, other students will ask in detail about the trip.

Example questions:

どこに行きましたか。

天気はどうでしたか。

だれと行きましたか。

飛行機の切符はいくらでしたか。

C. Role Play—Using Dialogue Ⅱ as a model, buy some stamps and postcards.

郵便局で
ゆうびんきょく

At the Post Office

Useful Expressions

これ、お願いします。————————— *Can you take care of this, please?*
　　　ねが

五十円切手を三枚ください。————— *Give me three 50-yen stamps, please.*
ごじゅうえんきって　さんまい

（航空便）でお願いします。————— *Make this (an airmail), please.*
こうくうびん　　ねが

何日ぐらいかかりますか。————— *How many days will it take?*
なんにち

百五十円になります。————————— *It will be 150 yen.*
ひゃくごじゅうえん

あと百円です。————————————— *Another 100 yen, please.*
ひゃくえん

Useful Vocabulary

窓口————————counter	切手————————stamp
まどぐち	きって
はがき————————postcard	エアログラム—aerogramme
小包————————parcel	封書————————letter
こづつみ	ふうしょ
航空便————————airmail	船便————————surface mail
こうくうびん	ふなびん
保険————————insurance	速達————————special delivery
ほけん	そくたつ
書留————————registered mail	
かきとめ	

Stamps

Postcard

写真屋で
しゃしんや

A t a P h o t o S h o p

Customer :	すみません。焼き増しお願いします。
	や ま ねが
	Excuse me. I'd like a reprint, please.

Shop clerk :	はい。光沢ありでよろしいですか。
	こうたく
	Certainly. Would the glossy finish be all right?

Customer :	はい。
	Yes.

Shop clerk :	ここに名前と電話番号をお願いします。
	なまえ でんわばんごう ねが
	Please fill in your name and telephone number here.

Customer :	いつできますか。
	When will it be ready?

Shop clerk :	仕上がりは十五日の三時です。
	し あ じゅうごにち さんじ
	It will be ready at three o'clock on the 15th.
	この引き換え券を持ってきてください。
	ひ か けん も
	Please bring this receipt.

Customer :	わかりました。じゃ、お願いします。
	ねが
	All right. Thank you.

Shop clerk :	ありがとうございました。
	Thank you very much.

Useful Vocabulary

焼き増し———————reprint
や ま

現像————————development
げんぞう

光沢あり——————glossy finish
こうたく

光沢なし——————mat finish
こうたく

パノラマ——————panoramic

スライド——————slide

プリント——————print

仕上がり——————date/time something is ready
し あ

24枚撮り—————24-print roll
まいど

使い捨てカメラ——disposable camera
つか す

ネガ———————negative

フィルム—————film

電池————————battery
でんち

引き換え券————receipt
ひ か けん

第6課 | L E S S O N ……6

ロバートさんの一日 A Day in Robert's Life

会話 Dialogue 🔊

Ⅰ In the class.

1 山下先生： ロバートさん、次のページを読んでください。

2 ロバート： ……

3 山下先生： ロバートさん、起きてください。クラスで寝てはいけませんよ。

4 ロバート： 先生、教科書を忘れました。

5 山下先生： 教科書を持ってきてくださいね。毎日使いますから。

6 ロバート： はい、すみません。

Ⅱ After class.

1 スー： ロバートさん、今日は大変でしたね。

2 ロバート： ええ。後でスーさんのノートを借りてもいいですか。

3 スー： ええ、いいですよ。

4 ロバート： ありがとう。すぐ返します。

5 スー： ロバートさん、あしたテストがありますよ。

6 ロバート： えっ。本当ですか。

7 スー： ええ。ロバートさん、金曜日に休みましたからね。

8 ロバート： じゃあ、今日は家に帰って、勉強します。

Ⅲ On the bus.

1 おばあさん： あの、すみません。このバスは市民病院へ行きますか。

2 ロバート： ええ、行きますよ……あの、おばあさん、どうぞ座ってください。

3 おばあさん： いいえ、けっこうです。すぐ降りますから。

4 ロバート：　　そうですか。じゃあ、荷物を持ちましょうか。

5 おばあさん：　あ、どうもすみません。

Ⅰ

Prof. Yamashita: Robert, please read the next page.

Robert: . . .

Prof. Yamashita: Robert, please wake up. You cannot sleep in the class.

Robert: Mr. Yamashita, I forgot to bring the textbook.

Prof. Yamashita: Please bring your textbook with you. We use it everyday.

Robert: I understand. I'm sorry.

Ⅱ

Sue: Robert, you had a hard time today.

Robert: Yes. May I borrow your notebook later, Sue?

Sue: Yes.

Robert: Thank you. I'll return it soon.

Sue: Robert, we will have a test tomorrow.

Robert: Really?

Sue: Yes. You were absent from the class last Friday. (That's why you didn't know about it.)

Robert: Well then, I'll go home and study today.

Ⅲ

Old woman: Excuse me. Does this bus go to the city hospital?

Robert: Yes, it does. Take this seat, ma'am.

Old woman: No, thank you. I'll get off soon.

Robert: Is that so? Then, shall I carry your bag?

Old woman: Thank you.

単語
たん ご

Vocabulary

Nouns

おかね	お金	money
* おばあさん		grandmother; old woman
おふろ	お風呂	bath
かんじ	漢字	kanji; Chinese character
* きょうかしょ	教科書	textbook
こんしゅう	今週	this week
* しみんびょういん	市民病院	Municipal Hospital
* つぎ	次	next
テレビゲーム		video game
でんき	電気	electricity
でんしゃ	電車	train
* にもつ	荷物	baggage
* ページ		page
まど	窓	window
よる	夜	night
らいしゅう	来週	next week
らいねん	来年	next year

な-adjective

* たいへん（な）	大変	tough (situation)

U-verbs

あそぶ	遊ぶ	to play; to spend time pleasantly
いそぐ	急ぐ	to hurry
おふろにはいる	お風呂に入る	to take a bath
* かえす	返す	to return (things) (*person* に *thing* を)
けす	消す	to turn off; to erase （〜を）
しぬ	死ぬ	to die
* すわる	座る	to sit down (*seat* に)
たつ	立つ	to stand up
たばこをすう	たばこを吸う	to smoke
* つかう	使う	to use （〜を）
てつだう	手伝う	to help (*person/task* を)

* Words that appear in the dialogue

はいる	入る	to enter （～に）
* もつ	持つ	to carry; to hold （～を）
* やすむ	休む	(1) to be absent (from . . .) （～を）
		(2) to rest

Ru-verbs

あける	開ける	to open (something) （～を）
おしえる	教える	to teach; to instruct (*person* に *thing* を)
* おりる	降りる	to get off （～を）
* かりる	借りる	to borrow (*person* に *thing* を)
しめる	閉める	to close (something) （～を）
つける		to turn on （～を）
でんわをかける	電話をかける	to make a phone call (*person* に)
* わすれる	忘れる	to forget; to leave behind （～を）

Irregular Verbs

| つれてくる | 連れてくる | to bring (a person) （～を） |
| * もってくる | 持ってくる | to bring (a thing) （～を） |

Adverbs and Other Expressions

* あとで	後で	later on
おそく	遅く	(do something) late
* ～から		because . . .
* けっこうです	結構です	That would be fine.; That wouldn't be necessary.
* すぐ		right away
* ほんとうですか	本当ですか	Really?
ゆっくり		slowly; leisurely; unhurriedly

文 法 G r a m m a r
ぶん ぼう

1 Te-form

The main topic of this lesson is a new conjugation of verbs called the "*te*-form." *Te*-forms are a *very* important part of Japanese grammar. In this lesson, we will learn, among their various uses, to use them in:

- making requests (". . . , please.")
- giving and asking for permission ("You may . . ./May I . . .")
- stating that something is forbidden ("You must not . . .")
- forming a sentence that describes two events or activities. ("I did this and did that.")

The conjugation paradigm of *te*-forms is fairly complex, as we need to learn separate rules for *ru*-, *u*-, and irregular verbs. Furthermore, the rule for *u*-verbs is divided into five subrules.

First, with *ru*-verbs, the rule is very simple: Take る off and add て.

ru-verbs
食べる → 食べて
た　　　　た

U-verbs come in several groups, based on the final syllable of their dictionary forms.

u-verbs with final う, つ, and る[1]
会う → 会って
あ　　　あ
待つ → 待って
ま　　　ま

---

[1]As we discussed in Lesson 3, some verbs that end with the *hiragana* る are *ru*-verbs and some others are *u*-verbs. The rule of thumb for determining which verb is which is to examine the vowel before the final る syllable. If the vowel is *a*, *o*, or *u*, the verb, without any exceptions, is an *u*-verb. If the vowel is either *i* or *e*, the verb can be either an *u*-verb or a *ru*-verb. Statistically speaking, there are many more *ru*-verbs, than *u*-verbs in the *iru* and *eru* camp, but there are many important verbs in the minority, such as 入る (to enter), and 帰る (to return).
はい　　　　　　　　　　　　かえ

$$\left.\begin{array}{l} \ldots \textit{aru} \\ \ldots \textit{oru} \\ \ldots \textit{uru} \end{array}\right\} = \text{always } \textit{u}\text{-verbs} \qquad \left.\begin{array}{l} \ldots \textit{iru} \\ \ldots \textit{eru} \end{array}\right\} = \text{often, but not always, } \textit{ru}\text{-verbs}$$

As far as *te*-forms are concerned, we observe that *u*-verbs that end with る will have a small つ, *ru*-verbs that end with る do not.

とる → とって

u-verbs with final む, ぶ, and ぬ

読む → 読んで
遊ぶ → 遊んで
死ぬ → 死んで

u-verbs with final く

書く → 書いて

There is an important exception in this class:

行く → 行って

u-verbs with final ぐ

泳ぐ → 泳いで

u-verbs with final す

話す → 話して

The irregular verbs する and くる, and compound verbs built with them, conjugate as follows.

irregular verbs

する → して
くる → きて

Note that *te*-forms and stems (the forms you find before ます) are totally different constructs in the *u*-verb camp. A common mistake is to assume that the simple paradigm provided by the *ru*-verbs (食べて and 食べます) covers the *u*-verbs also, thus coming up with unwarranted forms such as ×会いて (see 会います) and ×読みて (see 読みます). It is probably easier, at this stage of learning, to memorize each verb as a set, as in 書く—書きます—書いて, than to apply the conjugation rules on the spot. Refer to the verb conjugation table at the end of this volume.

2 ～てください

Use a verbal *te*-form together with ください to make a polite request to another person "please do . . . for me.[2]"

教科書のテープを聞いてください。
Please listen to the tape that goes with the textbook.

すみません。ちょっと教えてください。
Excuse me. Please teach me a little. (= Tell me, I need your advice.)

3 ～てもいいです／～てはいけません

A verbal *te*-form plus もいいです means "you may do . . . ," which describes an activity that is permitted. To ask for permission, you can turn it into a question sentence, ～てもいいですか.

教科書を見てもいいですか。　　　　*May I see the textbook?*

はい、見てもいいですよ。　　　　*Yes, you may.*

To deny somebody permission to do something, you can use the *te*-form plus はいけません.

いいえ、教科書を見てはいけません。　*No, you may not see the textbook.*

4 Describing Two Activities

You can use a *te*-form if you want to combine two or more verbs, as in describing a sequence of events or actions ("I did this and then I did that"). In other words, the *te*-form does the work of "and" with verbs. (Note that two verbs cannot be joined by と, which only connects nouns.)

ノートを借りて、コピーします。
I will borrow her notebook and xerox it.

---

[2] If you are talking to a very close friend or a member of your family, a *te*-form, by itself, can be used as a request.

窓を開けて。　　　*Open the window, will you?*

今日は、六時に起きて、勉強しました。
Today I got up at six and studied.

食堂に行って、昼ごはんを食べましょう。
Let's go to the cafeteria and have lunch.

The *te*-form of a verb can also be used to connect a verb more "loosely" with the rest of a sentence. In the first example below, the verb in the *te*-form describes the manner in which the action described by the second verb is performed. In the second example, the *te*-form describes the situation for which the apology is made.

バスに乗って、会社に行きます。
I go to work by bus. (I take a bus to work.)

教科書を忘れて、すみません。
I am sorry for not bringing in the textbook. (I left the book at home, and I am sorry.)

5   〜から

A sentence that ends with から (because) explains the reason or the cause of a situation, a proposal, and so forth.

> (situation)。(explanation) から。[3]

私は今晩勉強します。あしたテストがありますから。
I will study this evening. (Because) we will have an exam tomorrow.

バスに乗りましょう。タクシーは高いですから。
Let's go by bus. (Because) taxis are expensive.

6   〜ましょうか

In Lesson 5 we learned ましょうか meaning "let's . . . ." ましょうか is also used in the sense of "let me do . . . ," in offering assistance. If you see somebody having a hard time opening the lid of a bottle, for example, you can offer help by saying:

（私が）やりましょうか。   *I'll do it.*

---

[3]The explanation clause may also precede the situation clause. Thus the first example above can also be paraphrased as :

   あしたテストがありますから、私は今晩勉強します。
We will discuss this further in Lesson 9.

Or to a person who is carrying a heavy bag:

荷物を持ちましょうか。　　　　　*Shall I carry your bag?*
に もつ　 も

表現ノート
ひょうげん

遅く/遅い▶ Although both 遅い and 遅く mean "late," they have different
おそ　おそ　　　　　　　　　　　　　　　おそ　　　　　　　おそ
usages, since 遅い is an adjective and 遅く is an adverb. 遅い modifies nouns
　　　　　　　おそ　　　　　　　　　　　　おそ　　　　　　　　　おそ
or works as a predicate, and 遅く modifies verbs.
　　　　　　　　　　　　　　　おそ

    A: きのう一時に寝ました。　　*I went to bed at one o'clock yesterday.*
　　　　　　いちじ　ね
    B: 遅いですね。　　　　　　　*It's late.*
　　　　おそ

    週末には、十時ごろ起きて、遅い朝ごはんを食べます。
　　しゅうまつ　　じゅうじ　　お　　　おそ　あさ　　　た
                      On weekends, I get up around 10:00
                      and eat late breakfast.

    きのう、遅く寝ました。　　　*I went to bed late yesterday.*
　　　　　おそ　ね

You can also apply this rule to 早く／早い.
　　　　　　　　　　　　　　　　　はや　　はや

どうも▶ どうも is normally used with ありがとう, as in どうもありがとう
(Thank you very much), or with すみません, as in どうもすみません (I am
very sorry/Thank you very much). When used alone, it is an abbreviation
of どうもありがとう or どうもすみません. Therefore, when you want to show
your gratitude or regret, you can just say どうも instead of saying a long
sentence. どうも functions in many ways, depending on the situation. Some
people use どうも as "hello" or "good-bye."

お▶ Many words that begins with お can also be used without it. お in such
words simply adds smoothness and nuance of social refinement, without
changing the meaning of the words.

    Example： お酒　　お金　　お風呂
　　　　　　　　　　さけ　　　かね　　　ふろ

練習 Practice
れん しゅう

I 窓を開けてください
まど あ

A. Change the following verbs into *te*-forms. 🔊

Example: おきる → おきて

1. たべる　2. かう　　3. よむ　　4. かく　　5. くる　　6. まつ

7. あそぶ　8. とる　　9. する　　10. いそぐ　11. いく　　12. ねる

13. しぬ　14. はなす　15. かえる

B. Let's sing a *te*-form song!　(Battle Hymn of the Republic) 🔊

♪1.　あう　あって　まつ　まって　とる　とって
　　よむ　よんで　あそぶ　あそんで　しぬ　しんで
　　かく　かいて　けす　けして　いそぐ　いそいで
　　みんな　*u*-verb　*te*-form

♪2.　うつる　って　むぶぬ　んで　く　いて　ぐ　いで

　　(repeat twice)

　　す　して　*u*-verb　*te*-form

C. What will you say when you want someone to do the following things? 🔊

Example: to speak slowly　→　ゆっくり話してください。
はな

1. to call you tomorrow　　　2. to write a letter

3. to open the window　　　4. to drink tea

5. to teach you kanji　　　6. to bring a drink

7. to wait for you　　　8. to come with you

9. to go to a hospital　　　10. to return your book

11. to bring a friend　　　12. to stand up

D. What would you say in the following situations?

Example: 窓を開けてください。
まど　あ

Ex.　　　　　(1)　　　　　(2)

(3)　　　　　(4)　　　　　(5)

E. Pair Work—Make your own request, such as "Please stand up" and "Please take a picture," and ask your partner to act it out.

Example:　A：コーヒーを飲んでください。　→　B pretends to drink coffee.
の

Ⅱ テレビを見てもいいですか／テレビを見てはいけません
み　　　　　　　　　　　み

A. You are staying with a host family. Ask your host family for permission to do the following things. 🔊

Example:　テレビを見る　→　テレビを見てもいいですか。
み　　　　　　　　　　　み

1. たばこを吸う
す
2. 電話をかける
でんわ
3. 朝、お風呂に入る
あさ　ふろ　はい

4. 遅く帰る
おそ　かえ
5. 友だちを連れてくる
とも　つ
6. 音楽を聞く
おんがく　き

7. 夜、出かける
よる　で
8. テレビゲームをする

B. What would you say in the following situations? Make sentences with ～てもいいですか.

1. You are in class. You realize you need to go to the bathroom as soon as possible.
2. You are in class. You feel sick and want to return home.
3. You have forgotten to do the homework. You are sure you can bring it in tomorrow.
4. You want to ask your teacher something, but you cannot phrase it in Japanese.
5. You want to smoke in a coffee shop, and there is someone sitting nearby.
6. You are at a friend's house，and suddenly remember that you need to make a phone call.
7. You have run into a celebrity. Conveniently, you have a camera with you.
8. You have arrived at a classroom. The air is stuffy.
9. You and your friend are in a dark room, and you feel somewhat uncomfortable.

C. You are a strict parent. Tell your child not to do the following things using the cues in A.

Example: テレビを見る　→　テレビを見てはいけません。

D. Tell the class what we can and can't do at school and at a host family's house.

Example: 学校でたばこを吸ってはいけません。
ホストファミリー (host family) のうちで朝お風呂に入ってもいいです。

Ⅲ 朝起きて、コーヒーを飲みます

A. Look at the pictures below and combine the pictures using *te*-forms.

Example: 朝起きて、コーヒーを飲みます。

(2)

(3)

(4)

(5)

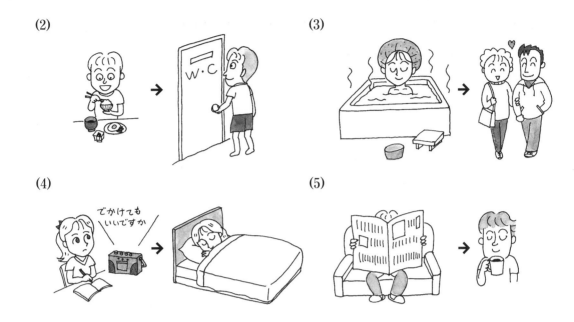

B. Change the following into *te*-forms and make the rest of the sentences.

Example: 朝起きる　→　朝起きて、新聞を読みます。
　　　　　あさお　　　　　あさお　　　しんぶん　よ

1. 友だちのうちに行く　　2. うちに帰る　　　　3. 電車を降りる
　とも　　　　　　　い　　　　　　かえ　　　　　　でんしゃ　お
4. 友だちに会う　　　　　5. お風呂に入る　　　6. 大学に行く
　とも　　　あ　　　　　　　　ふ　ろ　はい　　　だいがく　い

Ⅳ バスに乗ります。時間がありませんから。
　　　　　　の　　　　　じかん

A. Add reasons to the following sentences.

Example: バスに乗ります。　→　バスに乗ります。時間がありませんから。
　　　　　　　　の　　　　　　　　　　の　　　　　じかん

1. 先週は大変でした。　　　　　　2. あの映画を見ません。
　せんしゅう　たいへん　　　　　　　えいが　み
3. あのレストランに行きました。　4. きのうクラスを休みました。
　　　　　　　　　い　　　　　　　　　　　　　　やす
5. (name of a friend) が大好きです。
　　　　　　　　　　　だい す

B. Pair Work—Ask each other why you think the following.

Example: 朝ごはんを食べません。
→ Ａ：私は朝ごはんを食べません。
Ｂ：どうしてですか。
Ａ：あまりお金がありませんから。Ｂさんは？
Ｂ：私も朝ごはんを食べません。朝、忙しいですから。

1. 今週は大変です。
2. あしたはひまです。
3. 週末、（name of a movie）を見ます。
4. きのう、（name of a restaurant）に行きました。
5. お金がぜんぜんありません。
6. 来年は日本語を勉強しません。
7. 来週、（name of a place）に行きます。
8. 自転車を買います。

Ⓥ テレビを消しましょうか

Pair Work—Propose to do the following things, using ましょうか.

Example: テレビを消す
→ Ａ：テレビを消しましょうか。
Ｂ：すみません。お願いします。／いいえ、けっこうです。

1. 窓を開ける
2. テレビをつける
3. 手伝う
4. 先生に聞く
5. 電話をかける
6. 荷物を持つ
7. 飲み物を持ってくる
8. 電気を消す
9. 写真を撮る
10. 窓を閉める

Ⅵ まとめの練習 (Review Exercises)

A. Role Play—Play the roles of A and B with your partner.

Example:

Example-A	Example-B
You are short of money and want to borrow some money from your friend.	You are going on a trip tomorrow. You don't have money to lend to your friend.

A：すみませんが、お金を借りてもいいですか。

B：お金ですか。どうして。

A：あしたは友だちの誕生日ですから。

B：でも、私もお金がありません。あした、旅行に行きますから。

(1)

1-A	1-B
You have a date tomorrow and want to borrow a car from your friend.	You just bought a brand-new car and don't want anyone to use it.

(2)

2-A	2-B
You lost your Japanese textbook, but you need to study for a test tomorrow.	You have a big test in Japanese and need your textbook to prepare for the test.

(3)

3-A	3-B
You are asked to return your friend's video today, but you forgot to bring it. You want to return it tomorrow.	You asked your friend to return your video today. You need it today because you want to watch it together with another friend.

(4)

4-A	4-B
You are now in your friend's house. You see a cake that looks very delicious. You love cakes.	You just baked a cake for your mother's birthday. Your friend is in your house now.

B. Answer the following questions.

1. 今週の週末、何をしますか。　　（Answer with "〜て、〜。"）
2. 子供の時、よく何をしましたか。　　（Answer with "〜て、〜。"）
3. 図書館で何をしてはいけませんか。
4. 電車の中でたばこを吸ってもいいですか。
5. 大学に何を持ってきますか。
6. よく電車に乗りますか。
7. 先週、宿題を忘れましたか。
8. 子供の時、どこで遊びましたか。
9. 子供の時、よくお母さんを手伝いましたか。
10. 図書館でよく本を借りますか。
11. よくクラスを休みますか。

道を聞く／教える
みち　き　　おし

Directions

Useful Expressions

まっすぐ行く
い

(go straight)

右に曲がる
みぎ　ま

(turn right)

左に曲がる
ひだり　ま

(turn left)

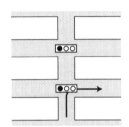

一つ目の信号を右に曲がる
ひと　め　しんごう　みぎ　ま

(turn right at the first signal)

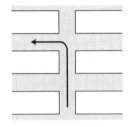

二つ目の角を左に曲がる
ふた　め　かど　ひだり　ま

(turn left at the second corner)

道を渡る
みち　わた

(cross the street)

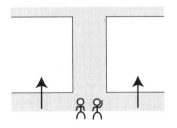

道の左側　　　道の右側
みち　ひだりがわ　　みち　みぎがわ

(left side of the street)　(right side of the street)

Directions

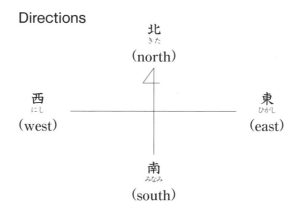

北
きた
(north)

西
にし
(west)

東
ひがし
(east)

南
みなみ
(south)

*　　　　　　*　　　　　　*

A：すみません。郵便局はどこですか。
　　ゆうびんきょく
Excuse me, where is a post office?

B：まっすぐ行って、三つ目の角を右に曲がって
　　　　い　　　　みっ　め　かど　みぎ　ま
　　ください。郵便局は道の右側にありますよ。
　　　　　　ゆうびんきょく　みち　みぎがわ
*Go straight and turn right at the third
corner. The post office is on the right
side of the street.*

A：どうもありがとうございます。
Thank you very much.

第7課 | L E S S O N ·····················7

家族の写真 Family Picture
かぞく　しゃしん

会話 D i a l o g u e 〔)))

Ⅰ Sue is showing a picture of her family to her roommate, Michiko.

1 みちこ： これはスーさんの家族の写真ですか。
かぞく　しゃしん

2 スー： ええ。

3 みちこ： スーさんはどれですか。

4 スー： これです。高校の時はめがねをかけていました。
こうこう　とき

5 みちこ： かわいいですね。

6 スー： これは父です。
ちち

7 アメリカの会社に勤めています。
かいしゃ　つと

8 みちこ： 背が高くて、ハンサムですね。
せ　たか

9 これはお姉さんですか。
ねえ

10 スー： ええ。姉は結婚しています。
あね　けっこん

11 今ソウルに住んでいます。
いま　す

12 子供が一人います。三歳です。
こども　ひとり　さんさい

13 みちこ： そうですか。あっ、猫がいますね。
ねこ

14 でも、ちょっと太っていますね。
ふと

15 スー： ええ、よく食べますから。
た

Ⅱ A phone rings in Sue and Michiko's room.

1 ロバート： みちこさん、今何をしていますか。
いまなに

2 みちこ： 別に何もしていません。今、スーさんの写真を見ています。
べつ　なに　いま　しゃしん　み

3 ロバート： そうですか。おもしろいビデオがありますから、よかったら見に来ま
み　き

4 せんか。

5 みちこ： いいですね。スーさんも一緒に行ってもいいですか。
いっしょ　い

6 ロバート： もちろん。

7 みちこ： じゃあ、すぐ行きます。

Ⅰ

Michiko: Is this your family picture, Sue?

Sue: Yes.

Michiko: Which is you?

Sue: This. I was wearing glassses when I was in high school.

Michiko: You are cute.

Sue: This is my father. He works for an American company.

Michiko: He is tall and handsome. Is this your elder sister?

Sue: Yes. My sister is married. She lives in Seoul now. She has one child. He is three years old.

Michiko: I see. Oh, there is a cat. But he is a little fat.

Sue: Yes, because he eats a lot.

Ⅱ

Robert: Michiko, what are you doing now?

Michiko: I'm not doing anything especially. I am looking at Sue's pictures.

Robert: I see. I have an interesting video, so if you like, would you like to come to see it?

Michiko: That sounds good. Is it all right if Sue comes with me?

Robert: Of course.

Michiko: We'll come right now.

単語
たんご

Vocabulary ▣))

Nouns

*	あね	姉	(my) older sister
	アパート		apartment
	いもうと	妹	younger sister
	うた	歌	song
	おとうと	弟	younger brother
	おとこのひと	男の人	man
	おにいさん	お兄さん	older brother
*	おねえさん	お姉さん	older sister
	おんなのひと	女の人	woman
*	かいしゃ	会社	company
*	かぞく	家族	family
	かみ	髪	hair
	きょうだい	兄弟	brothers and sisters
	くに	国	country; place of origin
	くるま	車	car
	コンビニ		convenience store
	しょくどう	食堂	cafeteria; dining commons
*	ちち	父	(my) father
	Tシャツ ティー		T-shirt
	め	目	eye
*	めがね	眼鏡	glasses

い-adjectives

	あたまがいい	頭がいい	bright; smart; clever (conjugates like いい)
	かっこいい		great-looking (conjugates like いい)
*	かわいい		cute
*	せがたかい	背が高い	tall
	せがひくい	背が低い	short (stature)
	ながい	長い	long
	はやい	速い	fast
	みじかい	短い	short (length)

* Words that appear in the dialogue

な-adjectives

しんせつ（な）	親切	kind
べんり（な）	便利	convenient

U-verbs

うたう	歌う	to sing
かぶる		to put on (a hat)
しる	知る	to get to know
しっています	知っています	I know
しりません	知りません	I do not know
* すむ	住む	to live　（〜にすんでいます）
はく		to put on (items below your waist)
* ふとる	太る	to gain weight
ふとっています	太っています	to be on the heavy side

Ru-verbs

* （めがねを）かける		to put on (glasses)
きる	着る	to put on (clothes above your waist)
* つとめる	勤める	to work for （〜につとめています）
やせる		to lose weight
やせています		to be thin

Irregular Verb

* けっこんする	結婚する	to get married　（〜と）

Adverbs and Other Expressions

が		but
* なにも ＋ negative	何も	not . . . anything
〜にん	〜人	[counter for people]
* ひとり	一人	one person
ふたり	二人	two people
* べつに ＋ negative	別に	not . . . in particular
* もちろん		of course
* よかったら		if you like

文法 G r a m m a r
ぶん ぽう

1 〜ている

A verbal "*te*-form," when followed by the helping verb いる, means either of the following:[1]

(a) *an action in progress,* or
(b) *a past event that is connected with the present.*

Which of these two senses a given verb is used in is to a large extent determined by the semantic characteristics of the verb. The verbs we have learned so far can be roughly divided into three groups based on their semantics.

(1) verbs that describe continuous *states*
(2) verbs that describe *activities* that last for some time
(3) verbs that describe *changes* that are more or less instantaneous

We have not seen many Group 1 verbs. So far we only have ある and いる. The *te*-forms of these verbs are never used together with the helping verb いる, so we will have nothing to say about them in this section.

Many verbs belong to Group 2. They include verbs such as 食べる, 読む, and 待つ. When
た　　　よ　　　　　ま
the *te*-form of a verb in this group is followed by the helping verb いる, we have a sentence describing *an action in progress.*

スーさんは今勉強しています。　　　*Sue is studying right now.*
　　　　いまべんきょう

たけしさんは英語の本を読んでいます。　　*Takeshi is reading a book in English.*
　　　　　　えいご　ほん　よ

You can also use a 〜ています sentence to describe what a person does by occupation. The first example below therefore has two interpretations: one, you are teaching English right at this moment; and two, you are an English language teacher (but are not necessarily in class right now).

---

[1]The distinction between いる and ある that we learned in Lesson 4 does not apply to this helping verb 〜ている: you can use 〜ている both for living things and for inanimate objects.

私は英語を教えています。
わたし　えいご　おし
I teach English. / I am teaching English (right now).

メアリーさんは日本語を勉強しています。
　　　　　　　にほんご　　べんきょう
Mary studies Japanese. / Mary is studying Japanese (right now).

Verbs in Group 3 describe changes from one state to another. If you get married, or 結婚
する, for example, your status changes from being single to being married. With these
verbs,[2] ている indicates a past occurrence of a change which has retained its significance
until the present moment. In other words, ている describes *the result of a change*.[3]

山下先生は結婚しています。　　　　　　　*Professor Yamashita is married.*[4]
やましたせんせい　けっこん

みちこさんは窓のそばに座っています。　　*Michiko is seated near the window.*
　　　　　　　まど　　　　すわ

Here are some more examples of verbs that are commonly used in the 〜ている frame-
work.

持つ も	→	持っている も (has)	スーさんはお金をたくさん持っています。 かね　　　　　　　　　　も *Sue has a lot of money.*
知る し	→	知っている し (knows)	山下先生は英語を知っています。 やましたせんせい　えいご　し *Professor Yamashita knows English.*
太る ふと	→	太っている ふと (is overweight)	トムさんはちょっと太っています。 ふと *Tom is a little overweight.*
やせる	→	やせている (is thin)	私の弟はとてもやせています。 わたし　おとうと *My younger brother is very thin.*

---

[2]Among the verbs we have learned so far, verbs such as 起きる, 行く, 帰る, 来る, わかる, 出かける, 乗る,
　　　　　　　　　　　　　　　　　　　　　　　　　お　　い　　かえ　　く　　　　　　　　　　　　　の
座る, 死ぬ, 消す, 忘れる, 借りる, 降りる, 持ってくる, 連れてくる, 結婚する, 太る, やせる, 着る belong to
すわ　し　　け　　わす　　か　　　お　　　　も　　　　　つ　　　　けっこん　　ふと　　　　　　き
Group 3. In most cases you can determine whether a verb belongs to Group 2 or 3 by checking if the verb
allows for a phrase describing duration, such as 一時間. Compare, for example,
　　　　　　　　　　　　　　　　　　　　いちじかん
　　○私はきのう一時間本を読みました。　*I read a book for an hour yesterday.*
　　　わたし　　　いちじかんほん　よ
　　×私は一時間死にました。(Ungrammatical, much as the English translation "I died for an hour" which
　　　わたし　いちじかんし　　　　　　is also odd.)
読む thus belongs to Group 2, and 死ぬ to Group 3.
よ　　　　　　　　　　　　　　　　し
[3]In Lesson 9, we will observe that this *result of a change* reading is actually not restricted to verbs in
Group 3, but can be associated with those in Group 2 in certain contexts.
[4]Note that the sentence does *not* mean Professor Yamashita *is getting married*.

着る き	→	着ている き (wears)

メアリーさんはＴシャツを着ています。
Mary is wearing/wears a T-shirt.

起きる お	→	起きている お (is awake)

お父さんは起きています。
Dad is up and awake.

住む す	→	住んでいる す (lives in)

父と母は東京に住んでいます。
My father and mother live in Tokyo.

勤める つと	→	勤めている つと (works for)

私の姉は日本の会社に勤めています。
My older sister works for a Japanese company.

Note that verbs like 行く and 来る belong to this group. Thus 行っている and 来ている indicate the current states that result from prior movements, *not* movements that are currently in progress. You may want to be careful with what the following sentences mean.

中国に行っています。
Somebody has gone to/is in China.
Not: *She is going to China.*

うちに来ています。
Somebody has come over to visit.
Not: *Somebody is coming over.*

Finally, a note on conjugation. The helping verb いる conjugates as a *ru*-verb. Thus we have long forms as in the following example.

食べ<u>ている</u> た		affirmative	negative
	present	食べ<u>ています</u> た *He is eating.*	食べ<u>ていません</u> た *He is not eating.*
	past	食べ<u>ていました</u> た *He was eating.*	食べ<u>ていませんでした</u> た *He was not eating.*

2　髪が長いです
かみ　なが

To describe somebody who has long hair, one could say:

トムさんの髪は長いです。
かみ　なが
Tom's hair is long.

But in fact it would be far more natural in Japanese to say:

トムさんは髪が長いです。　　*Tom has long hair.*
　　　　かみ　　なが　　　　　　*(＝As for Tom, he has long hair.)*

This applies not only to discussions of the length of one's hair, but to descriptions of a person's physical attributes in general.

A さんは ⎰目 耳 手 足 ⋮⎱ が ⎰大きい 小さい かわいい ⋮⎱ 　　*Person A has a body part which is . . .*

In idiomatic collocations, we also have:

背が高い　　*is tall*
せ　たか

背が低い　　*is short*
せ　ひく

頭がいい　　*is bright/smart*
あたま

3　*Te*-forms for Joining Sentences

In the last lesson, we discussed the use of verbal *te*-forms to join sentences. い- and な-adjectives and です after nouns also have *te*-forms, which can be used to combine two elements to form longer sentences.

The *te*-form of an い-adjective is formed by substituting くて for the final い. The *te*-form of a な-adjective and a noun＋です sequence is formed by adding で to the base or the noun.

い-adjectives:	安い やす	→	安くて やす
irregular :	いい	→	よくて
な-adjectives:	元気(な) げんき	→	元気で げんき
noun ＋ です:	日本人です に ほんじん	→	日本人で に ほんじん

あの店の食べ物は<u>安くて</u>、おいしいです。
The food at that restaurant is <u>inexpensive</u> <u>and</u> delicious.

あの人はいつも<u>元気で</u>、おもしろいです。
That person is always <u>energetic</u> <u>and</u> fun to be with.

山下先生は<u>日本人で</u>、四十歳ぐらいです。
Professor Yamashita is <u>a Japanese</u> <u>and</u> he is about forty years old.

4 verb stem ＋ に行く

If a person moves to another place in order to do something, we can describe their movement and its purpose this way:

The purpose of movement can either be a noun like 買い物 (shopping), or a phrase consisting of a verb, its object, and so forth. Verbs describing the purpose of a movement must be in their stem forms. Stems, as we learned in Lesson 3, are the part you get by removing ます from the verbs' present tense long forms.

> stems:
> 食べる　→　食べ（ます）
> 読む　→　読み（ます）
> etc.

デパートに　かばんを買い　に行きました。
I went to a department store to buy a bag.

メアリーさんは日本に　日本語を勉強し　に来ました。
Mary has come to Japan to study Japanese.

5 Counting People

The "counter" for people is 人, but "one person" and "two people" are irregular: 一人 and 二人.

ひとり （一人）	one person
ふたり （二人）	two people
さんにん （三人）	three people
よにん （四人）	four people
ごにん （五人）	five people
ろくにん （六人）	six people
しちにん／ななにん （七人）	seven people
はちにん （八人）	eight people
きゅうにん （九人）	nine people
じゅうにん （十人）	ten people

何人いますか。
なんにん

To count people in a class, for example, you can add 〜人 after the noun and the particle
にん
が, and say:

> person が　X 人　います
> にん

私のクラスに（は）スウェーデン人の学生が一人います。
わたし　　　　　　　　　　　　　　　じん　がくせい　　ひとり
There is one Swedish student in our class.

The place expressions are often followed by には instead of に in this type of sentence.

表現ノート　　　　　　　　　　　　Expression Notes ⑧
ひょうげん

遊ぶ▶ 遊ぶ means "to play," "to spend time pleasantly," or "to pay a social
あそ　　あそ
call."

子供の時、よく友だちと遊びました。	*When I was a child, I often played with friends.*
こ ど も　とき　　　とも　　　あそ	
遅くまで遊んではいけません。	*You must not play around until late.*
おそ　　あそ	
先週の週末は東京に遊びに行きました。	*I went to Tokyo to have fun last weekend.*
せんしゅう　しゅうまつ　とうきょう　あそ　い	
私のうちに遊びに来てください。	*Please come and see us.*
わたし　　　あそ　き	

Note that "to play" as used below requires different words.

Sports: to play tennis　テニスを<u>する</u>
　　　　 to play basketball　バスケットを<u>する</u>
Games: to play video games　テレビゲームを<u>する</u>
　　　　 to play cards　トランプを<u>する</u>
Music instruments: to play the guitar　ギターを<u>弾く</u>
　　　　　　　　　　　　　　　　　　　　　ひ

練習 Practice

① 何をしていますか

A. Look at the pictures below and answer the questions. 🔊

Example: Q：メアリーさんは何をしていますか。

A：メアリーさんはテレビを見ています。

Ex. (1) (2) (3)

(4) (5) (6) (7)

(8) (9) (10) (11)

B. Pair Work—What were you doing at the following times yesterday? Be as specific as possible (where, with whom, and so on).

Example: 2 P.M. → A：午後二時ごろ何をしていましたか。

B：友だちと部屋で勉強していました。

1. 6 A.M.　　　2. 8 A.M.　　　3. 10 A.M.　　　4. 12:30 P.M.

5. 6 P.M.　　　6. 8 P.M.　　　7. 11 P.M.

C. Class Activity—Let's play charades. The teacher gives a sentence card to each student. One of the students mimes the sentence. All other students guess what the person is doing and raise their hands when they recognize the action. The person that gets the most points is the winner.

Example: 田中さんは海で泳いでいます。

Ⅱ お父さんはどこに住んでいますか

A. This is Sue's family. Answer the following questions.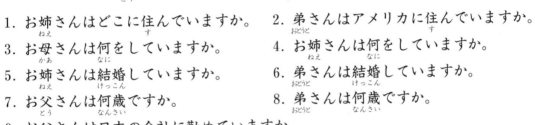

Example: Q：お父さんはどこに住んでいますか。
A：お父さんはニューヨークに住んでいます。

1. お姉さんはどこに住んでいますか。
2. 弟さんはアメリカに住んでいますか。
3. お母さんは何をしていますか。
4. お姉さんは何をしていますか。
5. お姉さんは結婚していますか。
6. 弟さんは結婚していますか。
7. お父さんは何歳ですか。
8. 弟さんは何歳ですか。
9. お父さんは日本の会社に勤めていますか。

Father	lives in N.Y.	works for an American company	48 years old
Mother		high school teacher	45 years old
Sister	lives in Seoul	works for a bank; married	27 years old
Brother	lives in London	student; not married	18 years old

B. Pair Work—Ask about your partner's family and fill in the blanks below.

	何歳ですか	何をしていますか	どこに住んでいますか	結婚していますか
お父さん				
お母さん				
お兄さん				
お姉さん				
弟さん				
妹さん				

Ⅲ 山田さんはやせています (Describing People)
やま だ

A. Look at the picture and answer the questions. 🕪

Example:　Q：山田さんはやせていますか。
　　　　　　　　やま だ
　　　　　　A：はい、山田さんはやせています。
　　　　　　　　　　　やま だ

1. 山田さんは太っていますか。
　やま だ　　　ふと
2. 山田さんはＴシャツを着ていますか。
　やま だ　　ティー　　　　き
3. 吉川さんは何を着ていますか。
　よしかわ　　なに　き
4. 山田さんはジーンズをはいていますか。
　やま だ
5. 吉川さんはめがねをかけていますか。
　よしかわ
6. 吉川さんはかさを持っていますか。
　よしかわ　　　　　も
7. 山田さんは背が高いですか。
　やま だ　　せ　たか
8. 吉川さんは背が低いですか。
　よしかわ　　せ　ひく
9. 山田さんは髪が長いですか。
　やま だ　　かみ　なが
10. 吉川さんは目が小さいですか。
　よしかわ　　め　ちい

山田　　　吉川
やま だ　　よしかわ

B. Look at the picture below and describe each person.

Example:　水野さんはぼうしをかぶっています。
　　　　　　みず の

川村
かわむら

山中
やまなか

中山　　小川　　水野
なかやま　おがわ　みず の

C. Class Activity—One student describes another student without mentioning the name. The rest of the class guesses who the student is.

Example:　髪が短いです。Ｔシャツを着ています。ジーンズをはいていません。
　　　　　　かみ みじか　　　　ティー　　　き

Ⅳ 大学は新しくて、きれいです
だいがく　あたら

A. Make sentences using two adjectives. 🔊

Example: 大学 ― 新しい／きれいな → 大学は新しくて、きれいです。
だいがく　あたら　　　　　　　　　　　　だいがく　あたら

1. 東京　　　　― 大きい／にぎやかな
とうきょう　　　おお

2. みちこさん ― きれいな／やさしい

3. たけしさん ― 背が高い／かっこいい
せ　たか

4. アパート　　― 静かな／大きい
しず　　おお

5. 新幹線 (Bullet Train) ― 速い／便利な
しんかんせん　　　　　　　はや　べんり

6. スーさん　　― 頭がいい／親切な
あたま　　しんせつ

7. 私の国の人 ― 元気な／にぎやかな
わたし　くに　ひと　げんき

B. Looking back on your childhood, make sentences using the given cues. 🔊

Example: my next-door neighbor ― tall & kind

→ となりの人は、背が高くて、親切でした。
ひと　せ　たか　　しんせつ

1. my town　　　― quiet & nice

2. my teacher　― big & scary

3. my house　　― old & not clean

4. classes　　　― long & not interesting

5. my friends　― kind & interesting

6. school　　　― lively & fun

7. homework　― difficult & tough

8. myself　　　― small & cute

C. Describe the following items using two or more adjectives.

Example: my roommate

→ 私のルームメート (roommate) は親切でおもしろいです。
わたし　　　　　　　　　　　　　　しんせつ
私のルームメートは親切ですが、つまらないです。
わたし　　　　　　　　しんせつ

1. my hometown　　　　2. my country

3. my Japanese class　　4. one of my family members

5. Japanese people　　　6. people of my country

Ⓥ 映画を見に行きます
えい が   み   い

A. Sue is going to the following places to do the things below. Make sentences like the example. 🔊

Example: 京都 ― かぶき (Kabuki) を見る
きょう と   み

→ スーさんは京都にかぶきを見に行きます。
きょう と   み   い

1. LL   ― テープを聞く
エルエル   き
2. 図書館   ― 本を借りる
と しょかん   ほん か
3. 食堂   ― 昼ごはんを食べる
しょくどう   ひる   た
4. 郵便局   ― 切手を買う
ゆうびんきょく   きって か
5. 公園   ― 写真を撮る
こうえん   しゃしん と
6. 友だちのうち ― 勉強する
とも   べんきょう
7. 町   ― 遊ぶ
まち   あそ

8. デパート   ― くつを買う
か
9. 高校   ― 英語を教える
こうこう   えい ご おし
10. 喫茶店   ― コーヒーを飲む
きっ さ てん   の

B. For what purpose would you go to the following places?

1. コンビニに＿＿＿＿＿＿＿＿＿＿＿＿＿＿＿に行きます。
い

2. 東京に＿＿＿＿＿＿＿＿＿＿＿＿＿＿＿に行きました。
とうきょう   い

3. 図書館に＿＿＿＿＿＿＿＿＿＿＿＿＿＿に行きます。
と しょかん   い

4. 家に＿＿＿＿＿＿＿＿＿＿＿＿＿＿＿に帰ります。
いえ   かえ

5. 大学に＿＿＿＿＿＿＿＿＿＿＿＿＿＿に来ました。
だいがく   き

Ⓥ この部屋に女の人が何人いますか
へ や   おんな ひと なんにん

Pair Work―Ask your partner the following questions.

Example: A：この部屋に女の人が何人いますか。
へ や おんな ひと なんにん
B：二人います。
ふた り

1. この部屋に男の人が何人いますか。
　　へや　おとこ　ひと　　なんにん

2. この部屋に＿＿＿＿＿＿＿＿人が何人いますか。
　　へや　　　　(nationality)　　じん　なんにん

3. この部屋に髪が長い人が何人いますか。
　　へや　かみ　なが　ひと　なんにん

4. この部屋に元気な人が何人いますか。
　　へや　げんき　ひと　なんにん

⑦ まとめの練習
　　　　れんしゅう

A. Answer the following questions.

1. どこに住んでいますか。
　　　　す

2. 結婚していますか。
　　けっこん

3. 自転車／車を持っていますか。
　　じてんしゃ　くるま　も

4. 日本の歌を知っていますか。
　　にほん　うた　し

5. 日本語の先生は今日何を着ていますか／はいていますか。
　　にほんご　せんせい　きょうなに　き

6. 兄弟がいますか。何人いますか。
　　きょうだい　　　　なんにん

7. お父さん／お母さんはどこに勤めていますか。
　　とう　　　かあ　　　　　つと

8. 子供の時、自転車を持っていましたか。
　　こども　とき　じてんしゃ　も

9. 高校の時、日本語を知っていましたか。
　　こうこう　とき　にほんご　し

B. Class Activity—Show a picture of your family to the class and describe it.

体の部分
からだ　ぶ　ぶん
Parts of the Body

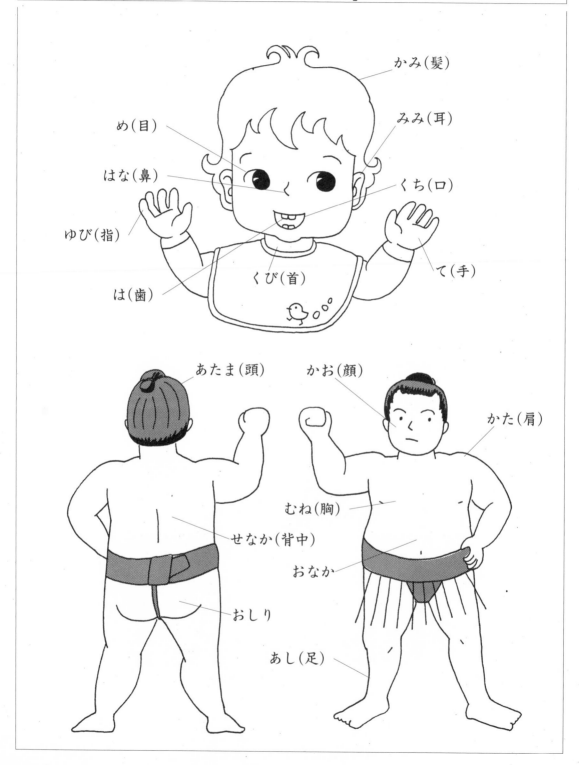

かみ（髪）

みみ（耳）

め（目）

はな（鼻）

くち（口）

ゆび（指）

て（手）

は（歯）

くび（首）

あたま（頭）

かお（顔）

かた（肩）

むね（胸）

せなか（背中）

おなか

おしり

あし（足）

家族
かぞく
F a m i l y

	I. Someone Else's Family	II. Own Family A: Formal Situation	B: Informal Situation
Father	お父さん とう	父 ちち	お父さん とう
Mother	お母さん かあ	母 はは	お母さん かあ
Older brother	お兄さん にい	兄 あに	お兄さん にい
Older sister	お姉さん ねえ	姉 あね	お姉さん ねえ
Younger brother	弟さん おとうと	弟 おとうと	
Younger sister	妹さん いもうと	妹 いもうと	
Husband	ご主人 しゅじん	主人／夫 しゅじん おっと	*(See below.)
Wife	奥さん おく	家内／妻 かない つま	*(See below.)
Grandfather	おじいさん	祖父 そ ふ	おじいさん
Grandmother	おばあさん	祖母 そ ば	おばあさん
Child	お子さん こ	うちの子 こ	

*Depending on each person, several words are used for spouses, e.g., for husband, だんな, うちの人, and for wife, 女房, ワイフ, かみさん, and so on.
　　　　　ひと　　　　　　　　　　にょうぼう

＊　　　　　　　＊　　　　　　　＊

A：田中さんのお父さんは何歳ですか。　　*How old is your father, Mr. Tanaka?*
　たなか　　　とう　　　なんさい

B：[formal]　父は五十歳です。　　*My father is 50 years old.*
　　　　　　ちち　ごじゅっさい

　　[informal]　お父さんは五十歳です。
　　　　　　　　とう　　　ごじゅっさい

A：田中さんのお兄さんはどこに住んでいますか。
　たなか　　　にい　　　　　　す
　Where does your older brother live, Mr. Tanaka?

B：[formal]　兄は東京に住んでいます。　　*My older brother lives in Tokyo.*
　　　　　　あに　とうきょう　す

　　[informal]　お兄さんは東京に住んでいます。
　　　　　　　　にい　　　とうきょう　す

Note that you can use お兄さん and お姉さん when you talk to your older brothers
　　　　　　　　　　　にい　　　　　ねえ
and sisters. The younger brothers and sisters are called by their names.

Younger brother:　お兄さん。　　*Hi, Big Brother.*
　　　　　　　　　にい

Older brother:　何？ たろう。　　*What is it, Taro?*
　　　　　　　　なに

第8課 LESSON 8

バーベキュー Barbecue

会話 Dialogue
_{かい わ}

Ⅰ At school.

1 みちこ： たけしさん、あしたみんなでバーベキューをしませんか。

2 たけし： いいですね。だれが来ますか。
_き

3 みちこ： スーさんとロバートさんが来ます。メアリーさんも来ると思います。
_き _{く おも}

4 たけし： けんさんは？

5 みちこ： けんさんはアルバイトがあると言っていました。
_い

6 たけし： 残念ですね。何か持っていきましょうか。
_{ざんねん なに も}

7 みちこ： 何もいらないと思います。
_{なに おも}

Ⅱ Robert is cooking at the barbecue.

1 みちこ： 上手ですね。ロバートさんは料理するのが好きですか。
_{じょうず りょうり す}

2 ロバート： ええ、よく家で作ります。
_{いえ つく}

3 みちこ： 何か手伝いましょうか。
_{なに てつだ}

4 ロバート： じゃあ、トマトを切ってください。
_き

    ＊   ＊   ＊

5 ロバート： 始めましょうか。
_{はじ}

6 みちこ： あっ、まだ飲まないでください。
_の

7 メアリーさんも来ると言っていましたから。
_{く い}

8 メアリー： 遅くなってすみません。
_{おそ}

9 みんな： じゃあ、乾杯！
_{かんぱい}

I

Michiko: Takeshi, would you like to have a barbecue party tomorrow?

Takeshi: That's nice. Who will come?

Michiko: Sue and Robert will come. I think Mary will come, too.

Takeshi: How about Ken?

Michiko: Ken said he had a part-time job.

Takeshi: Too bad. Shall I bring something?

Michiko: I think nothing is needed.

II

Michiko: You are good (at cooking). Do you like cooking, Robert?

Robert: Yes, I often cook at home.

Michiko: Shall I help you with something?

Robert: Well then, cut the tomatoes, please.

*   *   *

Robert: Shall we start?

Michiko: Don't drink yet. Mary said that she would come.

Mary: I'm sorry for being late.

Everyone: Well then . . . Cheers!

単語
たん　　ご
V o c a b u l a r y

N o u n s

あさって		the day after tomorrow
あめ	雨	rain
かいしゃいん	会社員	office worker
カメラ		camera
カラオケ		karaoke
くうき	空気	air
けさ	今朝	this morning
こんげつ	今月	this month
しごと	仕事	job; work; occupation
だいがくせい	大学生	college student
ディスコ		disco
てんきよほう	天気予報	weather forecast
ところ	所	place
* トマト		tomato
なつ	夏	summer
* なにか	何か	something
パーティー		party
* バーベキュー		barbecue
はし		chopsticks
ふゆ	冬	winter
ホームステイ		homestay; living with a local family
まいしゅう	毎週	every week
らいげつ	来月	next month

な - a d j e c t i v e s

* じょうず（な）	上手	skillful; good at . . .	（〜が）
へた（な）	下手	clumsy; poor at . . .	（〜が）
ゆうめい（な）	有名	famous	

U - v e r b s

あめがふる	雨が降る	it rains
あらう	洗う	to wash
* いう	言う	to say

* Words that appear in the dialogue

*	いる		to need （〜が）
*	おそくなる	遅くなる	to be late (for . . .) （〜に）
*	おもう	思う	to think
*	きる	切る	to cut
*	つくる	作る	to make
*	もっていく	持っていく	to take (something)

Ru-verbs

	じろじろみる	じろじろ見る	to stare (at . . .) （〜を）
*	はじめる	始める	to begin

Irregular Verbs

	うんてんする	運転する	to drive （〜を）
	せんたくする	洗濯する	to do laundry
	そうじする	掃除する	to clean
*	りょうりする	料理する	to cook

Adverbs and Other Expressions

	ううん		uh-uh; no
	うん		uh-huh; yes
*	かんぱい	乾杯	Cheers! (a toast)
*	ざんねん（ですね）	残念（ですね）	That's too bad.
*	まだ ＋ negative		not . . . yet
*	みんなで		all (of the people) together

文法 G r a m m a r

ぶん ぽう

1 Short Forms

In this and the next lesson, we will learn a new paradigm of conjugation, which we will call "short forms.[1]" Before we start worrying about their meaning and how they are used, let us first see what they look like. It should be obvious why they are called short forms. We will list the already familiar "long forms" to the right in the table below.

Present tense, affirmative		
	short forms	long forms
verbs:	読む[a]	読みます
い-adjectives:	かわいい[a]	かわいいです
な-adjectives:	静かだ[b]	静かです
noun ＋ です:	学生だ[b]	学生です
Present tense, negative		
	short forms	long forms
verbs:	読まない[c]	読みません
い-adjectives:	かわいくない[d]	かわいくありません
な-adjectives:	静かじゃない[d]	静かじゃありません
noun ＋ です:	学生じゃない[d]	学生じゃありません

The following rules summarize how short forms are constructed.

> Verbs and い-adjectives in the affirmative (a above)
> → same as their dictionary forms
> な-adjectives and noun ＋ です in the affirmative (b above)
> → replace です with だ
> い- and な-adjectives and noun ＋ です in the negative (d above)
> → replace ありません with ない

---

[1]Various names have been given to this paradigm. They include "plain forms," "informal forms," and "direct style." Long forms, on the other hand, are often called "polite forms," "formal forms," and "distal style."

As noted in Lesson 5, the adjective いい is irregular. Its negative short form is よくない.

Verbs in the negative need to be analyzed in more detail, because *ru-*, *u-*, and irregular verbs conjugate differently.

Negative short forms of verbs (c above)

ru-verbs: Take the final る off and add ない.

食べる　→　食べない

u-verbs: Take the final *-u* off and add *-anai*.

書く	→	書かない	作る	→	作らない
話す	→	話さない	泳ぐ	→	泳がない
待つ	→	待たない	呼ぶ	→	呼ばない
死ぬ	→	死なない	買う	→	買わない(1)
読む	→	読まない			

irregular verbs:

| する | → | しない | くる | → | こない(2) |

exception:

| ある | → | ない(3) |

With verbs in the negative, the following three points are worth noting.

(1) The negative short forms of verbs that end with the *hiragana* う are 〜 わない instead of 〜あない.[2]

(2) The vowel changes with the irregular verb くる.

(3) The verb ある in the negative is ない.

2　Uses of Short Forms

We now turn to discussion of how we utilize short forms. In this lesson, we will learn to use the short forms in the following four contexts:

- In represented, or quoted, speech ("I think . . . ," "She said . . .")
- In casual conversations, as signs of intimacy
- In making negative requests ("Please don't . . .") (See 3 on p. 157.)

---

[2] This suggests that the bases of verbs like 買う and 会う actually end with the consonant *w*. This consonant remains dormant when the base is followed by the vowel *i*, thus we have 買います, where *w* is lacking, but it surfaces with the vowel *a* following, 買わない. This mystery consonant also explains why the *te*-form of such a verb has the small つ, just like verbs whose bases obviously end with a consonant, such as とる and 待つ.

●In expressing ideas like "I like doing . . ." or "I am good at doing . . ."

(See 4 below.)

Quotations To quote a person's utterances or thoughts, you use a clause ending with a predicate in the short form, plus と言っていました (They said ". . ."), と思います (I think that . . .), and so forth. と is a quotation particle, which does the job of both the English word "that" in indirect quotation and of quotation marks (" ") in direct quotation.

スーさんは、あした試験があると言っていました。
Sue said that there would be an exam tomorrow.

(私は)たけしさんはメアリーさんが好きだと思います。[4]
I think Takeshi likes Mary.

Casual conversations Two people who are close friends or family members speak with short forms at the end of sentences, using them as a sign of intimacy. The use of long forms, in contrast, tends to imply the speaker's intention to "keep a proper distance" from the listener. Short forms, then, are like talking on a first name basis, while long forms are like using "Mr." and "Ms."

It may not be easy to decide when it is appropriate to switch to short forms. First of all, Japanese speakers are often very conscious of seniority. A year's difference in age may in many cases totally preclude the possibility of establishing a truly "equal" relationship.

---

[3]Note that the present tense in Sue's original utterance is preserved in Mary's report.
[4]To say that you *don't think* something is the case, it is more common in Japanese to say it like〜ない と思います (I *think* that something is *not* the case) than〜と思いません (I *don't think*). Therefore:
(私は)メアリーさんはたけしさんが好きじゃないと思います。
I don't think Mary likes Takeshi (=I think Mary doesn't like Takeshi.)

Second, license to use short forms is not mutual; senior partners may feel perfectly justified in using short forms while expecting their junior partners to continue addressing them with long forms. Thus if somebody who is older, say, your Japanese language professor, talks to you using short forms, they would be greatly surprised if you should return the favor.

Here are a few observations on the grammar of short forms as they are used in casual conversations.

- In the casual conversational use of short forms, question sentences do not end with the question particle か, but with rising intonation alone.
- The だ ending of な-adjectives and noun + です constructions (b in the previous section) is usually dropped.

In casual conversations, はい and いいえ are often replaced by the less formal うん and ううん.

3 ～ないでください

To request that someone refrain from doing something, one can use a negative verbal short form plus でください.

ここで写真を撮らないでください。
Please don't take pictures here.

| negative short form ＋ でください | *Please don't . . .* |

---

4 verb のが好きです

Short forms are used in constructions where verbs and adjectives are to be treated as nouns. Thus 私は～が好きです／きらいです can, besides describing your preference for items denoted by nouns, such as 猫, also describe your preference for activities, such as swimming, drinking coffee, and studying Japanese. Add の to a verbal short form to express the idea of "doing x."

（私は）日本語を勉強するのが好きです。
I like studying the Japanese language.

（私は）部屋を掃除するのがきらいです。
I don't like cleaning my room.

"To be good/bad at doing something" is 〜が上手です (is good at . . .) and 〜が下手です (is bad at . . .).[5]

ロバートさんは料理を作るのが上手です。
Robert is good at cooking meals.

たけしさんは英語を話すのが下手です。
Takeshi is not a good speaker of English.

person は	activity (verb) のが	好き きらい 上手 下手	です。	*like doing . . .* *doesn't like doing . . .* *is good at doing . . .* *is poor at doing . . .*

It is a common mistake to use the *te*-form of a verb in such contexts, misled by the association between 〜ている and the verb in the *-ing* form in English.

✕ たけしさんは英語を話してが下手です。

5　が

Consider what ロバートさんは沖縄に行きました means. This sentence of course is about Robert and describes what he did. It is likely to be uttered when the topic of Robert has already been breached. Grammatically speaking, (1) the noun ロバート stands as the subject in relation to the verb 行く (he was the person who performed the going), and (2) the noun is, per the function of the particle は, presented as the topic of the sentence (*as for* Robert, he went to Okinawa).

What if we both know that somebody went to Okinawa recently, and *I* know that it was Robert, but *you* don't. I will say:

ロバートさんが沖縄に行きました。　　*ROBERT went to Okinawa.*

---

[5]To describe one's skills or lack thereof, we also often use a different set of expressions, namely, 〜がとくいです (is comfortable with . . .) and 〜がにがてです (is uncomfortable with . . .).

私は日本語を話すのがとくいです。　*I am good at/comfortable with speaking Japanese.*

This sentence means that *Robert* went to Okinawa, which in English would be uttered with an extra emphasis on the name Robert. His identity is the new piece of information provided by this sentence. It is one of the functions of the particle が to (1) present the subject of a sentence in a way such that (2) the noun will "fill in the blank on the information sheet."

The "blank on the information sheet" is a question word like だれ and 何. The above sentence will fill in the blank left out by:

だれが沖縄に行きましたか。　　　　Compare: ✕ だれは沖縄に行きましたか。
Who went to Okinawa?

As we learned in Lesson 2, a question word that is the subject of a sentence is never followed by the particle は, but always by the particle が. As we have seen, a noun that will provide the answer to such a question is also followed by the particle が.

どのクラスがおもしろいですか。
Which class is (the most) interesting?

日本語のクラスがおもしろいです。
Japanese class is.

(このクラスで)だれがめがねをかけていますか。
Who wears glasses (in this class)?

山下先生がめがねをかけています。
Professor Yamashita does.

6　何か and 何も

The word for "something" is 何か, and the word for "anything" in negative sentences is 何も.

"Some" and "any" in:		
positive statements	何か	*something*
questions	何か	*anything?*
negative statements	何も ＋ negative	*not . . . anything*

These two words are used in places where the particles は, が, and を are expected. In these contexts, they are used on their own, without the help of particles. We will learn in Lesson 10 what to do in cases where particles other than these are expected.

猫が何か持ってきました。
The cat has brought something.

猫は何か食べましたか。
Did the cat eat anything?

いいえ、猫は何も食べませんでした。
No, the cat did not eat anything.

表現ノート　　　　　Expression Notes ⑨

〜する▶ Most irregular verbs are compounds of nouns and the verb する. If you have learned an irregular verb, therefore, you have also learned a noun.

verbs	nouns	
勉強する *to study*	勉強 *study*	ex. 日本語の勉強は楽しいです。 *Japanese language study is fun.*
料理する *to cook*	料理 *cooking*	ex. ロバートさんの料理はおいしいです。 *Robert's cooking is good.*

Some of these nouns can be used as the "object" of the verb する.

私は日本語の勉強をしました。　　*I studied Japanese.*
　　Compare: 私は日本語を勉強しました。

たけしさんは部屋の掃除をしました。　*Takeshi cleaned his room.*
　　Compare: たけしさんは部屋を掃除しました。

練習 Practice
れん しゅう

① Short Forms

A. Change the affirmatives into negatives. 🔊

Example: かく → かかない

1. みる
2. あける
3. すむ
4. かける
5. はく
6. はじめる
7. つくる
8. せんたくする
9. あらう
10. くる
11. わすれる
12. ある
13. おもう
14. もっていく
15. はいる
16. かえる
17. あめがふる

B. Change the affirmatives into negatives. 🔊

Example: たかい   → たかくない

　　げんきだ   → げんきじゃない

　　がくせいだ → がくせいじゃない

1. ゆうめいだ
2. あめだ
3. いそがしい
4. かわいい
5. みじかい
6. しんせつだ
7. やすい
8. きれいだ
9. たいへんだ
10. いい
11. かっこいい
12. すきだ
13. きらいだ

② Informal Speech

A. Answer the following questions in informal speech, first in the affirmative, then in the negative. 🔊

Example: Q：よく魚を食べる？
　　　　　　さかな た
　　　　A：うん、食べる。／ううん、食べない。
　　　　　　　た　　　　　　　　　　た

1. 今日、勉強する？
きょう べんきょう
2. 今日、友だちに会う？
きょう とも あ
3. よくお茶を飲む？
ちゃ の
4. よく電車に乗る？
でんしゃ の
5. 毎日、日本語を話す？
まいにち にほんご はな
6. 毎日、テレビを見る？
まいにち み

7. あした、大学に来る？　　　8. 今日、宿題がある？
　　　　だいがく　く　　　　　　　　きょう　しゅくだい

9. 自転車を持っている？　　　10. 来週、ディスコに行く？
　　じてんしゃ　も　　　　　　　　らいしゅう　　　　　い

11. 毎週、部屋を掃除する？　　12. 毎日、洗濯する？
　　まいしゅう　へや　そうじ　　　　まいにち　せんたく

B. Answer the following questions in informal speech, first in the affirmative, then in the negative.

　　Example:　Q：元気？
　　　　　　　　　　げんき
　　　　　　　　A：うん、元気。／ううん、元気じゃない。
　　　　　　　　　　　　げんき　　　　　　　げんき

1. ひま？　　　　　　　　　　　2. 忙しい？
　　　　　　　　　　　　　　　　　いそが

3. 日本語のクラスはおもしろい？　4. 日本語のクラスは難しい？
　　にほんご　　　　　　　　　　　　にほんご　　　　むずか

5. この教科書はいい？　6. 先生はこわい？　　7. 料理が上手？
　　きょうかしょ　　　　　せんせい　　　　　　りょうり　じょうず

8. お風呂が好き？　　9. スポーツがきらい？　10. 今日は月曜日？
　　ふろ　す　　　　　　　　　　　　　　　　　きょう　げつようび

(Ⅲ) 日本人だと思います
　　にほんじん　おも

A. Make a guess about Mary, using 〜と思います.
　　　　　　　　　　　　　　　おも

　　Example:　good at Japanese
　　　　　　　→　メアリーさんは日本語が上手だと思います。
　　　　　　　　　　　　　　　にほんご　じょうず　おも

1. often cooks　　　　　　　　　2. drives a car
3. doesn't smoke　　　　　　　　4. listens to a Japanese language tape every day
5. doesn't go home late at night　6. doesn't drink alcohol much
7. often goes to see movies　　　8. not married
9. likes Takeshi　　　　　　　　10. busy
11. a good student　　　　　　　12. not tall
13. not scary　　　　　　　　　14. not quiet
15. not a freshman

B. Make a guess about the person or place below and answer the following questions.

　　Example:　Q：この人は日本人ですか。
　　　　　　　　　　ひと　にほんじん
　　　　　　　　A：ええ、日本人だと思います。
　　　　　　　　　　　　にほんじん　おも
　　　　　　　　　いいえ、日本人じゃないと思います。
　　　　　　　　　　　　　にほんじん　　　　おも

Picture A

1. この人は会社員ですか。
2. 有名ですか。
3. ひまですか。
4. 頭がいいですか。
5. 背が高いですか。
6. 忙しいですか。
7. 結婚していますか。
8. お金をたくさん持っていますか。
9. よく食べますか。
10. よくスポーツをしますか。
11. フランス語を話しますか。

A

Picture B

1. ここは日本ですか。
2. 有名な所ですか。
3. 空気はきれいですか。
4. 暑いですか。
5. 冬は寒いですか。
6. 人がたくさん住んでいますか。
7. ここの人はよく泳ぎますか。
8. よく仕事をしますか。
9. 夏によく雨が降りますか。

B

C. Make a guess about the following things, using 〜と思います。

1. the weather tomorrow
2. the next test
3. what your classmates will do tomorrow

Ⅳ メアリーさんは忙しいと言っていました

A. Report what the following people said, using 〜と言っていました. 📶

Example: メアリー／今月は忙しいです。

→ Q：メアリーさんは何と言っていましたか。

A：今月は忙しいと言っていました。

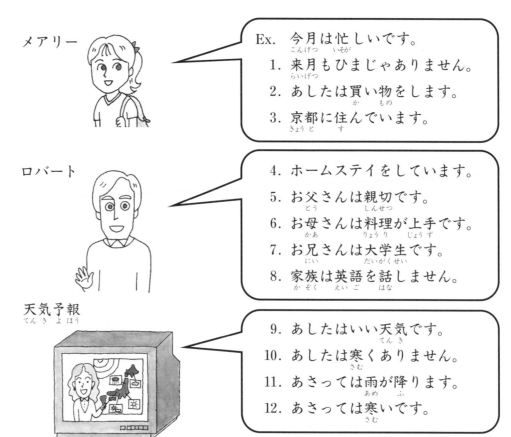

メアリー

Ex. 今月は忙しいです。
1. 来月もひまじゃありません。
2. あしたは買い物をします。
3. 京都に住んでいます。

ロバート

4. ホームステイをしています。
5. お父さんは親切です。
6. お母さんは料理が上手です。
7. お兄さんは大学生です。
8. 家族は英語を話しません。

天気予報

9. あしたはいい天気です。
10. あしたは寒くありません。
11. あさっては雨が降ります。
12. あさっては寒いです。

B. Pair Work—Ask your partner the following questions. Take notes and report to the class later, using 〜と言っていました.

1. 週末は何をしますか。
2. 日本はどうですか。
3. 日本の友だち／日本の家族はどんな人ですか。
4. どんな人が好きですか。

Ⅴ 食べ<ruby>た</ruby>ないでください

What would you say when you want someone . . .

Example: not to look at your photo → 写真を見ないでください。
<ruby>しゃしん</ruby> <ruby>み</ruby>

1. not to speak English
2. not to call you
3. not to come to your house
4. not to go
5. not to smoke
6. not to sleep in class
7. not to forget
8. not to stare at you
9. not to start the class yet
10. not to be late
11. not to erase the blackboard yet
    （こくばん）

Ⅵ 勉強するのが好きですか
べんきょう　　　す

A. Tell what Mary is good/poor at, using 上手です or 下手です.
じょう ず　　　　　 へ た

Example: tennis (good)

　　→　メアリーさんはテニスが上手です。
　　　　　　　　　　　　　　　　じょう ず

　　swimming (poor)

　　→　メアリーさんは泳ぐのが下手です。
　　　　　　　　　　　　　およ　　　 へ た

1. French (good)
2. video games (poor)
3. cooking (good)
4. making sushi (poor)
5. speaking Japanese (good)
6. taking pictures (good)
7. driving a car (good)
8. eating with chopsticks (good)
   （はしで）
9. writing love letters (good)
   （ラブレター）

B. Pair Work—Ask if your partner likes to do the following activities.

Example: studying

　　→　A：勉強するのが好きですか。
　　　　　　べんきょう　　　　　す

　　　　　B：はい、好きです／大好きです。
　　　　　　　　　す　　　　　　だい す

　　　　　　　　いいえ、きらいです／大きらいです。
　　　　　　　　　　　　　　　　　　　　だい

1. eating
2. sleeping
3. singing
4. doing shopping
5. playing sports
6. studying Japanese
7. doing cleaning
8. doing laundry
9. cooking
10. taking a bath
11. driving a car
12. washing a car

* If you neither like it nor dislike it, you can use 好きでもきらいでもありません。
す

Ⅶ だれがイギリス人ですか

A. Use the table below and answer the questions. 🔊

Example: Q：だれがイギリス人ですか。

A：ロバートさんがイギリス人です。

1. だれが韓国人ですか。
2. だれが料理をするのが上手ですか。
3. だれがいつも (always) 食堂で食べますか。
4. だれがデートをしましたか。
5. だれが犬が好きですか。

Robert	British	is good at cooking	cooks often	went to Okinawa last weekend	doesn't like cats
Mary	American	is good at skiing	does not cook	had a date last weekend	likes dogs
Sue	Korean	is good at singing	cooks sometimes	went to Tokyo last weekend	likes cats
Takeshi	Japanese	is good at swimming	always eats at cafeteria	had a date last weekend	doesn't like cats

B. Pair Work—Use the table above and ask your partner questions with だれが.

Ⅷ 週末、何もしませんでした

A. You went to a party but did nothing there. Make sentences using the cues. 🔊

Example: パーティーに行きましたが、(eat)

→ パーティーに行きましたが、何も食べませんでした。

1. パーティーに行きましたが、(drink)
2. カラオケがありましたが、(sing)
3. テレビがありましたが、(watch)
4. カメラを持っていましたが、(take)
5. ゆみさんに会いましたが、(talk)
6. パーティーに行きましたが、(do)

B. Answer the following questions.

Example: Q：きのうの晩ごはんは何か作りましたか。

A：はい、スパゲッティ (spaghetti) を作りました。

いいえ、何も作りませんでした。

1. けさ、何か食べましたか。
2. きのう、何か買いましたか。
3. きのう、テレビで (on TV) 何か見ましたか。
4. 今、何かいりますか。
5. 週末、何かしますか。
6. 週末、何か勉強しますか。

Ⅸ まとめの練習

A. Interview one of your classmates about any future plans and report to the class.

Example: スーさんは来年ソウルへ行くと言っていました。

B. Pair Work/Group Work—You are planning a party. Decide on the following points and fill in the chart.

いつですか	
どこでしますか	
どんなパーティーですか	
何を持っていきますか	
だれが来ますか	

C. Class Activity—Find someone who . . .

   1. likes to study Japanese   _____

   2. hates to do cleaning   _____

   3. likes to sing   _____

   4. is poor at driving   _____

   5. whose mother is good at cooking   _____

D. Pair Work—A and B are making plans for a one-day trip with two other friends C and D. A knows C's schedule and B knows D's schedule. Play the roles of A and B. Discuss your own and your friend's schedules using 〜と言っていました, and find out which days all four of you are available.

Example: A：十六日はひまですか。

          B：いいえ、買い物に行きます。十八日は、どうですか。

          A：私は、何もしません。でも、Cさんが映画を見に行くと言っていました。

          B：そうですか。じゃあ……

Student A

A's schedule						
16	17	18	19	20 study	21 quiz	22 party
23	24	25	26	27	28	29 part-time job

C told A that he would . . .
18th: go to see a movie
24th: meet friends
26th: go to Osaka to have fun

Student B

B's schedule

16	17	18	19	20	21	22
shopping	work					tennis
23	24	25	26	27	28	29
						work

D told B that she would . . .

  19th: do a part-time job

  27th: go to eat Japanese cuisine

  28th: go to Kyoto to see temples

第9課 L E S S O N 9

かぶき Kabuki

会話 D i a l o g u e 🔊

Ⅰ Mary and Takeshi are talking.

1 たけし：　メアリーさんはかぶきが好きですか。

2 メアリー：　かぶきですか。あまり知りません。でも、ロバートさんはおもしろかっ

3 　　　　　　たと言っていました。

4 たけし：　かぶきの切符を二枚もらったから、見に行きませんか。

5 メアリー：　ええ、ぜひ。いつですか。

6 たけし：　木曜日です。十二時から四時までです。

Ⅱ During intermission at a Kabuki theater.

1 メアリー：　きれいでしたね。

2 たけし：　出ている人はみんな男の人ですよ。

3 メアリー：　本当ですか。

4 たけし：　ええ。ところで、もう昼ごはんを食べましたか。

5 メアリー：　いいえ、まだ食べていません。

6 たけし：　じゃあ、買いに行きましょう。

Ⅲ At a concession stand.

1 たけし：　すみません。お弁当を二つください。

2 店の人：　はい。

3 たけし：　それから、お茶を一つとコーヒーを一つ。

4 店の人：　二千八百円です。どうもありがとうございました。

Ⅰ

Takeshi: Mary, do you like Kabuki?

Mary: Kabuki? I don't know it well. But Robert said it was interesting.

Takeshi: I got two tickets for Kabuki, so would you like to go to see it?

Mary: Sure. When is it?

Takeshi: On Thursday. From 12:00 to 16:00.

Ⅱ

Mary: It was beautiful.

Takeshi: The people who appear are all men.

Mary: Really?

Takeshi: Yes. By the way, did you already eat lunch?

Mary: No, I haven't eaten it yet.

Takeshi: Then, shall we go to buy it?

Ⅲ

Takeshi: Excuse me. Two box lunches, please.

Vendor: Here they are.

Takeshi: And then, one tea and one coffee.

Vendor: That is 2,800 yen. Thank you very much.

単語
たん　ご

Ｖｏｃａｂｕｌａｒｙ

Ｎｏｕｎｓ

いいこ	いい子	good child
いろ	色	color
* おべんとう	お弁当	boxed lunch
おんせん	温泉	spa; hot spring
* かぶき		Kabuki; traditional Japanese theatrical art
ギター		guitar
くすり	薬	medicine
くすりをのむ	薬を飲む	to take medicine
コンサート		concert
こんど	今度	near future
さくぶん	作文	essay; composition
しけん	試験	exam
しんかんせん	新幹線	Shinkansen; "Bullet Train"
スキー		ski
せんげつ	先月	last month
たんご	単語	word; vocabulary
ピアノ		piano
びょうき	病気	illness; sickness

い-ａｄｊｅｃｔｉｖｅｓ

あおい	青い	blue
あかい	赤い	red
くろい	黒い	black
さびしい	寂しい	lonely
しろい	白い	white
わかい	若い	young

な-ａｄｊｅｃｔｉｖｅ

いじわる(な)	意地悪	mean-spirited

U-ｖｅｒｂｓ

おどる	踊る	to dance
おわる	終わる	(something) ends　　（〜が）

* Words that appear in the dialogue

にんきがある	人気がある	to be popular
はじまる	始まる	(something) begins （〜が）
ひく	弾く	to play (a string instrument or piano)
* もらう		to get (from somebody) （*person* に *thing* を）

Ru-verbs

おぼえる	覚える	to memorize
* でる	出る	(1) to appear; to attend （〜に） (2) to exit （〜を）

Irregular Verbs

うんどうする	運動する	to do physical exercises
さんぽする	散歩する	to take a walk

Adverbs and Other Expressions

* 〜から		from . . .
* ぜひ	是非	by all means
* ところで		by the way
* みんな		all
* もう		already

Numbers (used to count small items)

* ひとつ	一つ	one
* ふたつ	二つ	two
みっつ	三つ	three
よっつ	四つ	four
いつつ	五つ	five
むっつ	六つ	six
ななつ	七つ	seven
やっつ	八つ	eight
ここのつ	九つ	nine
とお	十	ten

文法 G r a m m a r
ぶん ぽう

1 Past Tense Short Forms

We will now continue the discussion on short forms, which we started in the last lesson. Here we will learn the past tense paradigm of short forms.

Past tense, affirmative		compare with:
verbs:	読んだ [a] よ	読んで よ
い-adjectives:	かわいかった [b]	かわいい
な-adjectives:	静かだった [c] しず	静かだ しず
noun ＋ です:	学生だった [c] がくせい	学生だ がくせい
Past tense, negative		
verbs:	読まなかった [b] よ	読まない よ
い-adjectives:	かわいくなかった [b]	かわいくない
な-adjectives:	静かじゃなかった [b] しず	静かじゃない しず
noun ＋ です:	学生じゃなかった [b] がくせい	学生じゃない がくせい

Below is a brief discussion on the formation of past tense short forms.

Verbs in the affirmative (a above)
  → replace て/で in *te*-forms with た/だ
い-adjectives in the affirmative, and all categories in the negative (b above)
  → replace the final い with かった
な-adjectives and noun ＋ です in the affirmative (c above)
  → replace だ in the present tense short forms with だった

The two irregularities that we noted earlier are observed here once again. They are:

行く → 行った　　　　いい → よかった, よくなかった[1]
い　　　い

Short form predicates in the past tense can be used in the same way as the present tense forms, which we discussed in Lesson 8.

---

[1]See 行って in Lesson 6. See よかったです, よくありません, and よくありませんでした in Lesson 5.
い

● In represented, or quoted, speech

スーさんは、高校の時めがねをかけていたと言っていました。
Sue said that she wore (had worn) glasses in high school.

(私は)トムさんがやったと思います。
I think Tom did it.

● In casual conversations

晩ごはん、食べた？ ― うん、食べた。
Have dinner yet? *Uh-huh, I did.*

Note that in Japanese the tense of the original utterance is preserved when it is reported. If you are reporting somebody's utterance in which the present tense is used, you must also use the present tense inside the quote. Thus, if your friend Sue said 今、日本語を勉強しています, using the present tense, your report will be:

スーさんは日本語を勉強していると言っていました。
Sue said that she __was__ studying Japanese.

2 Qualifying Nouns with Verbs and Adjectives

The short forms of verbs can be used to qualify nouns, much like adjectives can. In the example below, the phrase あそこで本を読んでいる (reading a book over there) is used as a qualifier for the noun 学生.[2]

| あそこで本を読んでいる | 学生はみちこさんです。
The __student__ | who is reading a book over there | is Michiko.

The following table shows various forms of noun qualification. The phrases in the boxes qualify the noun 人 (person) to their right. Example 1 is a straightforward adjectival example. Example 2 contains a phrase describing a person's attribute (Lesson 7), example 3 has a verb in the short form (Lesson 8), and example 4 has a な-adjective, which is relational (Lesson 5).

---

[2]A qualifying phrase like this, which has a sentence-like structure of its own, is technically known as a "relative clause."

1.	おもしろい	人（ひと）	a person	who is interesting
2.	髪が長い（かみ なが）	人（ひと）	a person	who has long hair
3.	めがねをかけている	人（ひと）	a person	who wears glasses
4.	猫が好きな（ねこ す）	人（ひと）	a person	who likes cats

↑ adjectives and verbs used as qualifiers ↑ noun

Here are more examples of verbs used in descriptions of people.

あそこで写真を撮っている 人（はだれですか。）
（しゃしん と）（ひと）
(Who is) the person taking pictures over there?

毎日運動をする 人（は元気です。）
（まいにちうんどう）（ひと）（げん き）
People who do physical exercises every day (are healthy.)

たばこを吸わない 人（が好きです。）
（す）（ひと）（す）
(I like) people who do not smoke.

去年結婚した 友だち（から手紙が来ました。）
（きょねんけっこん）（とも）（て がみ き）
(A letter came from) a friend who got married last year.

3 まだ〜ていません

Consider first the following pair of sentences in English.

Zelda has lost her key.
Zelda lost her key.

These two sentences present the same fact, Zelda losing her key, in different ways. The first "present perfect" example describes the event as something that is connected with the present: hearing the sentence, one will understand that Zelda is still without her key. On the other hand, the second "simple past" example describes the event as something that is independent of the situation at the present moment; we do not know whether Zelda is still looking for her key or has later retrieved it.

In Japanese, past tense forms do double duty on the affirmative end of polarity, but the past tense and the ている construction share the work on the negative end. Thus in the affirmative, the past tense is used both with words like きのう (disconnected from the present) and もう ("already," connected with the present).

私はきのう宿題をしました。　　and　　私はもう宿題をしました。
I did the homework yesterday.　　　　　*I have already done the homework.*

With the negative, the past is used to talk about a finished time period like きのう, but ている is used if your intention is to talk about how things stand now ("not yet").

私はきのう宿題をしませんでした。　　and　　私はまだ宿題をしていません。
I did not do the homework yesterday.　　　　*I have not done the homework yet.*

まだ〜ていません	*have not . . . yet*

This use of ている can be found both with verbs describing *changes* and with verbs describing *activities*, as defined in Lesson 7.

スーさんはまだ起きていません。　　(change)
Sue has not woken up yet.

私はまだ昼ごはんを食べていません。　(activity)
I haven't eaten lunch yet.

4　〜から

We learned in Lesson 6 that から added to a sentence means "because."

私は朝ごはんを食べませんでした。忙しかったですから。
I didn't have breakfast. (Because) I was busy.

In this lesson, we learn to incorporate the explanation clauses in the statements themselves, rather than adding them as separate sentences. You can simply transpose the "explanation＋から" sequence to the beginning of a sentence for which the explanation is offered.

> (explanation) から、 (situation)。
> 　　　= (situation), *because* (explanation).
> 　　　= (explanation), *therefore*, (situation).

あした試験があるから、私は今晩勉強します。
I will study this evening, because we will have an exam tomorrow.
(＝We will have an exam tomorrow, therefore, I will study this evening.)

寒かったから、出かけませんでした。
We didn't go out, because it was cold.
(＝It was cold, therefore, I didn't go out.)

Note that the resulting order of elements resembles that of a "therefore" sentence more closely than that of a "because" clause in English.

Before the conjunction から, you find both the long and short forms. Thus the から clauses in the above examples can be rewritten as あした試験がありますから and 寒かったですから.[3] The long form before から is more polite, and is frequently found in request and suggestion sentences.

かぶきの切符がありますから、一緒に見に行きましょう。
Let's go to see Kabuki. I have tickets.

---

[3]The long form before から is inappropriate when the entire sentence ends in a short form, however. Thus it is inappropriate to say：×寒かったですから、出かけなかった。

練習 P r a c t i c e

れん しゅう

Ⅰ Short Forms Past

A. Verbs 🔊

(a) Change the following verbs into the past affirmatives.

Example: かく → かいた

1. はなす	2. しぬ	3. すむ	4. かける
5. いく	6. あそぶ	7. つくる	8. せんたくする
9. あらう	10. くる	11. ひく	12. まつ
13. いそぐ	14. もらう	15. おどる	16. でる

(b) Change the following verbs into the past negatives.

Example: かく → かかなかった

1. みる	2. すてる	3. すむ	4. かける
5. はく	(to throw away) 6. はじまる	7. つくる	8. せんたくする
9. あらう	10. くる	11. いう	12. うんどうする
13. おぼえる	14. うたう	15. かえる	16. やすむ

B. Adjectives and Nouns 🔊

(a) Change the following into the past affirmatives.

Example: たかい → たかかった
げんきな → げんきだった
がくせい → がくせいだった

1. ゆうめいな	2. あめ	3. あかい	4. かわいい
5. みじかい	6. しんせつな	7. やすい	8. きれいな
9. いいてんき	10. かっこいい	11. さびしい	12. ねむい

(b) Change the following into the past negatives.

Example:　たかい　　→　たかくなかった

　　　　　　げんきな　→　げんきじゃなかった

　　　　　　がくせい　→　がくせいじゃなかった

1. いじわるな　　2. びょうき　　　3. わかい　　　　4. かわいい

5. ながい　　　　6. べんりな　　　7. あおい　　　　8. しずかな

9. いいてんき　10. かっこいい　11. おもしろい　12. さびしい

Ⅱ Informal Speech

A. Using the cues below, make questions about yesterday in informal speech. How do you answer those questions? 〔⌐﹞

Example:　テレビを見る

　　　　　→　Q：きのうテレビを見た？

　　　　　　　A：うん、見た。／ううん、見なかった。

1. ピザを食べる
2. 散歩する
3. 図書館で本を借りる
4. うちを掃除する
5. うちで料理する
6. 友だちに会う
7. 単語を覚える
8. 学校に来る
9. 家族に電話をかける
10. コンピューターを使う
11. 手紙をもらう
12. 遊びに行く
13. 運動する
14. ディスコで踊る

B. Make questions about childhood in informal speech. How do you answer those questions?

Example: 元気
げんき
→ Q：子供の時、元気だった？
こども とき げんき
A：うん、元気だった。／ううん、元気じゃなかった。
げんき げんき

1. かわいい
2. 髪が長い
かみ なが
3. 背が高い
せ たか
4. 勉強が好き
べんきょう す
5. スキーが上手
じょうず
6. さびしい
7. 楽しい
たの
8. スポーツが好き
す
9. 宿題がきらい
しゅくだい
10. 頭がいい
あたま
11. 先生は親切
せんせい しんせつ
12. いじわる

Ⅲ 元気だったと思います
げんき おも

A. Make a guess about the childhoods of the people below.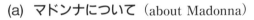

Example: 元気でしたか。
げんき
→ Q：この人は子供の時、元気でしたか。
ひと こども とき げんき
A：はい、元気だったと思います。
げんき おも
いいえ、元気じゃなかったと思います。
げんき おも

(a) マドンナについて（about Madonna）

1. きれいでしたか。
2. いじわるでしたか。
3. 歌が上手でしたか。
うた じょうず
4. 頭がよかったですか。
あたま
5. 背が高かったですか。
せ たか
6. 髪が黒かったですか。
かみ くろ
7. やせていましたか。
8. ピアノを弾きましたか。
ひ
9. よく勉強しましたか。
べんきょう
10. よくお母さんを手伝いましたか。
かあ てつだ

(b) 日本語の先生について（about your Japanese teacher）

1. かわいかったですか。　　　2. 学校が好きでしたか。

3. 太っていましたか。　　　　4. いじわるでしたか。

5. よく遊びましたか。　　　　6. 人気がありましたか。

B. Choose one classmate and guess what they were like as a child using the following characteristics.

Example: 頭がいい　→　ロバートさんは子供の時、頭がよかったと思います。

1. いい子　　　　　　　2. 元気　　　　　　　3. 背が高い／低い

4. 髪が長い／短い　　　5. 忙しい　　　　　　6. ひま

7. 静か　　　　　　　　8. いじわる　　　　　9. 学校が好き

10. かわいい

Ⅳ 子供の時遊んだと言っていました

A. Pair Work—Ask your partner the following questions about his/her childhood and report to the class using 〜と言っていました.

Example: いじわるでしたか。

→　Ａ：子供の時、いじわるでしたか。

Ｂ：はい、いじわるでした。

Ａ：Ｂさんは、子供の時いじわるだったと言っていました。

1. 学校が好きでしたか。　　　2. 頭がよかったですか。

3. 背が高かったですか。　　　4. かわいかったですか。

5. めがねをかけていましたか。　6. よく何をしましたか。

B. What would these people say/have said? Make up your own quote for the following people.

Example: シュワルツェネッガーは、きのうたくさん運動したと言っていました。

Ex. シュワルツェネッガー　(1) マイケル・ジャクソン　(2) エルビス・プレスリー

きのうたくさん
運動しました
うんどう

子供の時……
こども　とき

若い時……
わか　とき

(3) 友だち
とも

(4) 母（[my] mother）
はは

(5) 日本語の先生
にほんご　せんせい

先月……
せんげつ

高校の時……
こうこう　とき

大学の時……
だいがく　とき

Ⓥ めがねをかけている人です
ひと

A. Look at the picture below and answer the questions.

Example: 田中さん
たなか
→ 　Q：田中さんはどの人ですか。
たなか　　　　ひと
A：めがねをかけている人です。白いトレーナーを着ている人です。
ひと　　しろ　　　　　き　　ひと

1. 中村さん　2. 山口さん　3. 野村さん　4. 森さん　5. 大川さん　6. 鈴木さん
なかむら　　やまぐち　　　のむら　　　もり　　おおかわ　　すずき

B. Pair Work—One of you looks at picture A below and the other looks at picture B (p. 188). Ask each other questions and identify all the people in the picture.

Example: よしこ → A：よしこさんはどの人ですか。
B：テレビを見ている人です。

Picture A

えり

ゆたか

よしこ

じゅん

ちかこ

Ask which of the people are the following:

1. たろう
2. きょうこ
3. だいすけ
4. ようこ

C. Class Activity—Describe your classmates.

The class is divided into two groups, A and B. Each member of group A acts out something and freezes in the middle of doing so. Members of group B answer the teacher's questions, using 〜ている人です. Take turns when finished.

Example: Teacher：マイクさんはどの人ですか。
Student：車を運転している人です。

Ⓥ まだ食べていません

A. Answer the following questions using まだ〜ていません.

Example: Q：もう昼ごはんを食べましたか。
A：いいえ、まだ食べていません。

1. もう切符を買いましたか。
2. もう宿題をしましたか。
3. もう作文を書きましたか。

4. もう薬を飲みましたか。
   <ruby>薬<rt>くすり</rt></ruby> <ruby>飲<rt>の</rt></ruby>

5. もう晩ごはんを食べましたか。
   <ruby>晩<rt>ばん</rt></ruby> <ruby>食<rt>た</rt></ruby>

6. もう新しい単語を覚えましたか。
   <ruby>新<rt>あたら</rt></ruby> <ruby>単語<rt>たんご</rt></ruby> <ruby>覚<rt>おぼ</rt></ruby>

B. Pair Work—Ask if your partner has done . . . yet.

   Example: 天ぷらを食べる
   <ruby>天<rt>てん</rt></ruby> <ruby>食<rt>た</rt></ruby>
   → A：もう天ぷらを食べましたか。
     　　 <ruby>天<rt>てん</rt></ruby> <ruby>食<rt>た</rt></ruby>
   　　 B：ええ、もう食べました。／いいえ、まだ食べていません。
     　　 <ruby>食<rt>た</rt></ruby> <ruby>食<rt>た</rt></ruby>

1. 新幹線に乗る
   <ruby>新幹線<rt>しんかんせん</rt></ruby> <ruby>乗<rt>の</rt></ruby>

2. 温泉に入る
   <ruby>温泉<rt>おんせん</rt></ruby> <ruby>入<rt>はい</rt></ruby>

3. 十課 (Lesson 10) を読む
   <ruby>十課<rt>じゅっか</rt></ruby> <ruby>読<rt>よ</rt></ruby>

4. かぶきを見に行く
   <ruby>見<rt>み</rt></ruby> <ruby>行<rt>い</rt></ruby>

5. ＿＿＿＿＿＿＿＿＿＿＿＿＿＿＿＿を見る
   (a name of newly released movie) <ruby>見<rt>み</rt></ruby>

6. ＿＿＿＿＿＿＿＿＿＿＿＿＿＿＿＿を聞く
   (a name of newly released CD) <ruby>聞<rt>き</rt></ruby>

7. ＿＿＿＿＿＿＿＿＿＿＿＿＿＿＿＿を読む
   (a name of current best-selling novel) <ruby>読<rt>よ</rt></ruby>

Ⅶ 天気がいいから、遊びに行きます
<ruby>天気<rt>てんき</rt></ruby> <ruby>遊<rt>あそ</rt></ruby> <ruby>行<rt>い</rt></ruby>

A. Match up the phrases to make sense.

1. 魚がきらいだから　　　　　・　　　・今はひまです。
   <ruby>魚<rt>さかな</rt></ruby>　　　　　　　　　　　　　<ruby>今<rt>いま</rt></ruby>

2. 試験が終わったから　　　　・　　　・行きませんか。
   <ruby>試験<rt>しけん</rt></ruby> <ruby>終<rt>お</rt></ruby>　　　　　　　　<ruby>行<rt>い</rt></ruby>

3. 旅行に行ったから　　　　　・　　　・すしを食べません。
   <ruby>旅行<rt>りょこう</rt></ruby> <ruby>行<rt>い</rt></ruby>　　　　　　　　<ruby>食<rt>た</rt></ruby>

4. コンサートの切符を二枚もらったから・　・急ぎましょう。
   <ruby>切符<rt>きっぷ</rt></ruby> <ruby>二枚<rt>にまい</rt></ruby>　　　　<ruby>急<rt>いそ</rt></ruby>

5. 天気がよくなかったから　　・　　　・遊びに行きませんでした。
   <ruby>天気<rt>てんき</rt></ruby>　　　　　　　　　　　　<ruby>遊<rt>あそ</rt></ruby> <ruby>行<rt>い</rt></ruby>

6. クラスが始まるから　　　　・　　　・学校を休みました。
   <ruby>始<rt>はじ</rt></ruby>　　　　　　　　　　　　　<ruby>学校<rt>がっこう</rt></ruby> <ruby>休<rt>やす</rt></ruby>

B. Complete the following sentences adding reasons.

1. _____から、お金がぜんぜんありません。

2. _____から、日本語を勉強しています。

3. _____から、先週の週末は忙しかったです。

4. _____から、きのう学校を休みました。

Ⅷ まとめの練習

A. Role Play—One of you is working at a fast-food restaurant. The other is a customer. Using Dialogue Ⅲ as a model, order some food and drinks from the menu below. Be sure to say how many you want.

B. Answer the following questions.

1. ピアノを弾きますか。

2. ギターを弾くのが上手ですか。

3. 踊るのが好きですか。

4. 病気の時、よく薬を飲みますか。

5. よく散歩しますか。

6. 去年の誕生日（birthday）に何かもらいましたか。
   だれに何をもらいましたか。

7. 今日、クラスは何時に始まりましたか。何時に終わりますか。

8. 犬が好きですか。

9. 子供の時、よく友だちと遊びましたか。

10. どんな色のトレーナーを持っていますか。

11. 今度の試験は難しいと思いますか。

12. あなたの国では、どんなスポーツが人気がありますか。

13. どんな色が好きですか。

Pair Work Ⅴ B.

Example: よしこ

→ A：よしこさんはどの人ですか。

B：テレビを見ている人です。

Picture B

Ask which of the people are the following:

1. ゆたか
2. じゅん
3. ちかこ
4. えり

色

いろ

C o l o r s

There are two kinds of words for colors.

Group 1: い-adjectives

黒い —————— black		白い —————— white	
くろ		しろ	
赤い —————— red		青い —————— blue	
あか		あお	
黄色い —————— yellow		茶色い —————— brown	
きいろ		ちゃいろ	

These words become nouns without the い.

赤いかばん   *red bag*
あか

赤が一番好きです。   *I like red the best.*
あか　いちばん す

Group 2: nouns

緑／グリーン —————— green		紫 —————— purple	
みどり		むらさき	
灰色／グレー —————— gray		水色 —————— light blue	
はいいろ		みずいろ	
ピンク —————— pink		金色／ゴールド —————— gold	
		きんいろ	
銀色／シルバー —————— silver			
ぎんいろ			

There words need の in order to make noun phrases.

緑／グリーンのセーター   *green sweater*
みどり

Here are some words related to colors.

顔が青いですね。   *You look pale.*
かお　あお

白黒の写真   *black and white picture*
しろくろ　しゃしん

メアリーさんは金髪です。   *Mary has blonde hair.*
きんぱつ

第10課 | L E S S O N 10

冬休みの予定 Winter Vacation Plans
ふゆ やす　　　よ てい

会話 Dialogue
かい わ

(( ))

Ⅰ Winter vacation is approaching.

1 メアリー：　寒くなりましたね。
　　　　　　　さむ

2 たけし：　　ええ。メアリーさん、冬休みはどうしますか。
　　　　　　　　　　　　　　　　ふゆやす

3 メアリー：　韓国か台湾に行くつもりですが、まだ決めていません。
　　　　　　　かんこく たいわん い　　　　　　　　　　　　き

4 たけし：　　いいですね。

5 メアリー：　韓国と台湾とどっちのほうがいいと思いますか。
　　　　　　　かんこく たいわん　　　　　　　　　　　おも

6 たけし：　　うーん、台湾のほうが暖かいと思います。でも、スーさんは韓国の食べ
　　　　　　　　　　　たいわん　　　あたた　おも　　　　　　　　　　　　かんこく　た

7　　　　　　　物はおいしいと言っていましたよ。
　　　　　　　もの　　　　　　い

8 メアリー：　そうですか。ところで、たけしさんはどこかに行きますか。
　　　　　　　　　　　　　　　　　　　　　　　　　　　　い

9 たけし：　　どこにも行きません。お金がないから、ここにいます。
　　　　　　　　　　　い　　　　　　　かね

10 メアリー：　そうですか。じゃあ、たけしさんにおみやげを買ってきますよ。
　　　　　　　　　　　　　　　　　　　　　　　　　　　　　　　か

11 たけし：　　わあ、ありがとう。

Ⅱ At a travel agency.

1 メアリー：　　　　大阪からソウルまで飛行機の予約をお願いします。
　　　　　　　　　　おおさか　　　　　　　ひこうき　よやく　ねが

2 旅行会社の人：はい、いつですか。
　りょこうがいしゃ　ひと

3 メアリー：　　　　十二月十九日です。
　　　　　　　　　　じゅうにがつじゅうくにち

4 旅行会社の人：午前と午後の便がありますが……。
　りょこうがいしゃ　ひと　ごぜん　ごご　びん

5 メアリー：　　　　午前のをお願いします。
　　　　　　　　　　ごぜん　　　ねが

6　　　　　　　　　クレジットカードで払ってもいいですか。
　　　　　　　　　　　　　　　　　はら

7 旅行会社の人：はい。
　りょこうがいしゃ　ひと

8 メアリー：　　　　ソウルまでどのぐらいかかりますか。

9 旅行会社の人：一時間ぐらいです。
　りょこうがいしゃ　ひと　いちじかん

I

Mary: It is getting cold.

Takeshi: Yes. Mary, what will you do at winter break?

Mary: I am planning to go to Korea or Taiwan, but I haven't decided yet.

Takeshi: That's nice.

Mary: Which do you think is better, Korea or Taiwan?

Takeshi: Mm . . . I think it is warmer in Taiwan. But Sue said that the food was delicious in Korea.

Mary: I see. By the way, are you going somewhere, Takeshi?

Takeshi: I won't go anywhere. I don't have money, so I will stay here.

Mary: Is that so? Then I'll buy some souvenir for you.

Takeshi: Wow, thank you.

Ⅱ

Mary: I'd like to reserve a plane ticket from Osaka to Seoul.

Travel agent: When is it?

Mary: December 19.

Travel agent: We have a morning flight and an afternoon flight.

Mary: A morning flight, please. Can I use a credit card?

Travel agent: Yes.

Mary: How long does it take to Seoul?

Travel agent: About one hour.

単語
たん ご

Vocabulary

Nouns

あき	秋	fall
いしゃ	医者	doctor
えき	駅	station
おかねもち	お金持ち	rich person
かお	顔	face
きせつ	季節	season
* クレジットカード		credit card
ことし	今年	this year
サッカー		soccer
シャツ		shirt
せいかつ	生活	life; living
せかい	世界	world
ちかてつ	地下鉄	subway
てぶくろ	手袋	gloves
とこや	床屋	barber's
はる	春	spring
パンツ		pants
びよういん	美容院	beauty parlor
* びん	便	flight
ふね	船	ship; boat
やきゅう	野球	baseball
ゆうめいじん	有名人	celebrity
* よやく	予約	reservation
らいがっき	来学期	next semester
りんご		apple

い-adjectives

* あたたかい	暖かい	warm
おそい	遅い	slow; late
すずしい	涼しい	cool (weather—not used for things)
つめたい	冷たい	cold (thing/people)
ねむい	眠い	sleepy

* Words that appear in the dialogue

な-adjective

かんたん（な）	簡単	easy; simple

U-verbs

* かかる		to take (amount of time/money) (*no particle*)
とまる	泊まる	to stay (at a hotel, etc.)　（〜に）
* なる		to become
* はらう	払う	to pay

Ru-verb

* きめる	決める	to decide

Irregular Verb

れんしゅうする	練習する	to practice

Adverbs and Other Expressions

あるいて	歩いて	on foot
いちばん	一番	best
* 〜か〜		or
〜かげつ	〜か月	for . . . months
〜ご	〜後	in . . . time; after . . .
このごろ		these days
〜しゅうかん	〜週間	for . . . weeks
〜で		by (means of transportation); with (a tool)
どうやって		how; by what means
どちら		which
* どっち		which
* どのぐらい		how much; how long
〜ねん	〜年	. . . years
はやく	早く	(do something) early; fast

文法 G r a m m a r
ぶん ぽう

1 Comparison

In Japanese, adjectives have the same shape in noncomparative and comparative sentences; there is no alteration as in "great/greater." The idea of comparison is expressed by adding something to the nouns that are compared.

> A のほうが　B より[1] (property)。　=　*A is more* (property) *than B.*

エルビス・プレスリーのほうがフランク・シナトラよりかっこいいです。
Elvis Presley is more hip than Frank Sinatra.

バーブラ・ストライザンドのほうがマドンナより歌が上手です。
うた　じょうず
Barbra Streisand is a better singer than Madonna.

You can ask for another person's opinion on two things in comparative terms.

> A と B と　どっちのほう[2]が　(property)。
> =　*Between A and B, which is more* (property)?

バスと電車とどっちのほうが安いですか。
でんしゃ　　　　　　　　　やす
Which is cheaper, (going by) bus or (by) train?

In comparison among three or more items, the degree qualifier いちばん is used.

> [(class of items) の中で] A がいちばん (property)。
> なか
> =　*A is the most* (property) [*among* (a class of items)].

パバロッティとカレーラスとドミンゴの中で、だれがいちばん歌が上手だと思い
なか　　　　　　　　　　　　うた　じょうず　おも
ますか。
Between Pavarotti, Carreras, and Domingo, who do you think is the best singer?

---

[1]In real life, the phrases A のほうが and B より often appear in the reverse order, making it very easy to be misled into believing the opposite of what is actually said. Don't rely on the word order, therefore, to decide which item is claimed to be superior. Listen carefully for the words のほうが and より.

[2]There are several alternates for どっちのほう. They are: どちらのほう、どっち、and どちら. Any one of these can be used in question sentences seeking comparisons between two items. どっち and どっちのほう are slightly more colloquial than どちら and どちらのほう.

もちろん、パバロッティがいちばん歌が上手です。
Pavarotti is best, naturally.

Note that the words のほう and どっち are not used in statements of comparison among three or more items. Normal question words like だれ, どれ, and 何 are used instead.[3]

2 adjective/noun ＋ の

When a noun follows an adjective, and when it is clear what you are referring to, you can replace the noun with the pronoun の, "one." You can use の to avoid repetition.

私は黒いセーターを持っています。赤いのも持っています。（の＝セーター）
I have a black sweater. I have a red one, too.

安い辞書を買いに行きました。でもいいのがありませんでした。（の＝辞書）
I went to buy an inexpensive dictionary, but there were no good ones.

い-adjective な-adjective ＋ noun	→	い-adjective な-adjective ＋ の

Similarly, a noun following another noun can be reduced. Here, a sequence of the form "noun₁ の noun₂" will be reduced to "noun₁ の." You simply omit the second noun.

これはスーさんのかばんですか。　　いいえ、それはメアリーさんの＿＿＿です。
Is this Sue's bag?　　*No, that is Mary's＿＿.*

アメリカのアイスクリームのほうが日本の＿＿＿よりおいしいです。
American ice cream is more delicious than Japanese one.

noun₁ の noun₂	→	noun₁ の＿＿＿

---

[3]The tendency is to use どれ when a list of items is presented, and to use 何 when a group is referred to collectively. Compare:
りんごとみかんとさくらんぼの中で、どれがいちばん好きですか。
Which do you like best, apples, tangerines, or cherries?
くだものの中で、何がいちばん好きですか。
What fruit do you like best?

3 ～つもりだ

つもり follows verbs in the present tense short forms to describe what a person is planning to do in the future. You can also use a verb in the negative plus つもり to describe what you are planning *not* to do, or what you do *not* intend to do.

| verb (present, short) ＋つもりだ | *(I) intend to do . . .* |

（私は）週末にたけしさんとテニスをする<u>つもりです</u>。
I intend to play tennis with Takeshi this weekend.

山下先生はあした大学に来ない<u>つもりです</u>。
Professor Yamashita does not intend to come to school tomorrow.

お寺を見に行く<u>つもりでした</u>けど、天気がよくなかったから、行きませんでした。
We were planning to visit a temple, but we didn't, because the weather was not good.

4 adjective ＋ なる

The verb なる means "to become," indicating a change. なる follows nouns and both types of adjectives.

い-adjectives:	暖かい	→	暖か<u>く</u>なる	*to become warm/warmer*
な-adjectives:	静か（な）	→	静か<u>に</u>なる	*to become quiet/quieter*
nouns:	会社員	→	会社員<u>に</u>なる	*to become a company employee*

日本語の勉強が楽しくなりました。
Studying the Japanese language is fun now (though it was like torture before).

日本語の勉強が好きになりました。
I have grown fond of studying the Japanese language.

With い-adjectives, the final い is dropped and く is added, as in their negative conjugations. A common mistake is to expand the pattern of な-adjectives and nouns and use に with い-adjectives. It is wrong to say, for example, ×暖かいになる.

When an adjective is used with なる, a question arises whether the sentence describes an absolute change (ex. "it has become warm, hence it is not cold any longer") or a relative change (ex. "it has become warmer, but it is still cold"). なる sentences are ambiguous in isolation. If you want to make clear that you are talking in relative terms, you can use the pattern for comparison together with なる.

メアリーさんは<u>前より</u>日本語が上手になりました。
Mary has become better in Japanese <u>than before</u>.

5 どこかに／どこにも

In Lesson 8 we learned the Japanese expressions for "something" and "not . . . anything," 何か and 何も. As you must have noticed, these expressions are made up of the question word for things, 何, plus particles か and も. Other expressions for "some" and "any" in Japanese follow this pattern. Thus,

| *something* | 何か__ | *someone* | だれか__ | *somewhere* | どこか__ |
| *not anything* | 何__も | *not anyone* | だれ__も | *not anywhere* | どこ__も |

As we noted in Lesson 8, these words are used by themselves, where particles は, が, or を would be expected. It is, then, interesting to observe how these expressions interact with other particles, such as に, へ, and で. These particles appear in the places shown with underscores above. Let us look at some examples.

どこか<u>へ</u>行きましたか。
Did you go anywhere?

いいえ、どこ<u>へ</u>も行きませんでした。
No, I didn't go anywhere.

だれか<u>に</u>会いましたか。
Did you see anybody?

いいえ、だれ<u>に</u>も会いませんでした。
No, I didn't see anybody.

何かしましたか。
Did you do anything?

いいえ、何もしませんでした。
No, I didn't do anything.

6 で

You can use the particle で with nouns that describe the means of transportation and the instruments you use.

はしでごはんを食べます。　　We eat our meals <u>with chopsticks</u>.

日本語で話しましょう。　　Let's talk <u>in Japanese</u>.

バスで駅まで行きました。　　I went to the station <u>by bus</u>.

テレビで映画を見ました。　　I saw a movie <u>on TV</u>.

表現ノート　　Expression Notes ⑩

午前と午後の便がありますが……▶ We sometimes use が and けど at the end of a sentence when we want our partners to treat what we have just said as a given, common ground to build upon. These words often indicate the speaker's intention to give her partner a chance to react and speak up. By relegating the right to speak to one's partner, they also contribute to the politeness of one's utterance.

In the dialogue, the travel agent lays out the relevant information on the table; there are two flights, one leaving in the morning and another in the afternoon. が attached to her sentence indicates that she wants to build upon, and move forward with, these pieces of information. Instead of asking the obvious question, namely, どちらがいいですか, the agent chooses not to finish her sentence, and lets her customer come forward with an answer immediately.

練習 Practice
れん しゅう

① 電車のほうがバスより速いです
でんしゃ　　　　　　　　　　　　　はや

A. Look at the pictures below and answer the following questions. 🔊

Example:　Q：電車とバスとどちらのほうが速いですか。
　　　　　　　　でんしゃ　　　　　　　　　　　　はや
　　　　　　A：電車のほうがバスより速いです。
　　　　　　　　でんしゃ　　　　　　　　はや

Picture (a)

(a)

1. 新幹線とバスとどちらのほうが速いですか。
　しんかんせん　　　　　　　　　　　　はや
2. 新幹線と電車とどちらのほうが遅いですか。
　しんかんせん　でんしゃ　　　　　　　　おそ
3. 新幹線とバスとどちらのほうが安いですか。
　しんかんせん　　　　　　　　　　　　やす
4. 電車とバスとどちらのほうが高いですか。
　でんしゃ　　　　　　　　　　　　　たか

Picture (b)

5. 東京と大阪とどっちのほうが大きいですか。
　とうきょう　おおさか　　　　　　　　おお
6. 京都と大阪とどっちのほうが小さいですか。
　きょうと　おおさか　　　　　　　　ちい

Picture (c)

7. 田中さんと山田さんとどっちのほうが背が高いですか。
　たなか　　やまだ　　　　　　　　　せ　たか
8. 山田さんと鈴木さんとどっちのほうが背が低いですか。
　やまだ　　すずき　　　　　　　　　せ　ひく
9. 田中さんと鈴木さんとどっちのほうが若いですか。
　たなか　　すずき　　　　　　　　　わか
10. 山田さんと鈴木さんとどっちのほうが髪が短いですか。
　　やまだ　　すずき　　　　　　　　かみ　みじか

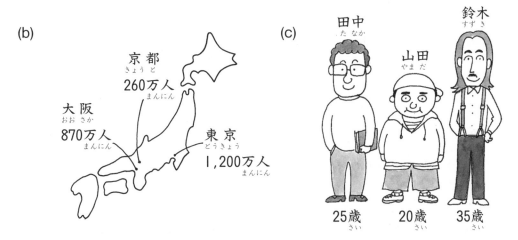

B. Pair Work—Make questions using the following cues and ask your partner. When you answer the questions, add reasons for your answers, if possible.

Example: 夏／冬 （好き）

→ A：夏と冬とどちら（のほう）が好きですか。

B：夏のほうが（冬より）好きです。

（or 夏も冬も好きです。／夏も冬もきらいです。）

A：どうしてですか。

B：泳ぐのが好きですから。

1. すし／天ぷら （おいしい）
2. 頭がいい人／かっこいい人 （好き）
3. 野球／サッカー （人気がある）
4. 中国料理／日本料理 （好き）
5. 船／飛行機 （好き）
6. 日本の車／ドイツ (Germany) の車 （いい）
7. 漢字／カタカナ （かんたん）
8. シュワルツェネッガー／スタローン （頭がいい）
9. マイケル・ジャクソン／マドンナ （お金持ち）
10. 春／秋 （好き）
11. 日本の冬／あなたの国の冬 （暖かい）
12. 日本の生活／あなたの国の生活 （大変 or 楽しい）

Ⅱ 新幹線がいちばん速いです

A. Look at the pictures on the previous page and answer the questions below. 🔊

Example: Q：この中で、どれがいちばん速いですか。

A：新幹線がいちばん速いです。

Picture (a)

1. この中で、どれがいちばん遅いですか。
2. この中で、どれがいちばん安いですか。

Picture (b)

3. この中で、どこがいちばん大きいですか。

4. この中で、どこがいちばん小さいですか。

Picture (c)

5. この中で、だれがいちばん背が高いですか。

6. この中で、だれがいちばん若いですか。

7. この中で、だれがいちばん髪が長いですか。

B. Answer the following questions.

Example: 食べ物／好き
→ Q：食べ物の中で、何がいちばん好きですか。
A：すしがいちばん好きです。

1. 飲み物／好き　　2. 世界の町／好き　　3. 有名人／好き

4. 日本料理／きらい　5. 音楽／好き　　6. 季節／好き

7. クラス／いい学生　8. クラス／背が高い　9. クラス／たくさん食べる

C. Group Work—Make a group of three or four people. Ask each other questions and make as many superlative sentences as possible about the group.

Example: この中で、Aさんがいちばん若いです。
Bさんがいちばん背が高いです。
Cさんがいちばんよく遅くクラスに来ます。

D. Class Activity—First form pairs and make comparative and superlative question sentences with your partner. (You should know the answers.) Then ask questions to the class. The rest of the class answer the questions.

Example: 富士山とエベレストとどちらのほうが高いですか。
田中さんと山田さんとどちらのほうが若いですか。
クラスの中で今日だれがいちばんお金を持っていますか。
世界の国の中でどこがいちばん小さいですか。

Ⅲ これは私のです

A. This is a refrigerator in a dormitory. Tell whose each thing is, using の.

Example:　このりんごはリーさん<u>の</u>です。

B. You are a customer. Look at the picture and tell which you want.

Example:

Store attendant：どちらのコーヒーがいいですか。

Customer：　　　熱いのをください。

熱い　　　冷たい

(1) どちらの辞書がいいですか。　　(2) どちらのかばんがいいですか。

大きい　　　小さい　　　　　高い　　　安い

(3) どちらの手袋がいいですか。

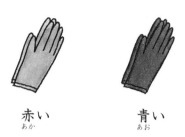

赤い
あか

青い
あお

(4) どちらのパンツがいいですか。

長い
なが

短い
みじか

(5) どちらのシャツがいいですか。

白い
しろ

黒い
くろ

Ⅳ 見に行くつもりです
み　い

A. You are planning to do/not to do the following things next week. Tell what you will/will not do using ～つもりです.

Example: 月曜日に本を読むつもりです。
げつようび　ほん　よ

月曜日 げつようび	Ex. to read books	(1) to practice the piano
火曜日 かようび	(2) to do exercises	
水曜日 すいようび	(3) to do laundry	
木曜日 もくようび	(4) to write letters to friends	(5) not to go out
金曜日 きんようび	(6) to eat dinner with friends	(7) not to study Japanese
土曜日 どようび	(8) to stay at a friend's	(9) not to go home
日曜日 にちようび	(10) to clean a room	(11) not to get up early

B. Answer the following questions.

Example:　Q：週末、映画を見に行きますか。
　　　　　　A：ええ、見に行くつもりです。
　　　　　　　　いいえ、見に行かないつもりです。

1. 今日の午後、勉強しますか。
2. 今晩、テレビを見ますか。
3. あさって、買い物をしますか。
4. 冬休みに旅行しますか。
5. 週末、料理を作りますか。
6. 三年後、日本にいますか。
7. 来学期も日本語を勉強しますか。

Ⓥ きれいになりました

A. Describe the following pictures. 🔊

Example:　きれい　→　きれいになりました。

Ex. きれい　　　　　　　　　　　　　　(1) 眠い

(2) 元気

(3) 大きい

(4) 髪が短い

(5) ひま

(6) 暑い

(7) 涼しい

(8) 医者
いしゃ

(9) 春
はる

(10) 円が安い
えん　やす

$1 =¥110 → $1 =¥150

B. Fill in the blanks with appropriate forms.

1. 掃除をしたから、部屋が＿＿＿＿＿＿＿なりました。
   そうじ　　　　　　　へや

2. 美容院／床屋に行ったから、髪が＿＿＿＿＿＿＿なりました。
   びょういん　とこや　い　　　　　　かみ

3. 円が＿＿＿＿＿＿＿なりました。
   えん

4. 毎日ピアノを練習しているから、＿＿＿＿＿＿＿なりました。
   まいにち　　　　れんしゅう

5. お酒をたくさん飲んで、顔が＿＿＿＿＿＿＿なりました。
   さけ　　　　　の　　　かお

6. 十一月は暖かかったですが、このごろ＿＿＿＿＿＿＿なりました。
   じゅういちがつ　あたた

7. 教えるのが好きだから、＿＿＿＿＿＿＿なるつもりです。
   おし　　　す

Ⅵ 自転車で行きます
じてんしゃ　い

A. Look at each picture and explain how to get to and from one place to another.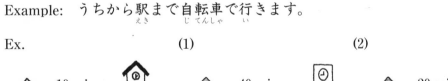

Example: うちから駅まで自転車で行きます。
えき　　じてんしゃ　い

Ex.　　　　　　　　(1)　　　　　　　　(2)

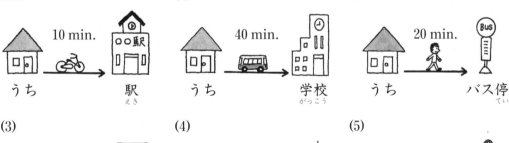

うち　　　　駅　　うち　　　　学校　　うち　　　　バス停
えき　　　　　　　　　がっこう　　　　　　　　　てい

(3)　　　　　　　　(4)　　　　　　　　(5)

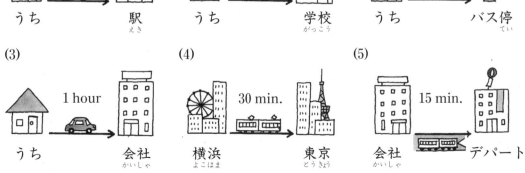

うち　　　　会社　　横浜　　　　東京　　会社　　　　デパート
かいしゃ　　よこはま　　とうきょう　　かいしゃ

(6)　　　　　　　　(7)　　　　　　　　(8)

B. Use the same pictures and describe how long it takes. 🔊

Example: うちから駅まで十分かかります。
えき　　じゅっぷん

C. Explain how you get from your house to school.

Example: うちから南駅まで自転車で行きます。五分かかります。
みなみえき　　じてんしゃ　い　　　　ごふん

南駅から西駅まで電車に乗ります。二十分かかります。
みなみえき　にしえき　　でんしゃ　の　　　　にじゅっぷん

西駅から学校まで歩いて行きます。十分ぐらいかかります。
にしえき　がっこう　　ある　い　　　　じゅっぷん

Ⅶ まとめの練習
れんしゅう

A. The chart below shows winter vacation plans for Mary and her friends. First, answer the following questions about Mary's plan.

Mary	will go to Korea with Sue	by plane	3 weeks	will stay at Sue's house	will do shopping and eat Korean foods
Robert	will go back to London	by plane	2 weeks		will meet friends
Ken	will go to Tokyo with a friend	by bullet train	3 days	will stay at a hotel	will play at Tokyo Disneyland
Tom	will go to the south pole（南極）なんきょく	by boat	2 months	doesn't know yet	will take pictures with penguins （ペンギン）
Takeshi	will go nowhere				

1. メアリーさんは今年の冬休みにどこかに行くつもりですか。
ことし　ふゆやす

2. どうやって韓国へ行きますか。だれと行きますか。
かんこく　い　　　　　　　い

3. どのぐらい行きますか。
い

4. どこに泊まりますか。

5. 韓国で何をするつもりですか。

How about the others' plans? Make pairs and ask questions.

B. Pair Work—Talk about your plans for the upcoming vacation.

C. Role Play—One of you works for a travel agency and the other is a customer. Using Dialogue Ⅱ as a model, make reservations for the following tickets.

(1) From Nagoya to Los Angeles	Jan. 1	1 person	smoking seat
(2) From Tokyo to Paris	Feb. 14	1 person	window seat
(3) From Osaka to Rome	Apr. 18	2 persons	aisle seats
(4) From Tokyo to Bangkok	Aug. 20	4 persons	nonsmoking seats

smoking seat = 喫煙席（きつえんせき）　　aisle seat = 通路側の席（つうろがわ　せき）

window seat = 窓側の席（まどがわ　せき）　　nonsmoking seat = 禁煙席（きんえんせき）

駅 で
えき
At the Station

Types of Trains

普通 ——————— local
ふつう

急行 ——————— express
きゅうこう

特急 ——————— super express
とっきゅう

Destination

～行き ——————— bound for . . .
い

～方面 ——————— serving . . . areas
ほうめん

Types of Tickets and Seats

乗車券 ——————— (boarding) ticket
じょうしゃけん

回数券 ——————— coupons
かいすうけん

定期券 ——————— commuter's pass
ていきけん

整理券 ——————— vouchers; zone tickets
せいりけん

学割 ——————— student discount
がくわり

指定席 ——————— reserved seat
していせき

自由席 ——————— general admission seat
じゆうせき

禁煙車 ——————— nonsmoking car
きんえんしゃ

往復 ——————— round trip
おうふく

片道 ——————— one way
かたみち

Places in Stations

～番線 ——————— track number . . .
ばんせん

切符売り場 ——————— ticket vending area
きっぷ う ば

改札 ——————— gate
かいさつ

ホーム ——————— platform

売店 ——————— kiosk
ばいてん

出口 ——————— exit
でぐち

入口 ——————— entrance
いりぐち

階段 ——————— stairs
かいだん

いちばん前 ——————— first car; front end
まえ

いちばん後ろ ——————— last car; tail end
うし

Miscellaneous Public Transportation Terms

乗り換え ——————— transfer
（の）（か）

次は〜 ——————— next (stop), . . .
（つぎ）

先発 ——————— departing first
（せんぱつ）

次発 ——————— departing second
（じ）（はつ）

終電 ——————— last train
（しゅうでん）

Announcements

まもなく発車します ——————— We will be leaving soon.
（はっしゃ）

電車が参ります ——————— A train is arriving.
（でんしゃ）（まい）

次は〜に止まります ——————— Next (we'll stop at) . . .
（つぎ）（と）

ドアが閉まります。ご注意ください —— The doors are closing. Please be careful.
（し）（ちゅう）（い）

Useful Expressions

この電車は秋葉原に止まりますか。——— Does this train stop at Akihabara?
（でんしゃ）（あき　は　ばら）（と）

終電は何時ですか。——————— What time is the last train?
（しゅうでん）（なん　じ）

東京までの指定席を一枚お願いします。— One reserved ticket to Tokyo, please.
（とうきょう）（し　ていせき）（いちまい）（ねが）

学割が使えますか。——————— Can I get a student discount?
（がくわり）（つか）

　　　　　　*　　　　　*　　　　　*

A：鎌倉行きの電車はどれですか。
（かまくら　い）　　（でんしゃ）
Which one is the train bound for Kamakura?

B：二番線です。
（に　ばんせん）
Track number two.

第11課 LESSON 11

休みのあと After the Vacation

会話 Dialogue 🔊

Michiko and Mary meet after the vacation.

Ⅰ

1 みちこ： メアリーさん、久しぶりですね。休みはどうでしたか。

2 メアリー： すごく楽しかったです。韓国で買い物をしたり、韓国料理を食べたり

3 しました。

4 みちこ： いいですね。私も旅行したいです。

5 メアリー： みちこさんの休みは楽しかったですか。

6 みちこ： まあまあでした。一日だけドライブに行きましたが、毎日アルバイト

7 をしていました。

Ⅱ

1 メアリー： みちこさん、友だちを紹介します。こちらはジョンさんです。ジョンさ

2 んは先月、日本に来ました。

3 ジョン： 初めまして。

4 みちこ： 初めまして、どうぞよろしく。

Ⅲ

1 みちこ： ジョンさん、出身はどこですか。

2 ジョン： オーストラリアのケアンズです。

3 みちこ： そうですか。

4 ジョン： みちこさんはケアンズに行ったことがありますか。

5 みちこ： いいえ、ありません。

6 ジョン： 山や海があって、きれいな所ですよ。グレートバリアリーフで有名です。

7　　　　　みちこさんはどこの出身ですか。
8 みちこ：　長野です。今度遊びに来てください。食べ物もおいしいですよ。
9 ジョン：　ぜひ、行きたいです。

Ⅰ

Michiko: Mary, I haven't seen you for a long time. How was your vacation?

Mary: It was really fun. I went shopping, ate Korean dishes, and things like that in Korea.

Michiko: Sounds good. I want to travel, too.

Mary: Did you have a fun vacation, Michiko?

Michiko: It was okay. I went for a drive just for one day, but I was working part-time every day.

Ⅱ

Mary: Michiko, I want to introduce you to a friend of mine. This is John. He came to Japan last month.

John: How do you do?

Michiko: How do you do? Nice to meet you.

Ⅲ

Michiko: John, where are you from?

John: I am from Cairns, Australia.

Michiko: Is that so.

John: Have you been to Cairns?

Michiko: No, I haven't.

John: It has mountains and the ocean and is a beautiful place. It's famous for the Great Barrier Reef. Where are you from, Michiko?

Michiko: I am from Nagano. Please come to visit me sometime. The food is good, too.

John: By all means, I would love to.

単語
たん　ご

Vocabulary

Nouns

* オーストラリア		Australia
おかし	お菓子	snack; sweets
おしょうがつ	お正月	New Year's
おとこのこ	男の子	boy
おもちゃ		toy
おんなのこ	女の子	girl
がいこく	外国	foreign country
かしゅ	歌手	singer
キャンプ		camp
* こちら		this person (polite)
こんがっき	今学期	this semester
しゃちょう	社長	president of a company
じゅぎょう	授業	class
しょうらい	将来	future
* ドライブ		drive
ビール		beer
びじゅつかん	美術館	art museum
ホストファミリー		host family
みずうみ	湖	lake
* やま	山	mountain
ゆめ	夢	dream
ルームメート		roommate

U-verbs

うそをつく		to tell a lie
おなかがすく		to become hungry
かう	飼う	to own (a pet)
サボる		to cut classes
とる	取る	to take (a class); to get (a grade)
ならう	習う	to learn
のぼる	登る	to climb　(place に)
はたらく	働く	to work

* Words that appear in the dialogue

Ru-verbs

つかれる	疲れる	to get tired
やめる		to quit

Irregular Verbs

けんかする		to have a fight; to quarrel
* しょうかいする	紹介する	to introduce (*person* に *person* を)
ダイエットする		to go on a diet
ちこくする	遅刻する	to be late (for an appointment)
りゅうがくする	留学する	to study abroad　(*place* に)

Adverbs and Other Expressions

あと	後	after (an event)　(*event* の)
* しゅっしん	出身	coming from　(*place* の)
* すごく		very
そして		and then
* ～だけ		just . . . ; only . . .
～てん	～点	. . . points
* ひさしぶり	久しぶり	it has been a long time
* まあまあ		okay; so-so
もっと		more

文法 Ｇ ｒ ａ ｍ ｍ ａ ｒ
ぶん　ぽう

1 〜たい

You can use a verb stem (the verb form that goes before ます) ＋たいです to describe your hope or aspiration.

今度の週末は、映画を見<u>たい</u>です。 *or* 映画が見<u>たい</u>です。
こん ど　 しゅうまつ　　　えい が　み　　　　　　　　　　　　えい が　み
I want to see a film this weekend.

いつか中国に行き<u>たい</u>です。
　　　ちゅうごく　 い
I want to go to China someday.

| verb stem ＋ たいです | *I want to do . . .* |

As you can see in the first example above, having たい attached to a verb slightly affects the composition of the sentence. A verb that takes the particle を can have either the particle を or が when it is followed by たい. Particles other than を remain the same.

The combination of a verb and たい conjugates as an い-adjective. Here are examples of negative and past tense たい sentences.

あの人にはもう会い<u>たくありません</u>。
　　ひと　　　　　　あ
I don't want to see that person any more.

セーターが買い<u>たかった</u>から、デパートに行きました。
　　　　　　か　　　　　　　　　　　　　い
I went to a department store, because I wanted to buy a sweater.

If your wish is one you have entertained for some time, that is, if you "have wanted to," you can use たいと思っています instead of たいです.
　　　　　　　　　　　　おも

たいです sentences are not usually used to describe wishes held by others. Somebody else's wishes are usually reported in Japanese either as quotations, observations, or guesses. To quote somebody, saying that she wants to do something, you can use と言っていました with たい.
　　　　　　　　　　　　　　　　　　い

メアリーさんはトイレに行き<u>たいと言っていました</u>。
　　　　　　　　　　　　　い　　い
Mary said she wanted to go to the bathroom.

To describe your observation to the effect that somebody wants to do something, you must use a special verb たがっている instead of たい. If a verb takes the particle を, the derived verb たがっている will retain the を, unlike たい, with which we had a choice between the particles が and を.

メアリーさんはコーヒーを飲みたがっています。
(It seems) Mary wants to drink coffee.

The verb たがっている, which comes from the dictionary form たがる, indicates "I think that she wants to, because of the way she is behaving." We will have more to say about this type of sentence in Lesson 14.

I want to . . . /Do you want to . . . ?	*They want to . . .*
• verb stem **＋** たいです	• verb stem **＋** たがっています
• たい conjugates as an い-adjective	• たがる conjugates as an *u*-verb
• が or を	• を only

2　〜たり〜たりする

You already know that you can connect two clauses with the *te*-form of predicates, as in:

大阪で買い物をして、韓国料理を食べます。
In Osaka, I will do some shopping and eat Korean food.

This sentence, however, tends to suggest that shopping and dining are *the only* activities you plan to perform in Osaka. If you want to avoid such implications and want to mention activities or events just *as exemplars*, thus leaving room for other things which are left unsaid, you can use a special predicate form 〜たり〜たりする.

大阪で買い物をしたり、韓国料理を食べたりします。
In Osaka, I will do such things as shopping and eating Korean dishes.

(activity A) たり　(activity B) たりする　　*do such things as A and B*

To get the たり form of a predicate, you just add り to the past tense short form of a predicate. (Thus we have したり for the verb する, whose past tense is した, and 食べたり for 食べる, past tense 食べた.) Note that the helping verb する at the end of the sentence indicates the tense of the sentence. You can change a 〜たり〜たりする sentence into the past tense, or incorporate it in a bigger sentence, by working on the helping verb part.

週末は、勉強したり、友だちと話したりしました。
I studied and talked with my friends, among other things, over the weekend.

踊ったり、音楽を聞いたりするのが好きです。
I like dancing, listening to music, and so forth.

3   ～ことがある

The past tense short form of a verb + ことがある describes that you did something, or something happened, in earlier times.

ヨーロッパに行ったことがありますか。 ― はい、行ったことがあります。
Have you ever been to Europe?   *Yes, I have.*

たけしさんは授業を休んだことがありません。
Takeshi has never been absent from classes (in his life).

verb (past, short) + ことがある	*have the experience of . . .*

4   noun A や noun B

や connects two nouns, as does と. や suggests that the things referred to are proposed as examples, and that you are not citing an exhaustive list.

A や B	*A and B, for example*

京都や奈良に行きました。
I went to Kyoto and Nara (for example, and may have visited other places as well).

表現ノート
ひょうげん

は in negative sentences▶ In negative sentences, you often find the particle は where you expect が or を. Observe the reply sentences in the following dialogues:

Q：山下先生はテレビを見ますか。 *Do you watch TV, Prof. Yamashita?*
やましたせんせい　　　　　み
A：いいえ、テレビは見ません。 *No, I don't.*
　　　　　　　　み

Q：コーヒーが飲みたいですか。 *Do you want to have a cup of coffee?*
　　　　　　の
A：いいえ、コーヒーは飲みたくありません。*No, I don't.*
　　　　　　　　　の

を and が, respectively, would not be ungrammatical in the above examples. Many Japanese speakers, however, find the は versions more natural.

　The rule of thumb is that negative Japanese sentences tend to contain at least one は phrase. If you add 私は to the sentences above, therefore, the
わたし
need for は is already fulfilled, and Japanese speakers feel much less compelled to use は after テレビ and コーヒー.

は may also follow particles like で and に.

英語では話したくありません。 *I don't want to speak in English.*
えいご　　はな
広島には行ったことがありません。 *I have never been to Hiroshima.*
ひろしま　　い

だけ▶ You can add だけ to numbers to talk about having just that many items. だけ implies that you have something up to the amount needed, but not more than that.

私はその人に一回だけ会ったことがあります。
わたし　　ひと　いっかい　　あ
　　　　　　　　　　I have met that person <u>just</u> once.
一つだけ質問があります。 *I have <u>just</u> one question.*
ひと　　しつもん
三十分だけ寝ました。 *I slept for <u>just</u> thirty minutes.*
さんじゅっぷん　　ね

だけ suggests that you can live with that few, though the number admittedly could have been higher. We will learn another word in Lesson 14, namely, しか, which means "only" in the sense that you do not have enough of.

に▶ You can use the particle に to indicate the occasion on which you do something.

晩ごはんにサラダを食べました。 *I ate salad <u>at</u> dinner.*
ばん　　　　　　た

に can also indicate the role you want something to play.

おみやげに絵葉書を買いました。 *I bought a postcard <u>as</u> a souvenir.*
　　　　えはがき　か

ドライブ▶ ドライブ is used when you go somewhere by car for pleasure. To say "to have a drive" or "to go for a drive," use ドライブに行く or ドライブする.

> 湖までドライブに行きました／ドライブしました。
> みずうみ　　　　　　　　　　　い
> *I went for a drive to the lake.*

When you simply want to say "to drive a car" (not necessarily for pleasure), use 運転する instead.
うんてん

> 日本で車を運転したことがありますか。
> に ほん　くるま　うんてん
> *Have you ever driven a car in Japan?*

夢▶ 夢, like the English word "dream," has two meanings. One is the dream
ゆめ　　ゆめ
you have while sleeping; the others the dream that you wish would come true. To say "I have a dream," in Japanese, you use the verb 見る for
み
sleeping dreams, and 持っている or ある for your visions.
　　　　　　　　　　　　　　　　　　も

> ゆうべこわい夢を見ました。　　　*I had a scary dream last night.*
> 　　　　　　　ゆめ　み
> 夢を持っています／夢があります。　*I have a dream.*
> ゆめ　も　　　　　　ゆめ
> あなたの将来の夢は何ですか。　　　*What is your future dream?*
> 　　　　しょうらい　ゆめ　なん

には▶ The particle は often follows the particle に in sentences describing a place in terms of the things that are found there.

> 東京には大きいデパートがたくさんあります。
> とうきょう　　　おお
> 　　　　*There are lots of big department stores <u>in</u> Tokyo.*

> 私の大学にはいい日本語の先生がいます。
> わたし　だいがく　　　に ほん ご　せんせい
> 　　　　*We have a good Japanese teacher <u>in</u> my college.*

These sentences would be okay without は, but there is a subtle difference between the versions with and without は. The は sentences are *about* the places; they answer questions (either explicitly asked, or implicit) like "What is Tokyo like?"

　　The sentences without は after に, on the other hand, are answers to a question like "Where do you find good teachers of Japanese?"

　　See the grammar note discussing the difference between が and は in Lesson 8. In the case of the particle に, the contrast is between the simple に and the combination には. (See also the grammar note on counting people in Lesson 7.)

練習 Practice
れん しゅう

① ハンバーガーが食べたいです
た

A. Change the following phrases into 〜たい sentences. 🔊

Example: ハンバーガーを食べる
た

（はい） → ハンバーガーが食べたいです。
た

（いいえ） → ハンバーガーが食べたくありません。
た

1. 湖に行く （はい）
みずうみ い

2. 日本語のテープを聞く （はい）
に ほん ご き

3. 旅行をする （はい）
りょこう

4. ゆっくり休む （いいえ）
やす

5. 会社の社長になる （いいえ）
かいしゃ しゃちょう

6. 日本で働く （はい）
に ほん はたら

7. 車を買う （はい）
くるま か

8. 日本に住む （いいえ）
に ほん す

9. 留学する （はい）
りゅうがく

10. 山に登る （いいえ）
やま のぼ

B. Pair Work—Ask if your partner wants to do the things above. When you answer, give reasons as in the example.

Example: A：ハンバーガーが食べたいですか。
た

B：はい、食べたいです。おなかがすいていますから。
た

いいえ、食べたくありません。さっき食べましたから。
た た

C. Change the following phrases into 〜たい sentences in the past tense. 🔊

Example:

おもちゃの電車で遊ぶ
でんしゃ あそ

（はい） → 子供の時、おもちゃの電車で遊びたかったです。
こ ども とき でんしゃ あそ

（いいえ） → 子供の時、おもちゃの電車で遊びたくありませんでした。
こ ども とき でんしゃ あそ

1. テレビを見る （はい）
み

2. 飛行機に乗る （はい）
ひ こう き の

3. お風呂に入る （いいえ）
ふ ろ はい

4. 犬を飼う （はい）
いぬ か

5. 学校をやめる （いいえ）
がっこう

6. 魚を食べる （いいえ）
さかな た

7. 男の子／女の子と話す （いいえ）
おとこ こ おんな こ はな

8. ピアノを習う （いいえ）
なら

9. 車を運転する （はい）　　　10. 有名になる （はい）
11. ミッキー・マウスに会う （はい）

D. Pair Work—Ask if your partner wanted to do the things above during their childhood.

E. Pair Work—Ask your partner the following questions and report the answers as in the example.

Example:　Ａ：けんさんは何が食べたいですか。
　　　　　Ｂ：ピザが食べたいです。
　　→　　Ａ：けんさんはピザが食べたいと言っていました。
　　　　　　けんさんはピザを食べたがっています。

1. 昼ごはんに何が食べたいですか。
2. 何がいちばん買いたいですか。
3. どこにいちばん行きたいですか。
4. だれにいちばん会いたいですか。
5. 何が習いたいですか。
6. 今週の週末、何がしたいですか。
7. 何がしたくありませんか。
8. 子供の時、何になりたかったですか。
9. 将来、何になりたいですか。
10. 今学期の後、何がしたいですか。

Additional Vocabulary——職業 (Occupations)

さっか（作家）	writer	ジャーナリスト	journalist
けいさつかん（警察官）	police officer	しゅふ（主婦）	housewife
はいゆう（俳優）	actor/actress	じょゆう（女優）	actress
かんごし（看護師）	nurse	しょうぼうし（消防士）	firefighter
べんごし（弁護士）	lawyer		
やきゅうせんしゅ（野球選手）	baseball player		
だいとうりょう（大統領）	president of a country		

F. Complete the following sentences.

1. 今日はいい天気だから、＿＿＿＿＿＿＿＿＿＿たいです。

2. あしたは休みだから、＿＿＿＿＿＿＿＿＿＿たいです。

3. 疲れたから、＿＿＿＿＿＿＿＿＿たくありません。

4. 田中さんはいじわるだから、一緒に＿＿＿＿＿＿＿たくありません。

5. 高校の時、もっと＿＿＿＿＿＿＿＿たかったです。

Ⅱ 掃除したり、洗濯したりします

A. Tell what the following people did on the weekend using 〜たり〜たりする. 🔊

Example:　ジョン: saw temples in Kyoto, went to a museum, etc.

→　ジョンさんはお寺を見たり、美術館に行ったりしました。

1. たけし: went camping, went for a drive, etc.

2. きょうこ: made sweets, read books at home, etc.

3. スー: went to Osaka to have fun, went to eat, etc.

4. けん: cleaned his room, did laundry, etc.

5. ロバート: met friends, watched videos, etc.

6. 山下先生: went to a hot spring, rested, etc.

B. Look at the pictures and make your own sentences using 〜たり〜たりする.

C. Pair Work—Ask your partner the following questions. When you answer, use ～たり～たりする as in the example.

Example:　A：日本で何をしたいですか。
　　　　　　B：日本のお菓子を食べたり、富士山 (Mt. Fuji) に登ったりしたいです。

1. 週末よく何をしますか。
2. デートの時、何をしますか。
3. あなたの国ではお正月に何をしますか。
4. 子供の時、よく何をしましたか。
5. 日本で何をしますか／しましたか。
6. 冬休み／夏休みに何をしましたか。
7. クラスで何をしてはいけませんか。
8. 今度の週末、何をするつもりですか。
9. 何をするのが好きですか／きらいですか。

Ⅲ　有名人に会ったことがありますか

A. The following are what John has or hasn't done. Make the sentences using ～ことがある. 🔊

Example:　○ eat tempura　→　天ぷらを食べたことがあります。
　　　　　　✗ go to Tokyo　→　東京に行ったことがありません。

1. ○ eat sushi
2. ○ study French
3. ○ work at a restaurant
4. ✗ go to Hiroshima
5. ✗ write love letters
6. ○ sleep in class
7. ○ climb Mt. Fuji
8. ✗ drive a car in Japan
9. ✗ see Japanese movies

B. Pair Work—Make questions using ～ことがある and ask your partner.

Example:　日本のお酒を飲む
　　　　→　A：日本のお酒を飲んだことがありますか。
　　　　　　B：はい、あります。
　　　　　　A：どうでしたか。
　　　　　　B：おいしかったです。

1. ダイエットをする
2. テストで0点を取る
   <small>れいてん と</small>
3. 英語を教える
   <small>えいご おし</small>
4. 有名人に会う
   <small>ゆうめいじん あ</small>
5. カラオケに行く
   <small>い</small>
6. ふぐ (blowfish) を食べる
   <small>た</small>
7. 中国語を勉強する
   <small>ちゅうごくご べんきょう</small>
8. 新幹線に乗る
   <small>しんかんせん の</small>
9. うそをつく
10. 日本料理を作る
    <small>にほんりょうり つく</small>
11. 遅刻する
    <small>ちこく</small>
12. 授業をサボる
    <small>じゅぎょう</small>
13. 友だち／ルームメート／ホストファミリー とけんかする
    <small>とも</small>
14. 留学する
    <small>りゅうがく</small>

Ⅳ すしや天ぷらをよく食べます
<small>てん た</small>

Pair Work—Ask your partner the following questions. When you answer, use ～や～ as in the example.

Example:　Ａ：どんな日本料理をよく食べますか。
<small>にほんりょうり た</small>
　　　　　Ｂ：すしや天ぷらをよく食べます。
<small>てん た</small>

1. どんなスポーツをよく見ますか。
   <small>み</small>
2. どんな音楽が好きですか。
   <small>おんがく す</small>
3. どんな料理をよく作りますか。
   <small>りょうり つく</small>
4. あなたの大学の食堂には、どんな食べ物がありますか。
   <small>だいがく しょくどう た もの</small>
5. あなたの大学には、どこの国の人がいますか。
   <small>だいがく くに ひと</small>
6. 外国に行ったことがありますか。どこですか。
   <small>がいこく い</small>
7. 今、どんな授業を取っていますか。
   <small>いま じゅぎょう と</small>
8. 俳優 (actors) の中で、だれが好きですか。
   <small>はいゆう なか す</small>
9. 歌手の中で、だれが好きですか。
   <small>かしゅ なか す</small>

Ⅴ まとめの練習
れんしゅう

A. Talk about your dream for the future or what it was when you were a child.

1. あなたの夢は何ですか。
   ゆめ　なん

   Example: 私は将来、お金持ちになりたいです。そして、いろいろな国に行き
   わたし　しょうらい　かね も　　　　　　　　　　　　　　　　　くに い
   たいです。

2. 子供の時の夢は何でしたか。
   こども　とき　ゆめ　なん

   Example: 子供の時、歌手になりたかったです。
   こども　とき　か しゅ

B. Class Activity—Find someone who . . .

1. has seen celebrities　　　　　　　　　　　_____

2. has never used chopsticks　　　　　　　_____

3. wants to live in Japan in the future　_____

4. wanted to be a star（スター）as a child　_____

5. wants to cut classes tomorrow　　　　_____

6. doesn't want to go out today　　　　　_____

C. Class Activity—Bring pictures of your hometown and describe it.

Example:

私はニューヨークの出身です。ニューヨークはとても大きくてにぎやかです。
わたし　　　　　　　　　　しゅっしん　　　　　　　　　　　　　　　　　　　おお

きれいな公園や有名な美術館やたくさんの劇場 (theater) があります。
こうえん ゆうめい び じゅつかん　　　　　げきじょう

よくミュージカルを見たり、公園で散歩したりしました。
み　　こうえん さん ぽ

夏休みに帰って、友だちに会いたいです。
なつやす　かえ　とも　あ

日本語のクラスで
にほんご

In the Japanese Class

Useful Expressions

どちらでもいいです。——————Both are fine.

同じです。——————Same thing.
おな

だいたい同じです。——————More or less the same.
おな

ちょっと違います。——————A little different.
ちが

使えません。——————Can't use it.
つか

間違っています。——————It's wrong.
まちが

手をあげてください。——————Raise your hand.
て

読んできてください。——————Read it before coming to class.
よ

宿題を出してください。——————Hand in the homework.
しゅくだい だ

教科書を閉じてください。——————Close the textbook.
きょうかしょ と

となりの人に聞いてください。——————Ask the person sitting next to you.
ひと き

やめてください。——————The time is up. Please stop.

今日はこれで終わります。——————That's it for today.
きょう お

しつもんが
ありますか

Useful Vocabulary

宿題——————homework
しゅくだい

しめきり——————deadline

練習——————exercise
れんしゅう

意味——————meaning
いみ

発音——————pronunciation
はつおん

文法——————grammar
ぶんぽう

質問——————question
しつもん

答——————answer
こたえ

例——————example
れい

かっこ——————(　　)

まる——————○ (correct)

ばつ——————× (wrong)

くだけた言い方——————colloquial expression
いかた

かたい言い方——————bookish expression
いかた

ていねいな言い方——————polite expression
いかた

方言——————dialect
ほうげん

標準語——————standard Japanese
ひょうじゅんご

たとえば——————for example

ほかに——————anything else

〜番——————number . . .
ばん

〜ページ——————page number . . .

〜行目——————line number . . .
ぎょうめ

二人ずつ——————two people each
ふたり

第12課 | L E S S O N ⋯⋯⋯ 12

病 気 Feeling Ill
びょう き

会 話 D i a l o g u e
かい わ

🔊

Ⅰ Mary and Michiko are talking at school.

1 みちこ： メアリーさん、元気がありませんね。
げん き

2 メアリー： うーん。ちょっとおなかが痛いんです。
いた

3 みちこ： どうしたんですか。

4 メアリー： きのう友だちと晩ごはんを食べに行ったんです。たぶん食べすぎたん
とも ばん た い た

5 だと思います。
おも

6 みちこ： 大丈夫ですか。
だいじょう ぶ

7 メアリー： ええ。心配しないでください。……ああ、痛い。
しんぱい いた

8 みちこ： 病院に行ったほうがいいですよ。
びょういん い

Ⅱ At a hospital.

1 メアリー： 先生、のどが痛いんです。きのうはおなかが痛かったんです。
せんせい いた いた

2 医者： ああ、そうですか。熱もありますね。かぜですね。
い しゃ ねつ

3 メアリー： あの、もうすぐテニスの試合があるので、練習しなくちゃいけないん
し あい れんしゅう

4 ですが……。

5 医者： 二三日、運動しないほうがいいでしょう。
い しゃ に さんにち うんどう

6 メアリー： わかりました。

7 医者： 今日は薬を飲んで、早く寝てください。
い しゃ きょう くすり の はや ね

8 メアリー： はい、ありがとうございました。

9 医者： お大事に。
い しゃ だいじ

Ⅰ

Michiko: You don't look well, Mary.

Mary: Um . . . I have a little stomachache.

Michiko: What's the matter?

Mary: I went out to have dinner with my friend yesterday. I think maybe I ate too much.

Michiko: Are you all right?

Mary: Yes. Don't worry about it. Oh, it hurts.

Michiko: You had better go to a hospital.

Ⅱ

Mary: Doctor, I have a sore throat. I had a stomachache yesterday.

Doctor: I see. You have a fever, too. It is just a cold.

Mary: Well, I will have a tennis tournament soon, so I have to practice, though . . .

Doctor: You had better not exercise for a couple of days.

Mary: I understand.

Doctor: Take medicine and go to bed early tonight.

Mary: Yes. Thank you so much.

Doctor: Take care.

単 語
たん ご

V o c a b u l a r y

N o u n s

あし	足	leg; foot
いみ	意味	meaning
* おなか		stomach
* かぜ	風邪	cold
かのじょ	彼女	girlfriend
かれ	彼	boyfriend
きおん	気温	temperature (weather—not used for things)
くもり	曇り	cloudy weather
* しあい	試合	match; game
ジュース		juice
せいじ	政治	politics
せいせき	成績	grade (on a test, etc.)
せき		cough
* のど		throat
は	歯	tooth
はな	花	flower
はれ	晴れ	sunny weather
ふく	服	clothes
ふつかよい	二日酔い	hangover
プレゼント		present
ホームシック		homesickness
もの	物	thing (concrete object)
ゆき	雪	snow
ようじ	用事	business to take care of

い - a d j e c t i v e s

あまい	甘い	sweet
* いたい	痛い	hurt; painful
おおい	多い	there are many . . .
せまい	狭い	narrow; not spacious
つごうがわるい	都合が悪い	inconvenient; to have a scheduling conflict
わるい	悪い	bad

* Words that appear in the dialogue

な-adjective

すてき(な)	素敵	fantastic

U-verbs

かぜをひく	風邪をひく	to catch a cold
きょうみがある	興味がある	to be interested (in . . .) （*topic* に）
なくす		to lose
* ねつがある	熱がある	to have a fever
のどがかわく	のどが渇く	to become thirsty

Ru-verbs

せきがでる	せきが出る	to cough
わかれる	別れる	to break up; to separate （*person* と）

Irregular Verbs

きんちょうする	緊張する	to get nervous
* しんぱいする	心配する	to worry

Adverbs and Other Expressions

いつも		always
* おだいじに	お大事に	Get well soon.
* げんきがない	元気がない	don't look well
* たぶん	多分	probably; maybe
できるだけ		as much as possible
* ～でしょう		probably; . . . , right?
～ど	～度	. . . degrees (temperature)
* にさんにち	二三日	for two to three days
* ～ので		because . . .
はじめて	初めて	for the first time
* もうすぐ		very soon; in a few moments/days

文　法　G r a m m a r
ぶん　ぼう

1. 〜んです

There are two distinct ways to make a statement in Japanese. One way is to simply report the facts as they are observed. This is the mode of speech that we have learned so far. In this lesson, we will learn a new way: the mode of *explaining* things.

A *report* is an isolated description of a fact. When you are late for an appointment, you can already report in Japanese what has happened, バスが来ませんでした. This sentence, however, does not have the right apologetic tone, because it is not offered as an explanation for anything. If you want to mention the busses failing to run on time as an excuse for being late, you will need to use the *explanation* mode of speech, and say:

バスが来なかった<u>ん</u>です。　　　*(As it happens,) the bus didn't come.*
こ

An explanation has two components, one that is explicitly described in the sentence (the bus not coming), and another, which is implied, or explained, by it (you being late for the appointment). The sentence-final expression んです serves as the link between what the sentence says and what it accounts for. Compare:

あしたテストがあります。　　*I have an exam tomorrow.* (a simple observation)
あしたテストがある<u>ん</u>です。　*I have an exam tomorrow. (So I can't go out tonight.)*

トイレに行きたいです。　　*I want to go to the bathroom.* (declaration of one's wish)
い
トイレに行きたい<u>ん</u>です。　*I want to go to the bathroom. (So tell me where it is.)*
い

んです goes after the short form of a predicate. The predicate can be either in the affirmative or in the negative, either in the present tense or in the past tense. んです itself is invariant and does not usually appear in the negative or the past tense forms.[1] In writing, it is more common to find のです instead of んです.

成績がよくない<u>ん</u>です。(in response to the question, "Why do you look so upset?")
せいせき
(As a matter of fact) My grade is not good.

---

[1]In casual exchanges, んです appears in its short form, んだ. In casual questions, んですか is replaced by の. We will examine these further in Lesson 15.

試験が終わった<u>ん</u>です。(explaining to a person who has caught you smiling)
The exam is over. (<u>That's why</u> I'm smiling.)

When it follows a noun or a な-adjective, な comes in between.

	report sentences	explanation sentences
な-adjective:	静かです <small>しず</small>	静かなんです <small>しず</small>
noun:	学生です <small>がくせい</small>	学生なんです <small>がくせい</small>

You can use んです in questions to invite explanations and further clarifications from the person you are talking to. It is very often used together with question words, such as どうして (why) and どうした (what has happened).

Q：どうして彼と別れた<u>ん</u>ですか。
<small>かれ わか</small>
Why did you break up with your boyfriend? (You've got to tell me.)

A：彼、ぜんぜんお風呂に入らない<u>ん</u>です。
<small>かれ ふろ はい</small>
Oh, him. He never takes a bath. (That's a good enough reason, isn't it?)

Q：どうした<u>ん</u>ですか。
What happened? (You look shattered.)

A：猫が死んだ<u>ん</u>です。²
<small>ねこ し</small>
My cat died. (That should explain how I look today.)

You can also use んです to provide an additional comment on what has just been said.

A：とてもいい教科書ですね。
<small>きょうかしょ</small>
That's a great textbook that you are using.

B：ええ。私の大学の先生が書いた<u>ん</u>です。
<small>わたし だいがく せんせい か</small>
You bet. The professors at my university wrote it (for your information).

---

²A どうしたんですか question is best answered by a んです sentence with the subject marked with the particle が rather than は, as in this example. See Lesson 8 for a related discussion.

2　〜すぎる

Verb stems may be followed by the helping verb すぎる, which means "too much," or "to excess." すぎる conjugates as a regular *ru*-verb.

食べすぎてはいけません。 *You must not eat too much.*

早く起きすぎました。 *I got up too early.*

すぎる can also follow い- and な-adjective bases (the parts which do not change in conjugations); you drop the い and な at the end of the adjectives and then add すぎる.

（高い）　　この本は高すぎます。 *This book is too expensive.*

（親切な）　あの人は親切すぎます。 *That person is too nice.*

3　〜ほうがいいです

ほうがいいです "it is better (for you) to do . . ." is a sentence-final expression that you can use to give advice. When you suggest an activity with ほうがいいです, you are giving a very specific piece of advice; namely, that it is advisable to do it, and if one does not follow the advice, there is a danger or a problem.

ほうがいいです is peculiar in that it follows different tense forms, depending on whether the advice given is in the affirmative or the negative. When the advice is in the affirmative, ほうがいいです generally follows the past tense short form of a verb. When the advice is in the negative, however, the verb is in the *present* tense short form.

もっと野菜を食べたほうがいいですよ。 *You'd better eat more vegetables.*

授業を休まないほうがいいですよ。 *It is better not to skip classes.*

4　〜ので

You can use ので to give the reason for the situation described in the balance of the sentence. Semantically, ので is just like から. Stylistically, ので sounds slightly more formal than から.

(reason) ので (situation)。　　(situation), *because* (reason).

いつも日本語で話すので、日本語が上手になりました。
My Japanese has improved, because I always speak Japanese.

宿題がたくさんあったので、きのうの夜、寝ませんでした。
I did not sleep last night, because I had a lot of homework.

The reason part of a sentence ends in a short form predicate. When ので follows a な-adjective or a noun、な comes in between, as it did with the explanatory predicate んです.

その人はいじわるなので、きらいです。
I do not like that person, because he is mean.

今日は日曜日なので、銀行は休みです。
Banks are closed, because today is a Sunday.

5 　〜なくちゃいけません

We use なくちゃいけません[3] to say that it is necessary to do something, or "must."

来週テストがあるから、たくさん勉強しなくちゃいけません。
I have to study a lot, because there will be an exam next week.

なくちゃ means "if you do not do . . ." and いけません roughly means "you cannot go"; なくちゃいけません therefore means "you cannot go not doing . . ." with the double negatives giving rise to the affirmative sense of the mandate. To form a なくちゃいけません sentence, we substitute ない in the negative short form of a verb with なくちゃ.

verb	short negative	"must"
食べる	食べない	食べなくちゃいけません
言う	言わない	言わなくちゃいけません
する	しない	しなくちゃいけません
くる	こない	こなくちゃいけません

いけません is grammatically the negative long form of a verb in the present tense. You can change なくちゃいけません to なくちゃいけませんでした (past tense) to say you *had to*, and to なくちゃいけない (the short form, present tense) in casual speech and before elements like んです.

---

[3]In writing and in very formal speech、なくてはいけません is more common than なくちゃいけません.

けさは、六時に起き<u>なくちゃいけませんでした</u>。(long form, past)
I had to get up at six this morning.

毎日、練習し<u>なくちゃいけないんです</u>。(short form, present)
(The truth is,) I must practice every day.

6　〜でしょう

We use the sentence-final expression でしょう (probably) when we are making a guess or a prediction. でしょう follows verbs and い-adjectives in short forms, in the affirmative and in the negative.[4]

(verb)

あしたは雨が<u>降る</u>でしょう。　　　　　*It will probably rain tomorrow.*
　　　　<u>降らない</u>でしょう。　　　　　*It will probably not rain tomorrow.*

(い-adjective)

北海道は<u>寒い</u>でしょう。　　　　　*It is probably cold in Hokkaido.*
　　　<u>寒くない</u>でしょう。　　　　　*It is probably not cold in Hokkaido.*

でしょう may also follow な-adjective bases and nouns. Note that でしょう goes directly after these elements; we do not use ×〜<u>な</u>でしょう, ×〜<u>の</u>でしょう, or ×〜<u>だ</u>でしょう.

(な-adjective)

山下先生は魚が<u>好き</u>でしょう。　　*Professor Yamashita probably likes fish.*
　　　　　<u>好きじゃない</u>でしょう。　*Professor Yamashita probably doesn't like fish.*

(noun)

あの人は<u>オーストラリア人</u>でしょう。　*That person is probably an Australian.*
　　　<u>オーストラリア人じゃない</u>でしょう。*That person is probably not an Australian.*

---

[4] でしょう may also follow predicates in the past tense. We will, however, concentrate on the present tense examples in this lesson.

でしょう sentences can be turned into questions (～でしょうか), which can be used to invite another person's opinion or guess.

日本語と韓国語と、どっちのほうが難しいでしょうか。
Which would you say is more difficult, Japanese or Korean?

The short form of でしょう is だろう. You can use it to cautiously phrase a prediction or an analysis.

たけしさんは興味がある<u>だろう</u>と思います。
I think Takeshi would be interested in it.

In casual exchanges, you can use でしょう (with the question intonation, and most often pronounced as somewhat shorter でしょ) when you want to check if your partner agrees that you have the correct understanding about what you have just said.

ジョン、中国語がわかるでしょ？ これ、読んで。
John, you understand Chinese, right? Can you read this for me?

練習 P r a c t i c e
れん しゅう

Ⅰ どうしたんですか

A. You are in the following situations. Explain them using ～んです.

Example: 頭が痛いです
あたま　いた
→　Q：どうしたんですか。
A：頭が痛いんです。
あたま　いた

(1) 彼から電話が
かれ　てんわ
ありました

(2) プレゼントを
もらいました

(3) あしたは休みです
やす

(4) きのうは
誕生日でした
たんじょうび

(5) テストが難しく
むずか
ありませんでした

(6) のどが痛いです
いた

(7) かぜをひきました

(8) 切符をなくしました
きっぷ

(9) あしたテストがあります

(10) せきが出ます
_で

(11) 彼女と別れました
_{かのじょ} _{わか}

B. Respond to the comments using 〜んです.

Example:

すてきな車ですね。
_{くるま}

My father's → 父のなんです。
_{ちち}

(1)

きれいな花ですね。
_{はな}

I received them
from my friend.

(2)

新しい靴ですね。
_{あたら} _{くつ}

Italian ones

(3)

すてきなセーター
ですね。

My mother made it.

(4)

いいかばんですね。

It was cheap.

(5)

かっこいい彼ですね。
_{かれ}

kind

C. Pair Work—Your partner has said something nice about what you have. Respond using 〜んです.

Example:　B：すてきな時計ですね。
　　　　　　A：友だちにもらったんです。

D. Pair Work—Make up dialogues asking for reasons.

Example:　I went to Tokyo last week.

→　A：先週東京に行きました。
　　B：どうして東京に行ったんですか。
　　A：母がアメリカから来たんです。

1. I am very tired.
2. I have no money.
3. It is not convenient today.（都合が悪い）
4. I want to marry my boyfriend/girlfriend.
5. I am going to Japan to study.
6. He speaks Chinese very well.（中国語が上手です）
7. I don't want to watch that movie.

Ⅱ 食べすぎました

A. Describe the following pictures using 〜すぎる. Use "verb ＋ すぎる" for (1) through (4) and "adjective ＋ すぎる" for (5) through (10).

Example:

→　作りすぎました。

→　この部屋はせますぎます。

(1) (2) (3) (4) (5) (6) (7) (8) (9) (10)

B. Look at the verbs below. Think about the results of over doing these things and make sentences as in the example.

Example: 食べる　→　食べすぎたから、おなかが痛いんです。

1. 飲む
2. 勉強する
3. コンピューターを使う
4. 本を読む
5. テニスをする
6. 甘い物を食べる
7. 歌を歌う
8. 緊張する

Ⅲ 薬を飲んだほうがいいです
くすり の

A. Using the cues below, give advice to a friend who has a headache. Decide if you should use the affirmative or the negative. 🔊

Example: 薬を飲む → B：頭が痛いんです。
　　　　　くすり の　　　　あたま いた
　　　　　　　　　　　　A：薬を飲んだほうがいいですよ。
　　　　　　　　　　　　　　くすり の

1. 早く寝る　　　　　　2. 遊びに行く　　　　3. 病院に行く
　はや ね　　　　　　　　あそ い　　　　　　びょういん い
4. 仕事を休む　　　　　5. うちに帰る　　　　6. 運動する
　しごと やす　　　　　　　　　かえ　　　　　うんどう

B. Pair Work—Give advice to your partner in the following situations, using 〜ほうがいい.

Example: 日本語が上手になりたい
　　　　　にほんご じょうず
　　→　　B：日本語が上手になりたいんです。
　　　　　　にほんご じょうず
　　　　　A：日本人の友だちを作ったほうがいいですよ。
　　　　　　にほんじん とも つく
　　　　　　できるだけ英語を話さないほうがいいですよ。
　　　　　　　　　　えいご はな

1. ホームシックだ　　　2. やせたい　　　　　3. 友だちとけんかした
　　　　　　　　　　　　　　　　　　　　　　とも
4. お金がない　　　　　5. 成績が悪い　　　　6. 二日酔いだ
　かね　　　　　　　　せいせき わる　　　　ふつか よ
7. 歯が痛い　　　　　　8. 教科書をなくした　9. いつも授業に遅刻する
　は いた　　　　　　きょうかしょ　　　　じゅぎょう ちこく

C. Pair Work—You are a health counselor. Someone who hasn't been feeling well is at your office. Ask the following questions. Complete this form first, then give your advice using 〜ほうがいい.

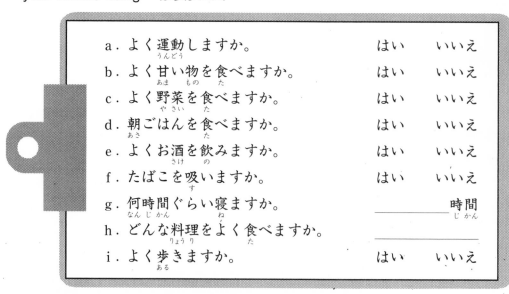

a. よく運動しますか。　　　　　　はい　　　いいえ
　　うんどう
b. よく甘い物を食べますか。　　　　はい　　　いいえ
　　あま もの た
c. よく野菜を食べますか。　　　　　はい　　　いいえ
　　やさい た
d. 朝ごはんを食べますか。　　　　　はい　　　いいえ
　　あさ た
e. よくお酒を飲みますか。　　　　　はい　　　いいえ
　　さけ の
f. たばこを吸いますか。　　　　　　はい　　　いいえ
　　す
g. 何時間ぐらい寝ますか。　　　　　＿＿＿＿＿時間
　　なんじかん ね　　　　　　　　　　　　　　じかん
h. どんな料理をよく食べますか。　　＿＿＿＿＿
　　りょうり た
i. よく歩きますか。　　　　　　　　はい　　　いいえ
　　ある

Ⅳ いい天気なので、散歩します

A. Connect the two sentences using 〜ので. 🔊

Example: いい天気です／散歩します
→ いい天気なので、散歩します。

1. 安いです／買います

2. あの映画はおもしろくありません／見たくありません

3. 今週は忙しかったです／疲れています

4. 病気でした／授業を休みました

5. 彼女はいつも親切です／人気があります

6. 政治に興味がありません／新聞を読みません

7. あしたテストがあります／勉強します

8. のどがかわきました／ジュースが飲みたいです

9. 歩きすぎました／足が痛いです

B. Make sentences using the cues below as reasons, according to the example.

Example: かぜをひきました → かぜをひいたので、授業を休みました。

1. お金がありません

2. おなかがすいています

3. ホームシックです

4. 用事があります

5. 単語の意味がわかりません

6. 疲れました

C. Fill in the blanks with appropriate words.

1. ＿＿＿＿＿＿＿＿＿＿＿＿＿＿＿＿＿ので、中国に行きたいです。

2. ＿＿＿＿＿＿＿＿＿＿＿＿＿＿＿＿＿ので、人気があります。

3. ＿＿＿＿＿＿＿＿＿＿＿＿＿＿＿＿＿ので、かぜをひきました。

4. ＿＿＿＿＿＿＿＿＿＿＿＿＿＿＿＿＿ので、別れました。

5. ＿＿＿＿＿＿＿＿＿＿＿＿＿＿＿＿＿ので、日本に住みたくありません。

6. ＿＿＿＿＿＿＿＿＿＿＿＿＿＿＿＿＿ので、遅刻しました。

7. ＿＿＿＿＿＿＿＿＿＿＿＿＿＿＿＿＿ので、緊張しています。

Ⓥ 七時に起きなくちゃいけません
しち じ　　　お

A. Look at Tom's schedule and make sentences, according to the example. 🔊

Example: 7:00 A.M.／起きる　→　トムさんは七時に起きなくちゃいけません。
お　　　　　　　　　　　　　　　　しち じ　お

7:00 A.M.	Ex. 起きる
8:00 A.M.	(1) うちを出る
9:00 A.M.	(2) 授業に出る
1:00 P.M.	(3) 山下先生に会う
2:00 P.M.	(4) 英語を教える
3:00 P.M.	(5) ＬＬに行って、テープを聞く
5:00 P.M.	(6) うちに帰る
6:00 P.M.	(7) ホストファミリーと晩ごはんを食べる
8:00 P.M.	(8) 宿題をする
9:00 P.M.	(9) お風呂に入る
10:00 P.M.	(10) 薬を飲む
11:00 P.M.	(11) うちに電話をかける

B. Pair Work—Invite the partner to do the following things together. Turn down the invitation and give an explanation using ～なくちゃいけない.

Example:　play tennis

　　　→　A：あしたの朝、一緒にテニスをしませんか。
　　　　　　　　あさ　いっしょ
　　　　　B：ちょっと都合が悪いんです。あしたは授業に出なくちゃいけ
　　　　　　　　　　つごう　わる　　　　　　　　　じゅぎょう　で
　　　　　ないんです。

1. do homework　　　2. eat lunch　　　3. drink coffee
4. study in the library　　5. go to karaoke

C. Answer the following questions.

1. 日本語の授業で何をしなくちゃいけませんか。
　にほんご　じゅぎょう　なに

2. 日本で外国人は何をしなくちゃいけませんか。
　にほん　がいこくじん　なに

3. かっこよくなりたいんです。何をしなくちゃいけませんか。
　　　　　　　　　　　　　　　　なに

4. 友だちが遊びに来ます。何をしなくちゃいけませんか。
　とも　　あそ　き　　　　なに

5. あしたは初めてのデートです。何をしなくちゃいけませんか。
　　　　はじ　　　　　　　　　なに

6. 子供の時、何をしなくちゃいけませんでしたか。
　こども　とき　なに

Ⅵ あしたは晴れでしょう
　　　　　　　は

A. Here is tomorrow's weather forecast (天気予報). Play the role of a meteorologist
　　　　　　　　　　　　　　　　　　　てんきよほう
and tell the weather forecasts for each city.

Examples:　Tokyo/snow

→　東京はあした雪でしょう。
　　とうきょう　　ゆき

temperature in Tokyo/around 2℃

→　東京の気温は、二度ぐらいでしょう。
　　とうきょう　きおん　　にど

city	weather		temperature
Tokyo	Ex. snow		Ex. around 2℃
Sydney	(1) sunny	(2) hot	(3) around 30℃
Hong Kong	(4) rain	(5) cool	(6) around 18℃
Rome	(7) cloudy	(8) warm	(9) around 20℃

B. Pair Work—Play the role of a meteorologist. Predict the weather for your favorite
city. The other person fills in the blanks. Switch roles and do the same thing.

city	weather	temperature

Ⅶ まとめの練習
れんしゅう

A. Using Dialogue Ⅰ as a model, make skits in the following situations.

　　―Your friend looks sad.
　　―Your friend looks happy.

B. Pair Work―A and B are deciding when they can play tennis together. Play the role of A and B. Discuss your schedules and find the day on which both of you are available. Refer to p. 245 for B's schedule.

Example:　A：来週の月曜日に一緒にテニスをしませんか。
らいしゅう げつよう び いっしょ

　　　　　　B：来週の月曜日はちょっと都合が悪いんです。英語を教えなくちゃ
らいしゅう げつよう び つごう わる えい ご おし
いけないんです。日曜日はどうですか。
にちよう び

A's schedule

Sunday	go shopping
Monday	
Tuesday	read books
Wednesday	
Thursday	
Friday	meet friends
Saturday	

C. Role Play―Visiting a Doctor's Office

Using Dialogue Ⅱ as a model, act the role of a doctor or a patient.

Doctor―Fill out the medical report on p. 245 and give advice to the patient.

Patient―Describe the symptoms you have and answer the doctor's questions.

Sex: ☐ Male   ☐ Female
Age:

Symptoms: ☐ Sore throat

           ☐ Headache

           ☐ Stomachache

           ☐ Any other pain

           ☐ Cough

           ☐ Fever

           ☐ Allergy（アレルギー）

           ☐ Others

Pair Work Ⅶ B.

Example: A：来週の月曜日に一緒にテニスをしませんか。

B：来週の月曜日はちょっと都合が悪いんです。英語を教えなくちゃ
いけないんです。日曜日はどうですか。

B's schedule

Sunday	
Monday	teach English
Tuesday	
Wednesday	clean rooms, do laundry, etc.
Thursday	
Friday	
Saturday	practice karate

健康と病気
けん こう びょう き
Health and Illness

At the Reception of the Clinic

Patient: すみません、初めてなんですが。
はじ
Excuse me, this is my first visit.

Receptionist: はい、保険証を見せてください。
ほ けんしょう み
OK. Please show me your health insurance certificate.

この紙に名前と住所を書いてください。
かみ なまえ じゅうしょ か
Please fill in your name and address on this paper.

       *   *   *

Patient: これは何の薬ですか。
なん くすり
What kinds of medicine are these?

Receptionist: 痛み止めです。食後に飲んでください。
いた ど しょくご の
These are painkillers. Please take one after meals.

Patient: わかりました。
I see.

Receptionist: お大事に。
だい じ
Please take care.

Useful Expressions for Illness（病気）and Injuries（けが）
びょう き

下痢です。————————————I have diarrhea.
げ り

便秘です。————————————I am constipated.
べん ぴ

生理です。————————————I have my period.
せい り

花粉症です。———————————I have hay fever.
か ふんしょう

(〜に)アレルギーがあります。———I have an allergy to . . .

虫歯があります。————————I have a bad tooth.
むし ば

くしゃみが出ます。———————I sneeze.
で

鼻水が出ます。—————————I have a runny nose.
はなみず で

背中がかゆいです。———————My back itches.
せ なか

発疹があります。————————I have rashes.
はっしん

めまいがします。————————I feel dizzy.

吐きました。————————I threw up.
は

気分が悪いです。————————I am not feeling well.
き ぶん   わる

やけどをしました。————————I burned myself.

足の骨を折りました。————————I broke my leg.
あし ほね お

けがをしました。————————I hurt myself.

Useful Vocabulary

● 医者 （Doctor's office）
  い しゃ

内科————————physician
ない か

皮膚科————————dermatologist
ひ ふ か

外科————————surgeon
げ か

産婦人科————————obstetrician and gynecologist
さん ふ じん か

整形外科————————orthopedic surgeon
せい けい げ か

眼科————————ophthalmologist
がん か

歯科————————dentist
し か

耳鼻科————————otorhinolaryngologist; ENT doctor
じ び か

● その他 （Miscellaneous）
    た

抗生物質————antibiotic
こうせいぶっしつ

レントゲン———X-ray

手術————operation
しゅじゅつ

注射————injection
ちゅうしゃ

体温計————thermometer
たいおんけい

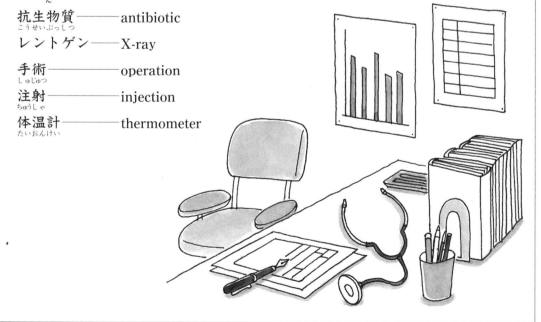

読み書き編
よ か へん

読み書き編 ● もくじ

第1課 L E S S O N 1
だい いっ か

ひらがな Hiragana

あ *a*	い *i*	う *u*	え *e*	お *o*
か *ka*	き *ki*	く *ku*	け *ke*	こ *ko*
さ *sa*	し *shi*	す *su*	せ *se*	そ *so*
た *ta*	ち *chi*	つ *tsu*	て *te*	と *to*
な *na*	に *ni*	ぬ *nu*	ね *ne*	の *no*
は *ha*	ひ *hi*	ふ *fu*	へ *he*	ほ *ho*
ま *ma*	み *mi*	む *mu*	め *me*	も *mo*
や *ya*		ゆ *yu*		よ *yo*
ら *ra*	り *ri*	る *ru*	れ *re*	ろ *ro*
わ *wa*				を *o*
ん *n*				

(Refer to "Japanese Writing System" on pages **18-22** for more details.)

Ⓘ Hiragana Practice

A. Choose the correct *hiragana*.

1. *yo*	ま	よ	2. *ho*	は	ほ	3. *me*	ぬ	め
4. *su*	む	す	5. *ki*	さ	き	6. *chi*	さ	ち
7. *ta*	た	に	8. *ro*	ろ	る	9. *e*	え	ん

B. Match the words.

Person's name

1. たなか　・　　・Akai
2. やまもと・　　・Nakamura
3. あかい　・　　・Takahashi
4. はしもと・　　・Tanaka
5. たかはし・　　・Morikawa
6. なかむら・　　・Sakuma
7. もりかわ・　　・Yamamoto
8. さくま　・　　・Hashimoto

Place name

9. さっぽろ・　　・Gifu
10. きょうと・　　・Beppu
11. かなざわ・　　・Sapporo
12. おおさか・　　・Osaka
13. ながさき・　　・Kyoto
14. ぎふ　　・　　・Kanazawa
15. べっぷ　・　　・Nagasaki
16. ちば　　・　　・Chiba

C. What's wrong with the *hiragana* below? Rewrite the correct *hiragana*.

(1)	(2)	(3)	(4)	(5)
ほ	む		∫	あ

D. Write as many *hiragana* as possible which contain the following parts.

(1)

(2)

(3)

(4)

(5)

(6)

E. Put the *hiragana* in the right order to make sense.

Example: だともち → <u>と</u><u>も</u><u>だ</u><u>ち</u>

1. わんで　＿＿＿＿＿＿＿　　　2. ごいえ　＿＿＿＿＿＿＿

3. んほに　＿＿＿＿＿＿＿　　　4. えなま　＿＿＿＿＿＿＿

5. んせせい　＿＿＿＿＿＿＿　　6. がだいく　＿＿＿＿＿＿＿

Ⅱ Reading Practice

Read what the following people are saying and answer the questions.

かいしゃいんです。

たなか　ゆうこ

だいがくせいです。せんもんは れきしです。

はらだ　りょう

だいがくいんせいです。せんもんは けいざいです。

かとう　やすお

こうこうの さんねんせいです。

きたの　ひろみ

だいがくせいです。せんもんは にほんごです。

やまだ　まこと

1. Who is an office worker?　　＿＿＿＿＿＿＿＿＿＿＿＿＿＿

2. Whose major is Japanese?　　＿＿＿＿＿＿＿＿＿＿＿＿＿＿

3. Who is a high school student?　＿＿＿＿＿＿＿＿＿＿＿＿＿＿

4. What is Harada's major?　　＿＿＿＿＿＿＿＿＿＿＿＿＿＿

ⅢWriting Practice

You received a letter from a Japanese friend. Read it and write a letter introducing yourself.

はじめまして、まえかわみちこです。

にほんじんです。

わたしはだいがくのいちねんせいです。

せんもんはえいごです。

どうぞよろしくおねがいします。

*どうぞよろしくおねがいします is more polite than どうぞよろしく.

第2課 だいにか LESSON 2

カタカナ Katakana

ア *a*	イ *i*	ウ *u*	エ *e*	オ *o*
カ *ka*	キ *ki*	ク *ku*	ケ *ke*	コ *ko*
サ *sa*	シ *shi*	ス *su*	セ *se*	ソ *so*
タ *ta*	チ *chi*	ツ *tsu*	テ *te*	ト *to*
ナ *na*	ニ *ni*	ヌ *nu*	ネ *ne*	ノ *no*
ハ *ha*	ヒ *hi*	フ *fu*	ヘ *he*	ホ *ho*
マ *ma*	ミ *mi*	ム *mu*	メ *me*	モ *mo*
ヤ *ya*		ユ *yu*		ヨ *yo*
ラ *ra*	リ *ri*	ル *ru*	レ *re*	ロ *ro*
ワ *wa*				ヲ *o*
ン *n*				

(Refer to "Japanese Writing System" on pages **22-24** for more details.)

① Katakana Practice

A. Choose the correct *katakana*.

1. *o*　オ　ア　　2. *nu*　ヌ　メ　　3. *sa*　テ　サ

4. *shi*　シ　ツ　　5. *ku*　ワ　ク　　6. *ma*　マ　ム

7. *ru*　レ　ル　　8. *ho*　モ　ホ　　9. *yu*　エ　ユ

B. Match the following words and pictures.

1. (　) オレンジジュース　　　7. (　) サンドイッチ

2. (　) フライドポテト　　　　8. (　) ステーキ

3. (　) ケーキ　　　　　　　　9. (　) スパゲッティ

4. (　) サラダ　　　　　　　10. (　) ピザ

5. (　) チョコレートパフェ　11. (　) トースト

6. (　) コーヒー　　　　　　12. (　) レモンティー

(a) 　(b) 　(c) 　(d)

(e) 　(f) 　(g) 　(h)

(i) 　(j) 　(k) 　(l)

C. Match each country with its capital city.

Countries	Capital Cities
1. マレーシア ・	・オタワ
2. オランダ ・	・ワシントンDC
3. アメリカ ・	・ニューデリー
4. エジプト ・	・アムステルダム
5. オーストラリア・	・クアラルンプール
6. スウェーデン ・	・ブエノスアイレス
7. インド ・	・キャンベラ
8. アルゼンチン ・	・カイロ
9. カナダ ・	・ストックホルム

D. Word Search—Find the following country names in the box of *katakana*.

ベトナム (Vietnam)

シンガポール (Singapore)

チェコ (Czech)

アメリカ (America)

スウェーデン (Sweden)

エクアドル (Ecuador)

メキシコ (Mexico)

ブラジル (Brazil)

ボスニア (Bosnia)

オランダ (Holland)

インドネシア (Indonesia)

カナダ (Canada)

ルワンダ (Rwanda)

タイ (Thailand)

オーストラリア (Australia)

イ	ン	ド	ネ	シ	ア	イ	ル	ワ	ン	ダ
コ	ウ	モ	リ	ブ	ク	ロ	ク	マ	チ	コ
オ	ー	ス	ト	ラ	リ	ア	ネ	コ	エ	イ
ラ	タ	ウ	ナ	ジ	ア	メ	キ	シ	コ	ヌ
ン	ヌ	エ	メ	ル	ヒ	リ	ネ	ズ	ミ	ベ
ダ	キ	ー	ク	ヘ	ル	カ	ナ	ダ	ラ	ト
カ	モ	デ	ジ	ビ	ボ	ス	ニ	ア	ク	ナ
ワ	シ	ン	ガ	ポ	ー	ル	パ	ン	ダ	ム
タ	イ	ゴ	リ	ラ	エ	ク	ア	ド	ル	メ

E. Put the *katakana* in the right order to make sense.

Example: キケー → ケーキ

1. トノー _____   2. ニュメー _____

3. ンペ ____   4. ンジーズ _____

5. プテー _____   6. レーナトー _____

Ⅱ Name Tags

Write your name in the box below and make your own name tag.

Example: マイケル・ジョーダン

マイケル・ジョーダン

Ⅲ Reading Practice

Mary wrote about the things below. Find out which item she wrote about.

1. (　　) これは わたしの ぼうしじゃありません。

    キャシーさんの ぼうしです。

    ニューヨークヤンキースの ぼうしです。

2. (　　) これは わたしの じてんしゃです。
　　　　 オーストラリアの じてんしゃです。
　　　　 たかいです。

3. (　　) これは ミシェルさんの じしょです。
　　　　 スペインごの じしょじゃありません。
　　　　 フランスごの じしょです。

4. (　　) これは ジャクソンさんの くつです。
　　　　 にほんの くつじゃありません。
　　　　 イタリアの くつです。

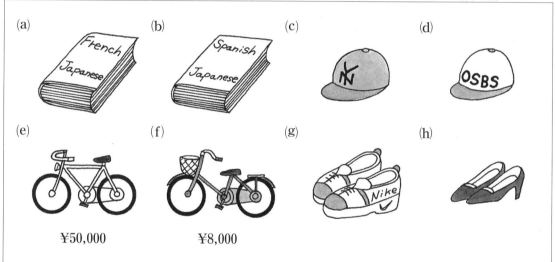

Ⅳ Writing Practice

Write about the things you or your classmates own. Use Mary's sentences in Ⅲ as a model.

第3課 │ L E S S O N ⋯⋯⋯⋯3
まいにちのせいかつ Daily Life

001	一 (one)	イチ イッ ひと	一 (イチ) one 　一時 (イチジ) one o'clock 一年生 (イチネンセイ) first-year student 一分 (イップン) one minute 　一つ (ひとつ) one
			(1) 一
002	二 (two)	ニ ふた	二 (ニ) two 　二時 (ニジ) two o'clock 二年生 (ニネンセイ) second-year student 二つ (ふたつ) two 　二日間 (ふつかカン) two days
			(2) 一 二
003	三 (three)	サン みっ	三 (サン) three 　三時 (サンジ) three o'clock 三年生 (サンネンセイ) third-year student 三つ (みっつ) three
			(3) 一 二 三
004	四 (four)	よん よ よっ シ	四 (よん) four 　四時 (よじ) four o'clock 四年生 (よネンセイ) fourth-year student 四つ (よっつ) four 　四月 (シガツ) April
			(5) 丨 冂 冂 四 四
005	五 (five)	ゴ いつ	五 (ゴ) five 　五時 (ゴジ) five o'clock 五つ (いつつ) five
			(4) 一 丆 五 五
006	六 (six)	ロク ロッ むっ	六 (ロク) six 　六時 (ロクジ) six o'clock 六百 (ロッピャク) six hundred 六分 (ロップン) six minutes 　六つ (むっつ) six
			(4) 丶 亠 亠 六
007	七 (seven)	シチ なな	七 (シチ／なな) seven 　七時 (シチジ) seven o'clock 七つ (ななつ) seven
			(2) 一 七
008	八 (eight)	ハチ ハッ やっ	八 (ハチ) eight 　八時 (ハチジ) eight o'clock 八百 (ハッピャク) eight hundred 八歳 (ハッサイ) eight years old 　八つ (やっつ) eight
			(2) 丿 八

009	九 (nine)	キュウ ク ここの (nine)	九（キュウ）nine　　九時（クジ）nine o'clock 九歳（キュウサイ）nine years old　　九つ（ここのつ）nine ⑵　ノ　九
010	十 (ten)	ジュウ ジュッ　とお (ten)	十（ジュウ）ten　　十時（ジュウジ）ten o'clock 十歳（ジュッサイ）ten years old　　十（とお）ten ⑵　一　十
011	百	ヒャク ピャク ビャク (hundred)	百（ヒャク）hundred　　三百（サンビャク）three hundred 六百（ロッピャク）six hundred 八百（ハッピャク）eight hundred ⑹　一　ア　ア　万　百　百
012	千	セン　ゼン (thousand)	千（セン）thousand　　三千（サンゼン）three thousand 八千（ハッセン）eight thousand ⑶　ノ　二　千
013	万	マン (ten thousand)	一万（イチマン）ten thousand 十万（ジュウマン）one hundred thousand 百万（ヒャクマン）one million ⑶　一　ブ　万
014	円	エン (yen; circle)	百円（ヒャクエン）one hundred yen 円（エン）circle ⑷　丨　冂　冂　円
015	時	ジ とき (time)	一時（イチジ）one o'clock 子供の時（こどものとき）in one's childhood 時々（ときどき）sometimes　　時計（トケイ）watch ⑽　丨　冂　日　日　旷　旷　旷　旷　時　時

(In this chart, *katakana* indicates the *on'yomi* [pronunciation originally borrowed from Chinese] and *hiragana* indicates the *kun'yomi* [native Japanese reading].)

Ⅰ 漢字の練習 (Kanji Practice)
かんじ　れんしゅう

A. Read the price of the following items in kanji and write it in numbers.

Example: チョコレート　(1) ハンカチ　(2) せんす

百五十円　　　　　　六百五十円　　　　　千八百円

（¥ 150 ）　　　　（¥＿＿＿＿）　　　（¥＿＿＿＿＿）

(3) きもの　(4) テレビ　(5) マンション

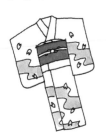　　

七十一万四千円　　　十二万三千円　　　　三千九百万円

（¥＿＿＿＿＿＿）　（¥＿＿＿＿＿＿）　（¥＿＿＿＿＿＿）

B. Write the following prices in kanji.

Example:　¥5,420　→　　五千四百二十円

1. ¥30 ＿＿＿＿＿　　2. ¥140 ＿＿＿＿＿　　3. ¥251 ＿＿＿＿＿＿

4. ¥6,070 ＿＿＿＿＿＿＿　　5. ¥8,190 ＿＿＿＿＿＿＿

6. ¥42,500 ＿＿＿＿＿＿＿　　7. ¥168,000 ＿＿＿＿＿＿＿

8. ¥3,200,000 ＿＿＿＿＿＿＿　　9. ¥57,000,000 ＿＿＿＿＿＿＿

Ⅱ まいにちのせいかつ

An international exchange student writes about his daily routine. Read the passage to find out about his schedule and fill in the blanks below.

> わたしはまいにち七時におきます。うちであさごはんをたべます。八時にだいがくへいきます。九時ににほんごをべんきょうします。十二時半にだいがくでひるごはんをたべます。ときどきコーヒーをのみます。四時にとしょかんでほんをよみます。六時ごろうちへかえります。十時にテレビをみます。十二時ごろねます。

      7:00   _____

(   )   go to the university

      9:00   _____

(   )   eat lunch

      4:00   _____

      6:00   _____

(   )   watch TV

(   )   _____

Ⅲ 書く練習 (Writing Practice)

Write about your daily routine. Use the above passage as a model.

第4課 LESSON 4

メアリーさんのしゅうまつ Mary's Weekend

016	日 (day; sun)	ニ ニチ び ひ ニッ	日本（ニホン）Japan　　日曜日（ニチヨウび）Sunday 毎日（マイニチ）every day　母の日（ははのひ）Mother's Day 日記（ニッキ）diary　　三日（ミッカ）three days
			(4) l 冂 月 日
017	本 (book; basis)	ホン もと	本（ホン）book　　日本（ニホン）Japan 日本語（ニホンゴ）Japanese language 山本さん（やまもとさん）Mr./Ms. Yamamoto
			(5) 一 十 オ 木 本
018	人 (person)	ジン ひと ニン	日本人（ニホンジン）Japanese people 一人で（ひとりで）alone　　この人（このひと）this person 三人（サンニン）three people
			(2) ノ 人
019	月 (moon; month)	ゲツ ガツ つき	月曜日（ゲツヨウび）Monday　　一月（イチガツ）January 月（つき）moon
			(4)) 刀 月 月
020	火 (fire)	カ ひ	火曜日（カヨウび）Tuesday 火（ひ）fire
			(4) 、 丷 少 火
021	水 (water)	スイ みず	水曜日（スイヨウび）Wednesday　　水（みず）water
			(4) 亅 키 才 水
022	木 (tree)	モク き	木曜日（モクヨウび）Thursday 木（き）tree
			(4) 一 十 オ 木
023	金 (gold; money)	キン かね	金曜日（キンヨウび）Friday お金（おかね）money
			(8) ノ 入 人 合 全 全 金 金

024	土	ド つち (soil)	土曜日 （ドヨウび） Saturday 土 （つち） soil
			⑶　一　十　土
025	曜	ヨウ (weekday)	日曜日 （ニチヨウび） Sunday
			⒅　l　ll　ⴼl　日　日ˈ　日ˈˈ　日ˈˈˈ　日ˈˈˈˈ　日ˈˈˈˈˈ　日ˈˈˈˈˈˈ　日ˈˈˈˈ　昭　昭ˈ　暚　暚ˈ　曜　曜　曜
026	上	うえ ジョウ (up)	上 （うえ） top; above 上手な （ジョウズな） good at 屋上 （オクジョウ） rooftop
			⑶　l　 ⵑ　 上
027	下	した カ (down)	下 （した） under 地下鉄 （チカテツ） subway　　下手な （へたな） poor at
			⑶　一　丁　下
028	中	なか チュウ　ジュウ (middle)	中 （なか） inside　　中国 （チュウゴク） China 中学 （チュウガク） junior high school 一年中 （イチネンジュウ） all year around
			⑷　l　ⵑ　ⵗ　中
029	半	ハン (half)	三時半 （サンジハン） half past three 半分 （ハンブン） half
			⑸　、　 ⵝ　ⵜ　ⵏ　半

(In this chart, *katakana* indicates the *on'yomi* and *hiragana* indicates the *kun'yomi*.)

Ⅰ 漢字の練習 (Kanji Practice)
かん じ れんしゅう

A. Match the kanji with the English equivalents.

1. 水曜日・　　　　　　　・Sunday
2. 金曜日・　　　　　　　・Monday
3. 日曜日・　　　　　　　・Tuesday
4. 月曜日・　　　　　　　・Wednesday
5. 土曜日・　　　　　　　・Thursday
6. 木曜日・　　　　　　　・Friday
7. 火曜日・　　　　　　　・Saturday

B. Look at the picture and choose the appropriate kanji for the blanks.

1. レストランはビルの＿＿＿です。
　　　　　　　(building)
2. 日本語学校はレストランの＿＿＿です。
　　ご がっこう
3. スーパーはレストランの＿＿＿です。

Ⅱ おかあさんへのメモ

メアリーさんはおかあさんにメモをかきました。
Read the memo and answer the questions.

1. メアリーさんはきょうなにをしますか。
2. うちでばんごはんをたべますか。
3. 何時ごろかえりますか。
　　なん

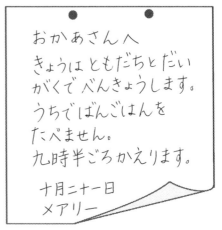

おかあさんへ
きょうは ともだちと だい
がくで べんきょうします。
うちで ばんごはんを
たべません。
九時半ごろ かえります。

十月二十一日
メアリー

Ⅲ メアリーさんのしゅうまつ

Read the following passage about Mary's weekend.

金曜日に日本人のともだちとこうえんにいきました。こうえんでともだちとはなしました。それから、レストランへいきました。たくさんたべました。

土曜日は一人でおてらへいきました。たくさんみせがありました。みせでおまんじゅうをかいました。

日曜日はおそくおきました。おかあさんもおそくおきました。わたしはあさテレビをみました。それから、おかあさんとひるごはんをたべました。ごごは日本語をべんきょうしました。本もよみました。

みせ　　store
おまんじゅう　sweet bun
おそく　late

Arrange the following activities in the order Mary did.

(　) → (　) → (　) → (　) → (　)

1. studied Japanese　　2. bought sweet buns　　3. went to a restaurant
4. watched TV　　5. went to a park

Ⅳ 書く練習 (Writing Practice)

A. You are going out. Write a memo to someone in your house, telling when you will be back and whether you will have dinner at home.

B. Write about your weekend.

第5課 LESSON 5
りょこう Travel

030	山	やま サン (mountain)	山（やま）mountain 富士山（フジサン）Mt. Fuji
			⑶ 丨 凵 山
031	川	かわ がわ (river)	川（かわ）river 小川さん（おがわさん）Mr./Ms. Ogawa
			⑶ 丿 刂 川
032	元	ゲン (origin)	元気な（ゲンキな）fine
			⑷ 一 二 テ 元
033	気	キ (spirit)	元気な（ゲンキな）fine　　天気（テンキ）weather 電気（デンキ）electricity
			⑹ 丿 ⺅ 气 气 気
034	天	テン (heaven)	天気（テンキ）weather 天国（テンゴク）heaven
			⑷ 一 二 チ 天
035	私	わたし シ (I; private)	私（わたし）I 私立大学（シリツダイガク）private university
			⑺ 一 二 千 禾 禾 私 私
036	今	いま コン (now)	今（いま）now　　今日（きょう）today 今晩（コンバン）tonight
			⑷ 丿 人 仐 今
037	田	た だ (rice field)	田中さん（たなかさん）Mr./Ms. Tanaka 山田さん（やまださん）Mr./Ms. Yamada 田んぼ（たんぼ）rice field
			⑸ 丨 冂 冊 田 田

038	女	おんな ジョ (woman)	女の人（おんなのひと）woman 女性（ジョセイ）woman
			(3) く 女 女
039	男	おとこ ダン (man)	男の人（おとこのひと）man 男性（ダンセイ）man
			(7) ┃ 冂 冂 田 田 田 男 男
040	見	み ケン (to see)	見る（みる）to see 見物（ケンブツ）sightseeing
			(7) ┃ 冂 日 日 目 見 見
041	行	い コウ　ギョウ (to go)	行く（いく）to go 銀行（ギンコウ）bank　　一行目（イチギョウめ）first line
			(6) ´ ク イ 彳 行 行
042	食	た ショク (to eat)	食べる（たべる）to eat 食べ物（たべもの）food　　食堂（ショクドウ）cafeteria
			(9) ノ 入 ハ 今 今 今 食 食 食
043	飲	の イン (to drink)	飲む（のむ）to drink 飲み物（のみもの）drink 飲酒運転（インシュウンテン）drunken driving
			(12) ノ 入 ハ 今 今 今 食 食 飣 飲 飲 飲

(In this chart, *katakana* indicates the *on'yomi* and *hiragana* indicates the *kun'yomi*.)

Ⅰ 漢字の練習 (Kanji Practice)
かんじ　れんしゅう

A. Using the parts below, make up the correct kanji.

Example:　目　→　見

1. 艮　　2. 欠　　3. ム　　4. 二　　5. 力

6. 气　　7. 人　　8. 良　　9. メ　　10. 田

B. Match the following sentences with the pictures.

1. (　　) えいがを見ます。　　2. (　　) コーヒーを飲みます。

3. (　　) ハンバーガーを食べます。　　4. (　　) 男の人と女の人がいます。

5. (　　) 山と川があります。　　6. (　　) 今日はいい天気です。

7. (　　) 銀行に行きます。
　　　　ぎんこう

C. Match the kanji with the reading.

1. (　　) 一日　　2. (　　) 二日　　3. (　　) 三日　　4. (　　) 四日

5. (　　) 五日　　6. (　　) 六日　　7. (　　) 七日　　8. (　　) 八日

9. (　　) 九日　　10. (　　) 十日　　11. (　　) 二十日

(a) いつか　(b) ここのか　(c) ついたち　(d) とおか　(e) なのか　(f) はつか

(g) ふつか　(h) みっか　(i) むいか　(j) ようか　(k) よっか

ⅠⅠ りょこうのはがき

A. Match the following *katakana* words with the English equivalents.

1. コーヒー　　・　　　　・cake
2. コンサート・　　　　　・coffee
3. ウィーン　　・　　　　・cafe
4. カフェ　　　・　　　　・classical
5. クラシック・　　　　　・concert
6. ケーキ　　　・　　　　・Vienna

B. ようこさんはみちこさんにはがきをかきました。

Read the postcard below. Write T for the things she did or does and write F for the things she didn't or doesn't do in Vienna.

1. (　　) see an old castle　　　2. (　　) go to see a ballet
3. (　　) take pictures　　　　　4. (　　) drink beer at the cafe
5. (　　) enjoy sweets　　　　　6. (　　) eat at McDonald's

みちこさんへ
元気ですか。私は今ウィーンにいます。ここはちょっとさむいです。ウィーンはとてもきれいなまちです。
　きのうはおしろを見ました。ふるかったですが、とてもきれいでした。たくさんしゃしんをとりました。よるはクラシックのコンサートに行きました。よかったです。
　ウィーンにはカフェがたくさんあります。まいにちカフェでコーヒーを飲みます。ケーキも食べます。とてもおいしいです。
　四日にかえります。また日本であいましょうね。
　　　　　山田 ようこ

〒305-0836
つくば市山中42-5
山川みちこさま
Japan

~さま　Mr./Ms. (used in letter writing)　　おしろ　castle
　　　　　が　but　　よる　night　　また　again

C. ロバートさんもはがきをかきました。

Read the postcard below and answer the following questions in Japanese.

1. ロバートさんは今どこにいますか。

2. どんな天気ですか。

3. きのうは なにをしましたか。

4. 今日は なにをしましたか。だれとしましたか。

5. おきなわの食べものはどうですか。

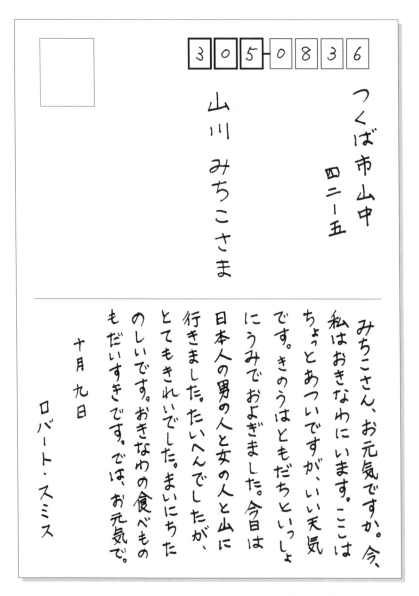

みちこさん、お元気ですか。今、私はおきなわにいます。ここはちょっとあついですが、いい天気です。きのうはともだちといっしょにうみでおよぎました。今日は日本人の男の人と女の人と山に行きました。たいへんでしたが、とてもきれいでした。まいにちたのしいです。おきなわの食べものもだいすきです。では、お元気で。

十月九日

ロバート・スミス

つくば市山中
四二一五

山川 みちこさま

305-0836

山 mountain 　たいへん tough
では、お元気で Take care.

Ⅲ 書く練習(かれんしゅう) (Writing Practice)

The following are your Japanese friends' addresses in your pocket notebook. Copy their addresses on the postcards and write about your vacation.

名前(なまえ)	住所(じゅうしょ)
今中ゆみ	〒753-0041　山口市東山(やまぐちしひがしやま)36-8
上田一男(うえだかずお)	〒112-0002　文京区小石川(ぶんきょうくこいしかわ)7-7

第6課 | L E S S O N ········· 6
私のすきなレストラン My Favorite Restaurant

044	東 (east)	ひがし トウ	東（ひがし）east　東口（ひがしぐち）east exit 東京（トウキョウ）Tokyo
			(8) 一 厂 厂 戸 同 申 東 東
045	西 (west)	にし セイ　サイ	西（にし）west　西口（にしぐち）west exit 北西（ホクセイ）northwest 関西（カンサイ）Kansai region
			(6) 一 厂 㽎 丙 西 西
046	南 (south)	みなみ ナン	南（みなみ）south　南口（みなみぐち）south exit 南東（ナントウ）southeast
			(9) 一 十 广 广 南 南 南 南 南
047	北 (north)	きた ホク　ホッ	北（きた）north　北口（きたぐち）north exit 東北（トウホク）Tohoku region 北海道（ホッカイドウ）Hokkaido
			(5) 一 十 土 北 北
048	口 (mouth)	ぐち くち　コウ	北口（きたぐち）north exit 口（くち）mouth　人口（ジンコウ）population
			(3) 丨 口 口
049	出 (to exit)	で だ　シュッ シュツ	出る（でる）to exit　出口（でぐち）exit 出す（だす）to take something out 出席（シュッセキ）attendance　輸出（ユシュツ）export
			(5) 丨 屮 屮 出 出
050	右 (right)	みぎ ウ　ユウ	右（みぎ）right 右折（ウセツ）right turn 左右（サユウ）right and left
			(5) ノ ナ 右 右 右
051	左 (left)	ひだり サ	左（ひだり）left 左折（サセツ）left turn
			(5) 一 ナ 左 左 左

052	分	フン　プン ブン (minute; to divide)	五分（ゴフン）five minutes 十分（ジュップン）ten minutes 自分（ジブン）oneself　半分（ハンブン）half
		(4)　ノ　ハ　分　分	
053	先	セン さき (ahead)	先生（センセイ）teacher 先週（センシュウ）last week　先に（さきに）ahead
		(6)　ノ　ᅩ　生　生　歩　先	
054	生	セイ う　ショウ (birth)	学生（ガクセイ）student　先生（センセイ）teacher 生まれる（うまれる）to be born 一生に一度（イッショウにイチド）once in a life time
		(5)　ノ　ᅩ　牛　牛　生	
055	大	ダイ　おお タイ (big)	大学生（ダイガクセイ）college student 大きい（おおきい）big 大変な（タイヘンな）tough　大人（おとな）adult
		(3)　一　ナ　大	
056	学	ガク ガッ　まな (learning)	大学（ダイガク）university　学生（ガクセイ）student 学校（ガッコウ）school　学ぶ（まなぶ）to study
		(8)　ゝ　ゞ　ゞ　ゞ　兴　学　学　学	
057	外	ガイ そと (outside)	外国（ガイコク）foreign country 外国人（ガイコクジン）foreigner 外（そと）outside
		(5)　ノ　ク　タ　列　外	
058	国	コク　ゴク くに (country)	外国（ガイコク）foreign country 中国（チュウゴク）China 国（くに）country
		(8)　丨　冂　冂　冂　用　国　国　国	

(In this chart, *katakana* indicates the *on'yomi* and *hiragana* indicates the *kun'yomi*.)

Ⅰ 漢字の練習 (Kanji Practice)
　　かん　じ　　れんしゅう

A. Combine the following kanji and make compound words. You can use the same kanji more than once.

Example: 外 ＋ 国 → 外国

気　生　外　先　学　天　日　国　今　大

B. Indicate where each place is located on the map.

1. (　) レストラン・アルデンテ：えきの中にあります。南口のそばです。
2. (　) ロイヤルホテル：えきの東口を出て、まっすぐ五分ぐらいです。
3. (　) 山下先生のうち：北口を出て、右へ十分ぐらいです。
4. (　) こうえん：西口をまっすぐ十五分ぐらい行ってください。
5. (　) 大学：北口を出て、左へ十分ぐらい行ってください。

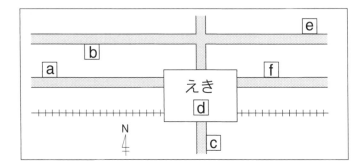

えき	station
出る	to exit
まっすぐ	straight

Ⅱ でんごんばん (Bulletin Board)

Look at the bulletin board on the next page and answer the questions.

1. If you want to buy a bicycle, who are you going to contact?
2. Where will the party be held? Are you going to bring anything?
3. How do you get to the concert hall?
4. What can you do for the winter break (from December to January)?

ホームステイ
プログラム

東北のまちでホームステイをしませんか。
<ruby>東北<rt>とうほく</rt></ruby>

十二月二十八日(日)〜一月三日(土)

きれいな山と川のそばです。

えいごをおしえてください。

日本人の大学生です。

９３１－２６８２

ようこ

セール!!
じてんしゃ

￥20,000

あたらしいです。
でんわしてください。

（よる7時〜11時）

山田　597-1651

ハロウィーン パーティー

ところ：山下先生のうち

じかん：6時〜

ともだちをつれてきてもいいですよ！

飲みものをもってきてください。

イタリアンレストラン
マンジャーレ

ランチスペシャル

1,200円

Aセット（サラダ・コーヒー）

Bセット（パン・コーヒー）

ギターコンサート

9月12日(金)

6：30〜

西コンサートホール

（西駅3出口を出て左へ3分）
<ruby>駅<rt>えき</rt></ruby>

Ⅲ 私のすきなレストラン

Mary writes about her favorite restaurant. Read the passage and answer the questions.

私のすきなレストラン

私のすきなレストランは、イタリアりょうりのマンジャーレです。えきの南口を出て、右へ五分ぐらいです。ちいさいレストランです。シェフはイタリア人のアントニオさんです。アントニオさんはとてもおもしろい人です。アントニオさんのりょうりはとてもおいしいです。私はよくマンジャーレに行きます。マンジャーレでワインを飲んで、ピザを食べます。アイスクリームもおいしいです。ここでいつもたくさん食べます。りょうりはやすいですから。外国人もたくさんきます。みなさんもきてください。

りょうり　cooking
いつも　　always
みなさん　everyone

A. Where is the restaurant?

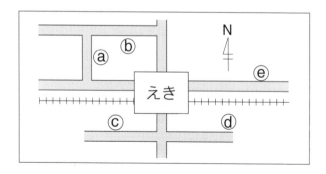

B. Circle the food or drink the writer has at the restaurant.

> ピザ　　スパゲッティ　　アイスクリーム
> ワイン　　ビール　　ステーキ

C. Choose the correct answer.

1. マンジャーレは $\left\{\begin{array}{l}大きい \\ ちいさい\end{array}\right\}$ レストランです。

2. マンジャーレは $\left\{\begin{array}{l}たかい \\ やすい\end{array}\right\}$ です。

3. アントニオさんは $\left\{\begin{array}{l}おもしろい \\ つまらない\end{array}\right\}$ 人です。

4. マンジャーレに外国人が $\left\{\begin{array}{l}きます。 \\ きません。\end{array}\right\}$

Ⅳ 書く練習 (Writing Practice)
か　　れんしゅう

A. You are organizing a party. Write a flyer about the party. Be sure to include: what kind of party it is, what time it starts, where it is held, what to bring, how to get there, and so on.

B. Write about your favorite restaurant.

第7課 L E S S O N 7
メアリーさんのてがみ Mary's Letter

059	京 (capital)	キョウ	東京 (トウキョウ) Tokyo　京子 (キョウこ) Kyoko 京都 (キョウト) Kyoto (8) ‵ 亠 宀 古 古 宁 京 京
060	子 (child)	こ シ	子ども (こども) child　京子 (キョウこ) Kyoko 女の子 (おんなのこ) girl　男の子 (おとこのこ) boy 電子メール (デンシメール) e-mail (3) 乛 了 子
061	小 (small)	ちい ショウ	小さい (ちいさい) small 小学校 (ショウガッコウ) elementary school 小学生 (ショウガクセイ) elementary school student (3) 亅 小 小
062	会 (to meet)	あ カイ	会う (あう) to meet　会社 (カイシャ) company 会社員 (カイシャイン) office worker (6) ノ 人 스 △ 会 会
063	社 (company)	シャ ジャ	会社 (カイシャ) company 神社 (ジンジャ) shrine (7) ‵ ラ オ ネ ネ‐ 社 社
064	父 (father)	ちち とう フ	父 (ちち) father　お父さん (おとうさん) father 父母 (フボ) father and mother (4) ′ ハ グ 父
065	母 (mother)	はは かあ ボ	母 (はは) mother　お母さん (おかあさん) mother 母語 (ボゴ) mother tongue (5) ㄥ 贝 贝 贝 母
066	高 (high)	たか コウ	高い (たかい) expensive; high 高校 (コウコウ) high school 高校生 (コウコウセイ) high school student (10) ‵ 亠 宀 古 古 戸 高 高 高 高

067	校	コウ	学校（ガッコウ）school　　高校（コウコウ）high school
			高校生（コウコウセイ）high school student
			中学校（チュウガッコウ）junior high school
	(school)	(10)	一　十　オ　オ　オ゙　オ゙　オ゙　オ゙　校　校
068	毎	マイ	毎日（マイニチ）every day
			毎週（マイシュウ）every week
			毎晩（マイバン）every night
	(every)	(6)	ノ　ト　ケ　勾　勾　毎
069	語	ゴ	日本語（ニホンゴ）Japanese (language)
			英語（エイゴ）English (language)
	(word)	(14)	丶　二　言　言　言　言　言　訂　訂　語　語　語　語
070	文	ブン	文学（ブンガク）literature
			作文（サクブン）composition
			文字（モジ）letter; character
	(sentence)	(4)	丶　一　ナ　文
071	帰	かえ	帰る（かえる）to return
		キ	帰国（キコク）going home
	(to return)	(10)	｜　リ　リ゙　リ゙　リ゙　リ゙　尸　帰　帰　帰
072	入	はい	入る（はいる）to enter　　入口（いりぐち）entrance
		いり　い	入れる（いれる）to put something in
		ニュウ	輸入（ユニュウ）import
	(to enter)	(2)	ノ　入

(In this chart, *katakana* indicates the *on'yomi* and *hiragana* indicates the *kun'yomi*.)

① 漢字の練習
かん じ　れんしゅう

A. Fill in the blanks with the appropriate kanji.

1. 日本＿＿＿＿学　高＿＿＿＿三年生　　＿＿＿＿と母　　　　| 父　文　校 |
ねん

2. ＿＿＿＿日、＿＿＿＿は六時におきます。　　　　| 母　毎 |

3. 日本＿＿＿＿はよくおふろに＿＿＿＿ります。　　　　| 人　入 |

4. 東＿＿＿＿に行きました。食べものは＿＿＿＿かったです。　　| 京　高 |

B. Which new kanji from this lesson include the *katakana* below?

Example:　エ　→　左

1. ヨ　→　　　　2. ネ　→　　　　3. ム　→　　　　4. ロ　→

C. What's wrong with the kanji below? Rewrite the correct kanji.

1.
母

2.
高

3.
卓

4.
話

5.
帰

6.
杦

Ⅱ メアリーさんのてがみ

京子さんは今アリゾナにすんでいます。メアリーさんは京子さんにてがみをかきました。

京子さんへ

京子さん、お元気ですか。アリゾナはあついですか。日本はすこしさむいです。今、私は日本のかぞくと大学のそばにすんでいます。ここは小さくて、しずかなまちです。

私のかぞくは四人です。みんなとてもしんせつで、たのしいです。お父さんは会社につとめています。いそがしくて、毎日おそく帰ります。お母さんはとてもおもしろい人です。いっしょによくはなします。いもうとは高校生です。らいねん大学ですから、よくべんきょうします。毎日学校から帰って、すぐじゅくへ行きます。日本の高校生はたいへんですね。おにいさんは東京の大学に行っていますから、あまり会いません。

私は今、日本語と日本文学のクラスをとって

います。テニスクラブにも入っています。とてもおもしろいです。

京子さんはいつ日本に帰りますか。いましょうね。たのしみにしています。日本で会からだに気をつけてください。

十一月三日

メアリー・ハート

すこし	a little
みんな	all
〜から	from . . .
じゅく	cram school
文学	literature
とる	to take (a class)
(〜を)たのしみにする	
	to look forward (to)
からだに気をつける	
	to take care of oneself

Summarize what Mary wrote about the following topics in Japanese.

1. Japan: _____

2. Her town: _____

3. Father: _____

4. Mother: _____

5. Sister: _____

6. Brother: _____

7. School: _____

⑪ 書く練習
か　　れんしゅう

A. Write about the following topics.

1. 日本は／私の国は_____

_____

2. 私のまちは_____

_____

3. かぞくは_____

_____

4. ともだちは_____

_____

B. Write letters to your Japanese friends. Describe your town, host family, friends, and so on.

第8課 | L E S S O N 8

日本の会社員 Japanese Office Workers

073	員 (member)	イン	会社員 (カイシャイン) office worker 店員 (テンイン) store clerk (10) ` ⼝ ⼝ ⼝ ⼝ 員 員 員 員 員
074	新 (new)	あたら シン	新しい (あたらしい) new 新聞 (シンブン) newspaper 新幹線 (シンカンセン) Bullet Train (13) ` ⼀ � 新 新 新
075	聞 (to listen)	き ブン	聞く (きく) to listen 新聞 (シンブン) newspaper (14) 聞
076	作 (to make)	つく サク	作る (つくる) to make 作文 (サクブン) composition 作品 (サクヒン) artistic piece (7) 作
077	仕 (to serve)	シ	仕事 (シごと) job (5) 仕
078	事 (thing)	ごと こと ジ	仕事 (シごと) job 事 (こと) thing 火事 (カジ) fire 食事 (ショクジ) meal (8) 事
079	電 (electricity)	デン	電車 (デンシャ) train 電気 (デンキ) electricity 電話 (デンワ) telephone (13) 電
080	車 (car)	くるま シャ	車 (くるま) car 電車 (デンシャ) train 自転車 (ジテンシャ) bicycle (7) 車

081	休	やす キュウ (to rest)	休む（やすむ）to be absent; to rest 休み（やすみ）holiday; absence 休日（キュウジツ）holiday
			(6) ノ イ 亻 什 休 休
082	言	い ゲン (to say)	言う（いう）to say 言語学（ゲンゴガク）linguistics
			(7) 丶 一 亠 三 言 言 言
083	読	よ ドク (to read)	読む（よむ）to read 読書（ドクショ）reading books
			(14) 丶 亠 亠 言 言 言 言 訁 計 訪 訪 誇 読 読
084	思	おも シ (to think)	思う（おもう）to think 不思議な（フシギな）mysterious
			(9) 丿 冂 田 田 田 甲 思 思 思
085	次	つぎ ジ (next)	次（つぎ）next 次女（ジジョ）one's second daughter
			(6) 丶 冫 冫 汐 次 次
086	何	なに　なん (what)	何（なに）what　　何時（なんジ）what time 何人（なんニン）how many people
			(7) ノ イ 亻 仁 何 何 何

(In this chart, *katakana* indicates the *on'yomi* and *hiragana* indicates the *kun'yomi*.)

① 漢字の練習
かんじ　れんしゅう

A. Using the parts below, make up as many kanji as possible.

Example: 乂 → 文　父

1. 言　　2. 木　　3. 日　　4. 田　　5. イ　　6. 口

B. Match the following phrases with an appropriate verb.

1. 新聞を　・　　　　　・作る
2. ラジオを・　　　　　・休む
3. 仕事を　・　　　　　・読む
4. 日本語はおもしろいと・　・する
5. カレーを・　　　　　・思う
6. 電車に　・　　　　　・聞く
7. クラスを・　　　　　・のる

② 日本の会社員

A. 留学生のマークさんはアンケートを作って、日本人の会社員に聞きました。
りゅう
Read the following questionnaire.

アンケート

1. 仕事のストレスがありますか。

　　□はい　　　　　□いいえ

2. よく残業をしますか。
　　ざんぎょう
　　□よくする　　□ときどきする　　□ぜんぜんしない

3. 仕事の後、何をしますか。
　　あと

4. 休みはたいてい何をしますか。

| アンケート | questionnaire | 残業（ざんぎょう） | overtime work |
| ストレス | stress | 〜の後（〜のあと） | after . . . |

B. How would you answer the above questions?

C. マークさんはアンケートについてレポートを書きました。
Read the report below and answer the questions.

日本の会社員

マーク・テイラー

　日本の会社員は、電車の中で、ときどき新聞を読んでいますが、たいていみんな寝ています。みんなとても疲れていると思います。私はアンケートを作って、会社員十人に聞きました。

　まず、「仕事のストレスがありますか」と聞きました。九人は「はい」と答えました。「仕事が大変で、休みがあまりない」と言っていました。次に、「よく残業をしますか」と聞きました。三人は「よく残業をする」と言っていました。五人は「ときどき残業をする」と言っていました。次に「仕事の後、何をしますか」と聞きました。六人は「お酒を飲みに行く」と言っていました。二人は「カラオケに行く」と言っていました。最後に「休みはたいてい何をしますか」と聞きました。七人は「疲れているから、家にいる」と言っていました。

　日本の会社員はたくさん仕事をして、ストレスもあります。だから、休みは何もしません。アンケートをして、日本の会社員はとても大変だと思いました。

〜について	about; regarding to	答える（こたえる）	to answer
疲れている（つかれている）	to be tired	次に	secondly
まず	first of all	最後に（さいごに）	lastly

1. どうしてマークさんはアンケートをしましたか。

2. 何人いましたか。

    (a) 仕事のストレスがある。 …… ＿＿＿＿＿人

    (b) よく残業_{ざんぎょう}をする。 …… ＿＿＿＿＿人

    (c) ときどき残業_{ざんぎょう}をする。 …… ＿＿＿＿＿人

    (d) 仕事の後_{あと}、お酒_{さけ}を飲む。 …… ＿＿＿＿＿人

    (e) 休みの日は出かけない。 …… ＿＿＿＿＿人

Ⅲ 書_かく練習_{れんしゅう}

Make a questionnaire and ask several people the questions. Then, write a report based on the result.

第9課 | L E S S O N 9

スーさんの日記 Sue's Diary
にっき

087	午 (noon)	ゴ	午前 (ゴゼン) A.M.　午後 (ゴゴ) P.M.; in the afternoon 午前中 (ゴゼンチュウ) in the morning
			(4) ノ 广 仁 午
088	後 (after)	ゴ あと うし	午後 (ゴゴ) P.M.; in the afternoon 〜の後 (のあと) after . . .　後で (あとで) later 後ろ (うしろ) back; behind　最後に (サイゴに) lastly
			(9) ノ ク イ 彳 袢 袢 移 移 後
089	前 (before)	まえ ゼン	前 (まえ) before; front　午前 (ゴゼン) A.M. 名前 (なまえ) name
			(9) ` ` 丷 丷 广 产 前 前 前
090	名 (name)	な メイ	名前 (なまえ) name 有名な (ユウメイな) famous　名刺 (メイシ) name card
			(6) ノ ク タ タ 名 名
091	白 (white)	しろ ハク	白い (しろい) white 白紙 (ハクシ) blank sheet
			(5) ノ イ 白 白 白
092	雨 (rain)	あめ ウ	雨 (あめ) rain 雨期 (ウキ) rainy season
			(8) 一 厂 冂 币 币 雨 雨 雨
093	書 (to write)	か ショ	書く (かく) to write 辞書 (ジショ) dictionary
			(10) フ ⁊ ⁊ ⁊ 聿 聿 書 書 書 書
094	友 (friend)	とも ユウ	友だち (ともだち) friend 親友 (シンユウ) best friend　友人 (ユウジン) friend
			(4) 一 ナ 方 友

095	間 (between)	カン　あいだ	時間（ジカン）time　　二時間（ニジカン）two hours 間（あいだ）between　　人間（ニンゲン）human being 一週間（イッシュウカン）one week
			⑿ 丨 冂 冂 冋 冋 門 門 門 門 問 間 間
096	家 (house)	いえ カ	家（いえ）house 家族（カゾク）family 家（うち）house; home
			⑽ 丶 宀 宁 宀 宁 宁 宀 宆 宆 家
097	話 (to speak)	はな　はなし ワ	話す（はなす）to speak　　話（はなし）talk; story 電話（デンワ）telephone 会話（カイワ）conversation
			⒀ 丶 丶 亠 亖 言 言 言 訁 訁 話 話 話
098	少 (little)	すこ すく　ショウ	少し（すこし）little 少ない（すくない）few　　少々（ショウショウ）a little
			⑷ 丿 小 小 少
099	古 (old)	ふる コ	古い（ふるい）old (for things) 中古（チュウコ）secondhand
			⑸ 一 十 十 古 古
100	知 (to know)	し チ	知る（しる）to know 知人（チジン）acquaintance
			⑻ 丿 二 二 チ 矢 矢 知 知
101	来 (to come)	く　き　こ ライ	来る（くる）to come　　来ます（きます）to come 来ない（こない）not to come 来週（ライシュウ）next week
			⑺ 一 ⼀ 冖 ⼕ 平 平 来 来

(In this chart, *katakana* indicates the *on'yomi* and *hiragana* indicates the *kun'yomi*.)

Ⓘ 漢字の練習
かん じ　れんしゅう

A. Fill in the blanks with the appropriate kanji.

1. この＿＿＿＿いTシャツは五＿＿＿＿円でした。　｜ 百　白 ｜

2. ＿＿＿＿さいケーキを＿＿＿＿し食べました。　｜ 小　少 ｜

3. 一時＿＿＿＿テープを＿＿＿＿きました。　｜ 聞　間 ｜

4. 日本＿＿＿＿を＿＿＿＿します。　｜ 話　語 ｜

B. Choose the most appropriate word for each blank.

1. はじめまして。私の＿＿＿＿＿＿＿はキムです。　｜ 名前　午前 ｜

2. 毎日たいてい＿＿＿＿＿＿＿＿七時ごろおきます。　｜ 午後　午前 ｜

3. このきものは古いから、＿＿＿＿＿＿＿きものをかいます。

　｜ 大きい　新しい ｜

4. 今日はいい＿＿＿＿＿＿＿だった。でも、あしたは＿＿＿＿＿＿＿がふると思う。

　｜ 元気　天気　白　雨 ｜

5. メアリーのお父さんを＿＿＿＿＿＿＿＿いますか。　｜ 帰って　知って ｜

Ⅱ スーさんの日記
にっ き

十一月二十五日（土）　雨

　　今日はあさから雨がふっていた。午前中は友だちに手紙を書いて、
　一時間ぐらい音楽を聞いた。昼ごろメアリーの家へ行った。白くて、
　　おんがく　　　　　　ひる
　大きい家だった。メアリーのホストファミリーの山本さんに会った。
　　　　　　　　　　　　　　　　　　　　　　　もと
　お父さんはせが高くて、やせている人だった。家で晩ごはんを食べ
　　　　　　　　　　　　　　　　　　　　　　　　ばん
　た。お母さんは「何もありませんが」と言っていたが、たくさんご

ちそうがあった。晩ごはんはとてもおいしかった。お母さんはとて
も料理が上手だと思う。晩ごはんの後、いろいろな話をした。そし
て、きれいなきものをもらった。お母さんは少し古いと言っていた
が、とてもきれいだ。メアリーのホストファミリーはとてもしんせ
つで楽しかった。

日記（にっき）	diary	いろいろな	various
午前中	in the morning	話をする	to have a talk
ホストファミリー	host family	そして	and
ごちそう	excellent food		

A. Put the following pictures in the right order according to Sue's diary.

(　　) → (　　) → (　　) → (　　) → (　　)

(a)

(b)

(c)

(d)

(e)

B. Mark T if the following statements are true. Mark F if not true.

1. (　　) スーさんは古いきものをもらった。
2. (　　) お父さんはせがひくくて、やせている。
3. (　　) 晩ごはんは何もなかった。

ばん
4. (　　) スーさんはお母さんの料理が好きだ。

りょうり　す
5. (　　) 天気がよくなかった。
6. (　　) メアリーさんのホストファミリーの名前は山田だ。

C. スーさんはメアリーさんのホストファミリーに手紙を書きました。

てがみ
   Read the following letter.

山本さま

　先日はどうもありがとうございました。
とても たのしかったです。りょうではあまり
日本のりょうりを食べませんが、お母さん
のりょうりはとてもおいしかったです。
それから、きものをありがとうございました。
とてもきれいなきものですね。
　どうぞかんこくに来てください。私は
ソウルのおもしろいところを知っています
から、あんないします。

　　　十一月二十八日
　　　　　スー・キム

先日（せんじつ）	the other day
りょう	dormitory
あんないする	to show someone around

Ⅲ 書く練習
れんしゅう

A. What did you do yesterday? Write a journal.

B. Write a thank-you letter to someone.

Useful Expressions for Letters and Cards:

いろいろおせわになりました。(Thank you for everything.)

体に気をつけてください。(Please take care of yourself.)
からだ

お会いできるのを楽しみにしています。(I am looking forward to seeing you.)
たの

〜おめでとう(ございます)。(Congratulations on . . .)

おたんじょうびおめでとう。(Happy Birthday)

第10課 LESSON 10

かさじぞう The Folktale *Kasajizo*

102	住 (to live)	す ジュウ	住む（すむ）to live 住所（ジュウショ）address (7) ノ イ イ 仁 仁 住 住
103	正 (right)	ショウ ただ	お正月（おショウガツ）New Year 正しい（ただしい）right (5) 一 丁 下 正 正
104	年 (year)	ネン　とし	三年生（サンネンセイ）third-year student 来年（ライネン）next year　　今年（ことし）this year 年（とし）year (6) ノ ゲ ヒ 仁 年 年
105	売 (to sell)	う バイ	売る（うる）to sell 売店（バイテン）stand; stall (7) 一 十 土 土 売 売 売
106	買 (to buy)	か	買う（かう）to buy 買い物（かいもの）shopping (12) 丶 丆 冂 皿 皿 罒 罒 胃 胃 買 買 買
107	町 (town)	まち チョウ	町（まち）town 北山町（きたやまチョウ）Kitayama town 町長（チョウチョウ）mayor of a town (7) 丿 冂 冂 用 田 田丁 町
108	長 (long)	なが チョウ	長い（ながい）long 長男（チョウナン）one's first son (8) 丨 厂 F F 手 長 長 長
109	道 (way)	みち ドウ	道（みち）way; road 書道（ショドウ）calligraphy　　柔道（ジュウドウ）judo 北海道（ホッカイドウ）Hokkaido (12) 丶 丷 丷 艹 艹 产 首 首 首 首 道 道

110	雪 (snow)	ゆき / セツ	雪（ゆき）snow 新雪（シンセツ）new snow
			⑾ 一 ⼀ ⼀ 户 ⾬ ⾬ ⾬ ⾬ 雪 雪 雪
111	立 (to stand)	た / リツ	立つ（たつ）to stand 国立大学（コクリツダイガク）national university 私立高校（シリツコウコウ）private high school
			⑸ 、 ⼀ ⼾ ⽴ 立
112	自 (self)	ジ	自分（ジブン）oneself 自動車（ジドウシャ）automobile 自転車（ジテンシャ）bicycle
			⑹ 、 ⼎ 冂 白 自 自
113	夜 (night)	よる / よ ヤ	夜（よる）night 夜中（よなか）midnight　今夜（コンヤ）tonight
			⑻ 、 ⼀ 广 广 疒 疒 夜 夜
114	朝 (morning)	あさ / チョウ	朝（あさ）morning　今朝（けさ）this morning 朝食（チョウショク）breakfast
			⑿ 一 十 ⼗ 市 吉 吉 直 卓 軌 朝 朝 朝
115	持 (to hold)	もつ / ジ	持つ（もつ）to hold　持ってくる（もってくる）to bring 所持品（ショジヒン）belongings
			⑼ 一 十 扌 扌 扩 护 拝 持 持

(In this chart, *katakana* indicates the *on'yomi* and *hiragana* indicates the *kun'yomi*.)

① 漢字の練習
かん じ　れんしゅう

A. Add strokes to the kanji below and turn them into new kanji from this lesson.

Example: 二 → 立

1. 上 →　　　2. 田 →　　　3. 雨 →　　　4. 月 →

5. 白 →　　　6. 土 →　　　7. 員 →　　　8. 自 →

B. Write each antonym in kanji.

1. 買う　　　⇔ _____　　　2. すわる　　⇔ _____

3. みじかい ⇔ _____　　　4. 夜　　　　⇔ _____

C. Fill in the blanks with the appropriate kanji from the list, and add *hiragana* where necessary.

売 雪 住 買 長 立 持

1. 町で_____をしました。
   shopping

2. かさを_____ていますか。
   have

3. 本屋では本を_____ています。
   や
   (are) sell(ing)

4. よく_____がふります。
   snow

5. おじいさんの話は_____。
   was long

6. アパートに_____でいます。
   live

7. 私の後ろに女の人が_____。
   was standing

Ⅱ かさじぞう

A. Answer the following questions.

1. 日本ではお正月に何をすると思いますか。

2. (Picture 1) これはおじぞうさんです。何だと思いますか。

3. (Picture 2) このおじいさんとおばあさんがこの話の主人公 (main characters) です。どんな人だと思いますか。どんな生活をしていると思いますか。

B. Read the Japanese folktale "かさじぞう" on pp. 302-3.

C. Put the following pictures in the right order.

(   ) → (   ) → (   ) → (   ) → (   ) → (   )

むかしむかし	once upon a time
かさ	bamboo hat
お正月	New Year's
年	year
おもち	rice cake
売る	to sell
かなしい	sad
山道	mountain road
じぞう	guardian deity of children
雪	snow
〜に〜をかぶせる	to put (a hat) on a person's head
自分	oneself
とる	to take off
いいこと	good deed
声（こえ）	voice
戸（と）	door
びっくりする	to be surprised
しあわせな	happy

ました。

うちに帰って、おじいさんはおばあさんにおじぞうさんの話をしました。

おばあさんは「おじいさん、いいことをしましたね。」と言いました。

その夜おそく、おじいさんはだれかの声を聞きました。

「おじいさん、おじいさん。」

おじいさんは戸を開けて、びっくりしました。六人のおじぞうさんが立っていました。おじぞうさんはお正月のおもちをたくさん持っていました。

お正月の朝になりました。おじいさんとおばあさんはおもちをたくさん食べました。二人はとてもしあわせでした。

D. Mark T if the following statements are true. Mark F if not true.

1. (　　) おじいさんとおばあさんはお金持ちだった。

2. (　　) だれもおじいさんのかさを買わなかった。

3. (　　) おじいさんはおじぞうさんにかさを売った。

4. (　　) 雪の中でおじいさんはおじぞうさんを六つ見た。

5. (　　) おじいさんは新しいかさを六つ持っていた。

6. (　　) おばあさんはおじいさんの話を聞いて、かなしくなった。

7. (　　) おじぞうさんはお金をたくさん持ってきた。

8. (　　) おじいさんとおばあさんのお正月はとてもよかった。

かさじぞう

むかしむかし、山の中におじいさんとおばあさんが住んでいました。おじいさんとおばあさんはうちでかさを作っていました。あしたはお正月です。新しい年がはじまります。でも、おじいさんとおばあさんはお金<ruby>金<rt>かね</rt></ruby>がなかったから、お正月のおもちもありませんでした。二人はかさを売って、おもちを買うつもりでした。

おじいさんはかさを持って、町に売りに行きました。でも、だれもかさを買いませんでした。おじいさんはかなしくなりました。

おじいさんは長い山道を歩<ruby>歩<rt>ある</rt></ruby>いて帰りました。雪がたくさんふっていました。

「あっ！ おじぞうさんだ！」

雪の中におじぞうさんが六つ立っていました。

おじいさんは「おじぞうさん、さむくありませんか。」と聞きました。

おじぞうさんは何も言いませんでした。

「どうぞかさを使<ruby>使<rt>つか</rt></ruby>ってください。」

おじいさんはおじぞうさんのあたまの上にかさをかぶせました。

「一つ、二つ、三つ、四つ、五つ」

かさは五つでした。一人のおじぞうさんはかさがありませんでした。

おじいさんは自分のかさをとりました。

「このかさは古いですが、どうぞ。」と言って、おじぞうさんにかぶせ

Ⅲ 書く練習<ruby>練習<rt>れんしゅう</rt></ruby>

Choose one topic from the list below and write a story about it. For example: What do people do on these days? Do you have good memories? Do you know unusual tales about these days?

クリスマス	お正月	ハロウィーン	誕生日<ruby>誕生日<rt>たんじょうび</rt></ruby> (Birthday)
感謝祭<ruby>感謝祭<rt>かんしゃさい</rt></ruby> (Thanksgiving Day)	13日の金曜日		

第11課 | L E S S O N ·····11
友だち募集 Looking for Friends
ぼ しゅう

116	手 (hand)	て シュ	手紙 (てがみ) letter　　歌手 (カシュ) singer 手 (て) hand　　手話 (シュワ) sign language 上手な (ジョウズな) good at
			(4) 一 二 三 手
117	紙 (paper)	がみ かみ シ	手紙 (てがみ) letter　　紙 (かみ) paper 和紙 (ワシ) Japanese paper
			(10) く 幺 幺 幺 糸 糸 糸 紅 紅 紙 紙
118	好 (favorite; to like)	す コウ この	好きな (すきな) to like 好意 (コウイ) good will　　好み (このみ) liking; taste
			(6) く 夕 女 女' 好' 好
119	近 (near)	ちか キン	近く (ちかく) nearby　　近所 (キンジョ) neighborhood 最近 (サイキン) recently 中近東 (チュウキントウ) the Middle and Near East
			(7) ′ ′ ′ 斤 斤 沂 近 近
120	明 (bright)	あか メイ	明るい (あかるい) cheerful; bright 明日 (あした) tomorrow 説明 (セツメイ) explanation
			(8) l 冂 日 日 日' 明 明 明
121	病 (ill; sick)	ビョウ	病院 (ビョウイン) hospital　　病気 (ビョウキ) illness 重病 (ジュウビョウ) serious illness 急病 (キュウビョウ) sudden illness
			(10) ′ 亠 广 广 疒 疒 疒 疔 病 病
122	院 (institution)	イン	病院 (ビョウイン) hospital 大学院 (ダイガクイン) graduate school 美容院 (ビヨウイン) beauty parlor
			(10) ' 了 阝 阝' 阝' 阝' 阡 阮 院 院
123	映 (to reflect)	エイ うつ	映画 (エイガ) movie 映画館 (エイガカン) movie theater 映る (うつる) to be reflected
			(9) l 冂 日 日 日' 叩 昢 映 映

124	画	ガ カク (picture)	映画（エイガ）movie 画家（ガカ）painter　計画（ケイカク）plan ⑻ 一 厂 厅 币 而 面 画 画
125	歌	うた カ (to sing)	歌う（うたう）to sing　歌（うた）song 歌手（カシュ）singer 国歌（コッカ）national anthem ⑭ 一 厂 厂 戸 可 哥 哥 哥 哥 哥 歌 歌 歌
126	市	シ いち (city)	川口市（かわぐちシ）Kawaguchi city 市役所（シヤクショ）city hall　市長（シチョウ）mayor 市場（いちば）market ⑸ 、 亠 广 方 市
127	所	ところ ジョ どころ ショ (place)	いろいろな所（いろいろなところ）various places 近所（キンジョ）neighborhood 台所（ダイどころ）kitchen　住所（ジュウショ）address ⑻ 一 ㇕ ㇕ ㇕ 戸 戸 所 所
128	勉	ベン つと (to make efforts)	勉強する（ベンキョウする）to study 勉める（つとめる）to try hard 勤勉な（キンベンな）diligent ⑽ ′ ㇇ ㇇ 召 召 召 勺 免 免 勉
129	強	キョウ つよ ゴウ (strong)	勉強する（ベンキョウする）to study 強い（つよい）strong 強情な（ゴウジョウな）obstinate ⑾ ㇇ ㇇ 弓 弦 弦 弦 弦 強 強 強 強
130	有	ユウ あ (to exist)	有名な（ユウメイな）famous 有料（ユウリョウ）toll; fee 有る（ある）to exist ⑹ ノ ナ 才 右 有 有
131	旅	リョ たび (travel)	旅行（リョコウ）travel 旅館（リョカン）inn 一人旅（ひとりたび）traveling alone ⑽ 、 亠 う 方 ㇰ 扩 扩 斻 旅 旅

(In this chart, *katakana* indicates the *on'yomi* and *hiragana* indicates the *kun'yomi*.)

Ⅰ 漢字の練習
かんじ れんしゅう

A. Combine the parts below to form the new kanji from this lesson.

B. Put one kanji in each box to make compunds.

(1) 歌□／□紙 (2) □□／所く (3) 有□／□前 (4) □院／気

Ⅱ 友だち募集
ぼ しゅう

A. 質問に答えてください。(Answer the following questions.)
しつもん こた

　1. あなたの国には友だち募集の雑誌がありますか。
　　　　　　　　　　ぼ しゅう　ざっし

　2. あなたは雑誌で友だちを募集したことがありますか。友だちを募集している人
　　　　　　ざっし　　　　　　ぼ しゅう　　　　　　　　　　　　　　　ぼ しゅう
　　に手紙を書いたことがありますか。

B. 雑誌の「友だち募集」を読みましょう。
ざっし　　　　ぼ しゅう

友だちになってください	手紙ください！
大学三年生です。専門はフランス文学 せんもん です。スポーツが大好きで、休みの日に は、テニスをしたり、サッカーをしたり しています。カラオケにもよく行きま す。今度いっしょに遊びませんか。 こんど　　　　あそ 　　　　　　水野　裕子（20歳／女） 　　　　　　みずの　ゆうこ　はたち	会社員です。川口市に住んでいます。 アウトドアが好きで、休みの日は車で 近くの山や川に行きます。将来は外国 しょうらい の山に登りたいと思っています。山に のぼ 登るのが好きな人、手紙ください。 のぼ 　　　　　　松本　明（23歳／男） 　　　　　　まつもと　あきら　さい

彼女募集！
20歳から25歳ぐらいで、明るくて、やさしくて、たばこを吸わない人。髪が長い人が好きです。ぼくは病院に勤めています。趣味はドライブと映画です。会って、いろいろ話しましょう。

中村　ひろし
（26歳／男）

いっしょにバンドをやりませんか
ロックが好きな女の子です。ギターをひくのが好きで、将来は歌手になりたいと思っています。私といっしょにバンドをやりませんか。それからコンサートにもいっしょに行きましょう！

岡田　香
（18歳／女）

〜募集（ぼしゅう）	looking for . . .	川	river
女（おんな）	woman	彼女（かのじょ）	girlfriend
男（おとこ）	man	明るい	cheerful
アウトドア	outdoor activities	趣味（しゅみ）	hobby
近く	near place	バンド	band

C. 次の人はだれですか。その人の名前を書いてください。

1. The person who is 18 years old　　　　　　（　　　　　　　　）さん

2. The person who is a college student　　　　（　　　　　　　　）さん

3. The person who likes movies　　　　　　　（　　　　　　　　）さん

4. The person who likes climbing mountains　（　　　　　　　　）さん

5. The person who is looking for a girlfriend　（　　　　　　　　）さん

D. 質問に答えてください。

1. 水野さんはどんなスポーツをしますか。

2. 水野さんの専門は何ですか。

3. 中村さんはどんな人が好きですか。

4. 松本さんは車を運転しますか。

5. 岡田さんは何になりたいと思っていますか。
   おか だ

6. あなたはどの人に手紙を書きたいですか。どうしてですか。

E. 雑誌を見て、カレンさんは松本さんに手紙を書きました。手紙を読んで、質問に答えてくだ
   ざっ し   まつもと   しつもん こた
   さい。

松本　明　様
まつもと あきら さま

　　はじめまして。雑誌を見ました。私も川口市に住んでいます。近所
　　　　　　　　ざっし
ですね。私はカナダ人の留学生です。一月に日本に来ました。今、
　　　　　　　　　　りゅう
日本語や日本文化を勉強しています。私もアウトドアが大好きで、
　　　　　ぶん か
山に登ったり、つりをしたりするのが好きです。旅行も好きです。
　　のぼ
外国は、シンガポールやニュージーランドに行ったことがあります。
日本では、まだあまり旅行していませんが、これからいろいろな所
に行くつもりです。古いお寺や神社を見たいと思っています。日本
　　　　　　　　　　てら じんじゃ
の有名な祭りも見たいです。スポーツはバスケットが好きです。日
　　　　まつ
本人の友だちをたくさん作って、日本語でいろいろなことを話した
いと思っています。よかったら、お返事ください。
　　　　　　　　　　　　　　　　へん じ

　　三月二十一日

　　　　　　　　　　　　　　　　　　　　　　カレン・ミラー

近所	neighborhood	神社（じんじゃ）	shrine
文化（ぶんか）	culture	祭り（まつり）	festival
つり	fishing	お返事（おへんじ）	reply

1. カレンさんはいつ日本に来ましたか。

2. カレンさんは何をするのが好きですか。

3. カレンさんは日本でどこに行きたいと思っていますか。

Ⅲ 書く練習
れんしゅう

A. 友だち募集の手紙を書きましょう。
ぼ しゅう

B. Ⅱ-B のどの人と友だちになりたいですか。その人に手紙を書きましょう。

第12課 | L E S S O N ·········· 12

七夕 Tanabata Festival
たな ばた

132	昔	むかし	昔（むかし）old times 昔話（むかしばなし）old tale
		(ancient times)	(8) 一 十 廿 苗 芹 苹 昔 昔
133	々	(symbol of repetition of a kanji)	昔々（むかしむかし）once upon a time 人々（ひとびと）people 時々（ときどき）sometimes　色々な（いろいろな）various
			(3) ノ ク 々
134	神	かみ　ジン シン	神さま（かみさま）God　　神社（ジンジャ）shrine 神道（シントウ）Shinto religion
		(God)	(9) ` ラ ネ ネ ネ 初 初 神 神
135	早	はや ソウ	早い（はやい）early 早起きする（はやおきする）to get up early 早朝（ソウチョウ）early morning
		(early)	(6) １ 口 日 日 旦 早
136	起	お キ	起きる（おきる）to get up 起こす（おこす）to wake someone up 起立する（キリツする）to stand up
		(to get up)	(10) 一 十 土 キ キ 走 走 起 起 起
137	牛	うし ギュウ	牛（うし）cow 牛乳（ギュウニュウ）milk　　牛肉（ギュウにく）beef
		(cow)	(4) ノ ゲ 二 牛
138	使	つか シ	使う（つかう）to use 大使（タイシ）ambassador 使用中（ショウチュウ）"Occupied"
		(to use)	(8) ノ イ イ 仁 仨 伊 使 使
139	働	はたら ばたら　ドウ	働く（はたらく）to work 共働き（ともばたらき）both husband and wife working for a living　　労働（ロウドウ）labor
		(to work)	(13) ノ イ イ 仁 伝 侮 侮 価 価 価 働 働

140	連	つ レン (to link)	連れて帰る（つれてかえる）to take home 国連（コクレン）United Nations 連休（レンキュウ）consecutive holidays ⑽ 一 厂 厂 宀 盲 亘 車 車 連 連
141	別	わか ベツ (to separate)	別れる（わかれる）to separate 別に（ベツに）not in particular 特別な（トクベツな）special 差別（サベツ）discrimination 別々に（ベツベツに）separately ⑺ 丶 冂 口 号 另 別 別
142	度	ド (time; degrees)	一度（イチド）once 今度（コンド）near future 温度（オンド）temperature 三十度（サンジュウド）30 degrees ⑼ 丶 亠 广 户 庐 庐 庐 度 度
143	赤	あか セキ (red)	赤（あか）red color 赤い（あかい）red 赤ちゃん（あかちゃん）baby 赤道（セキドウ）the equator 赤十字（セキジュウジ）the Red Cross ⑺ 一 十 土 チ 方 赤 赤
144	青	あお セイ (blue)	青（あお）blue color 青い（あおい）blue 青年（セイネン）youth ⑻ 一 十 キ 主 青 青 青 青
145	色	いろ シキ ショク (color)	色（いろ）color 色々な（いろいろな）various 景色（ケシキ）scenery 特色（トクショク）characteristic ⑹ 丿 勹 夕 刍 刍 色

(In this chart, *katakana* indicates the *on'yomi* and *hiragana* indicates the *kun'yomi*.)

Ⅰ 漢字の練習
かん じ れんしゅう

A. Match the reading, kanji, and translation.

Example: むかし　　・　　・早・　　・ to use

1. はや(い)　　・　　・青・　　・ cow

2. お(きる)　　・　　・昔・　　・ to get up

3. つか(う)　　・　　・牛・　　・ early

4. わか(れる)　　・　　・色・　　・ color

5. あか　　・　　・赤・　　・ ancient times

6. あお　　・　　・起・　　・ to separate

7. いろ　　・　　・別・　　・ blue

8. うし　　・　　・使・　　・ red

B. Which new kanji from this lesson include the *katakana* below?

1. マ →　　2. ネ →　　3. カ →　　4. ヌ →

C. Which new kanji from this lesson shares the same component as each pair of kanji below?

Example: 朝　前　→　青

1. 住　仕　　2. 道　近　　3. 万　旅

Ⅱ 七 夕
たな ばた

A. 絵 (picture) を見てください。これは何だと思いますか。七夕の日に作ります。
え　　　　　　　　　　　　　　　　　　　　　　　　　　　　　　たなばた

B. 七夕（たなばた）の話を読みましょう。

七月七日は七夕（たなばた）です。これは七夕（たなばた）の話です。

昔々、天に神さまが住んでいました。娘（むすめ）が一人いて、名前はおりひめでした。おりひめはとてもまじめで、毎日、朝早く起きてはた（お）を織っていました。

ある日、神さまは思いました。「おりひめはもう大人（おとな）だ。結婚（けっこん）したほうがいいだろう。」

神さまはまじめな男の人を見つけました。天（あま）の川（がわ）の向（む）こうに住んでいる人で、名前はひこぼしでした。ひこぼしは牛を使って、畑（はたけ）で働いていました。

おりひめとひこぼしは結婚（けっこん）しました。二人はとても好きになりました。いつもいっしょにいて、ぜんぜん働（おこ）きませんでした。

神さまは怒（おこ）りました。でも二人は仕事をしませんでした。

神さまはとても怒（おこ）って、おりひめを家に連れて帰りました。二人は別れなくてはいけま

せんでした。おりひめはひこぼしに会いたくて、毎日泣（な）いていました。

神さまは二人がかわいそうだと思って、言いました。

「おりひめ、ひこぼし、あなたたちは一年に一度だけ会ってもいい。それは七月七日の夜だ。おりひめ、あなたはその日、天（あま）の川（がわ）の向（む）こうに行ってもいい。でも、朝までに帰らなくちゃいけない。」

一年に一度、七夕（たなばた）の夜におりひめとひこぼしは会います。二人の願（ねが）いはかなうのです。

この日、私たちは赤や青などいろいろな色のたんざくに願（ねが）いを書きます。七夕（たなばた）の日の願（ねが）いはかなうと人々は言います。ある子供（ども）は「いい成績（せいせき）を取（と）りたい」と書きます。ある人は「すてきな人に会（あ）いたい」と書きます。あなたは七夕（たなばた）の日にどんな願（ねが）いを書きますか。

天	the heavens; the sky	怒る（おこる）	to get angry
神さま	God	連れて帰る	to take back
娘（むすめ）	daughter	泣く（なく）	to cry
まじめな	serious	かわいそうな	pitiful
はたを織る（おる）	to weave	一年に一度	once a year
ある〜	one . . .（ある日　one day）	〜までに	by . . .
大人（おとな）	adult	願い（ねがい）	wish
見つける	to find	かなう	to be realized
天の川（あまのがわ）	the Milky Way	私たち	we
向こう（むこう）	the other side; over there	〜など	and so forth
牛	cow	たんざく	strip of fancy paper
畑（はたけ）	farm	人々	people

C. 質問に答えてください。

1. おりひめはどんな人ですか。

2. ひこぼしはどんな人ですか。

3. どうして神さまは怒りましたか。

4. 七月七日におりひめは何をしますか。

5. どうして私たちは七夕の日にたんざくに願いを書きますか。

6. 神さまはやさしい人だと思いますか。どうしてですか。

Ⅲ 書く練習

あなたの願いを五つ書いてください。どうしてその願いを書きましたか。理由（reason）も書いてください。

巻末
かん　まつ

あいうえお　かきくけこ　さしすせそ　たちつてと　なにぬねの　はひふへほ　まみむめも　やゆよ　らりるれろ　わをん

さくいん1 Japanese-English

あいうえお　かきくけこ　さしすせそ　たちつてと　なにぬねの　はひふへほ　まみむめも　やゆよ　らりるれろ　わをん

いちねんせい　一年生　first-year student　会L1
いちねんにいちど　一年に一度　once a year
　　　　　　　　読L12-Ⅱ
いちばん　一番　best　会L10
いちばんうしろ　一番後ろ　last car; tail end
　　　　　　　　会L10(s)
いちばんまえ　一番前　first car; front end
　　　　　　　　会L10(s)
いつ　when　会L3
いつか　五日　the fifth day of a month　会L4(s)
いっさい　一歳　one year old　会L1(s)
いっしょに　一緒に　together　会L5
いつつ　五つ　five　会L9
いってきます　I'll go and come back.　会G
いってらっしゃい　Please go and come back.　会G
いっぷん　一分　one minute　会L1(s)
いつも　always　会L12, 読L6-Ⅲ
いぬ　犬　dog　会L4
いま　今　now　会L1
いみ　意味　meaning　会L11(s), 会L12
いもうと(さん)　妹(さん)　younger sister　会L1,
　　　　　　　　会L7, 会L7(s)
いらっしゃいませ　Welcome (to our store)　会L2
いりぐち　入口　entrance　会L10(s)
いる　(a person) is in . . .; stays at . . .　会L4
いる　to need　会L8
いろ　色　color　会L9
いろいろな　various　読L9-Ⅱ

ううん　uh-uh; no　会L8
うえ　上　on　会L4
うし　牛　cow　読L12-Ⅱ
うしろ　後ろ　back　会L4
うそをつく　to tell a lie　会L11
うた　歌　song　会L7
うたう　歌う　to sing　会L7
うち　home; house; my place　会L3
うちのこ　うちの子　(my) child　会L7(s)
うちのひと　うちの人　husband　会L7(s)
うみ　海　sea　会L5
うる　売る　to sell　読L10-Ⅱ
うん　uh-huh; yes　会L8
うんてんする　運転する　to drive　会L8
うんどうする　運動する　to do physical exercises
　　　　　　　　会L9

エアログラム　aerogramme　会L5(s)
えいが　映画　movie　会L3
えいご　英語　English (language)　会L1
ええ　yes　会L1
えき　駅　station　会L10, 読L6-Ⅰ
LL（エルエル）　language lab　会L3
〜えん　〜円　. . . yen　会L2
えんぴつ　鉛筆　pencil　会L2, 会L2(s)

おいしい　delicious　会L2
おうふく　往復　round trip　会L10(s)
おおい　多い　there are many . . .　会L12
おおきい　大きい　large　会L5
オーストラリア　Australia　会L1, 会L11
おかあさん　お母さん　mother　会L1, 会L2,
　　　　　　　　会L7(s)
おかえりなさい　Welcome home.　会G
おかし　お菓子　snack; sweets　会L11
おかね　お金　money　会L6
おかねもち　お金持ち　rich person　会L10
おきる　起きる　to get up　会L3
おくさん　奥さん　wife　会L7(s)
おこさん　お子さん　child　会L7(s)
おこる　怒る　to get angry　読L12-Ⅱ
おさけ　お酒　sake; alcohol　会L3
おじいさん　grandfather　会L7(s)
おしえる　教える　to teach; to instruct　会L6
おしょうがつ　お正月　New Year's　会L11,
　　　　　　　　読L10-Ⅱ
おしり　buttocks　会L7(s)
おしろ　お城　castle　読L5-Ⅱ
おそい　遅い　slow; late　会L10
おそく　遅く　(do something) late　会L6, 読L4-Ⅲ
おそくなる　遅くなる　to be late (for)　会L8
おだいじに　お大事に　Get well soon.　会L12
おちゃ　お茶　green tea　会L3
おっと　夫　husband　会L7(s)
おてあらい　お手洗い　restroom　会L2
おてら　お寺　temple　会L4
おとうさん　お父さん　father　会L1, 会L2, 会L7(s)
おとうと(さん)　弟(さん)　younger brother
　　　　　　　　会L1, 会L7, 会L7(s)
おとこ　男　man　読L11-Ⅱ

かようび　火曜日　Tuesday　会L4, 会L4(s)

カラオケ　karaoke　会L8

〜から　because . . .　会L6

〜から　from . . .　会L9, 読L7-Ⅱ

からだにきをつける　体に気をつける
　　to take care of oneself　読L7-Ⅱ

かりる　借りる　to borrow　会L6

かれ　彼　boyfriend　会L12

かわ　川　river　読L11-Ⅱ

かわいい　cute　会L7

かわいそうな　pitiful　読L12-Ⅱ

がんか　眼科　ophthalmologist　会L12(s)

かんこく　韓国　Korea　会L1, 会L2

かんじ　漢字　kanji; Chinese character　会L6

かんたん(な)　簡単　easy; simple　会L10

かんぱい　乾杯　Cheers! (a toast)　会L8

きいろい　黄色い　yellow　会L9(s)

きおん　気温　temperature (weather)　会L12

きく　聞く　to listen; to hear　会L3

きく　聞く　to ask　会L5

きせつ　季節　season　会L10

きた　北　north　会L6(s)

ギター　guitar　会L9

きっさてん　喫茶店　cafe　会L2

きって　切手　postal stamps　会L5, 会L5(s)

きっぷ　切符　ticket　会L5

きっぷうりば　切符売り場　ticket vending area
　　　　　　　会L10(s)

きのう　昨日　yesterday　会L4, 会L4(s)

きめる　決める　to decide　会L10

キャンプ　camp　会L11

きゅうこう　急行　express　会L10(s)

きゅうさい　九歳　nine years old　会L1(s)

きゅうふん　九分　nine minutes　会L1(s)

きょう　今日　today　会L3, 会L4(s)

きょうかしょ　教科書　textbook　会L6

きょうだい　兄弟　brothers and sisters　会L7

きょうみがある　興味がある　to be interested (in)
　　　　　　　会L12

〜ぎょうめ　〜行目　line number . . .　会L11(s)

きょねん　去年　last year　会L4(s)

きらい(な)　嫌い　disgusted with; to dislike　会L5

きる　着る　to put on (clothes above your waist)
　　会L7

きる　切る　to cut　会L8

きれい(な)　beautiful; clean　会L5

きんいろ　金色　gold　会L9(s)

ぎんいろ　銀色　silver　会L9(s)

きんえんしゃ　禁煙車　nonsmoking car　会L10(s)

ぎんこう　銀行　bank　会L2

きんじょ　近所　neighborhood　読L11-Ⅱ

きんちょうする　緊張する　to get nervous　会L12

きんぱつ　金髪　blonde hair　会L9(s)

きんようび　金曜日　Friday　会L4, 会L4(s)

くうき　空気　air　会L8

くがつ　九月　September　会L4(s)

くじ　九時　nine o'clock　会L1(s)

くすり　薬　medicine　会L9

くすりをのむ　薬を飲む　to take medicine　会L9

くだけたいいかた　くだけた言い方
　　colloquial expression　会L11(s)

ください(〜を)　Please give me . . .　会L2

くち　口　mouth　会L7(s)

くつ　靴　shoes　会L2

くに　国　country; place of origin　会L7

くび　首　neck　会L7(s)

くもり　曇り　cloudy weather　会L12

〜ぐらい　about (approximate measurement)
　　　　　会L4

クラス　class　会L4

グリーン　green　会L9(s)

くる　来る　to come　会L3

くるま　車　car　会L7

グレー　gray　会L9(s)

クレジットカード　credit card　会L10

くろい　黒い　black　会L9, 会L9(s)

けいざい　経済　economics　会L1, 会L2

けが　injury　会L12(s)

げか　外科　surgeon　会L12(s)

けさ　今朝　this morning　会L8

けしゴム　消しゴム　eraser　会L2(s)

けす　消す　to turn off; to erase　会L6

けっこうです　結構です　That would be fine.;
　　　　　　　That wouldn't be necessary.　会L6

けっこんする　結婚する　to get married　会L7

げつようび　月曜日　Monday　会L4, 会L4(s)

あいうえお　かきくけこ　**さしすせそ**　たちつてと　なにぬねの　はひふへほ　まみむめも　やゆよ　らりるれろ　わをん

けんかする　to have a fight; to quarrel　会 L11
げんき（な）　元気　healthy; energetic　会 L5
げんきがない　元気がない　don't look well　会 L12
げんぞう　現像　development　会 L5(s)

〜ご　〜語　language　会 L1
〜ご　〜後　in . . . time; after . . .　会 L10
こうえん　公園　park　会 L4
こうくうびん　航空便　airmail　会 L5(s)
こうこう　高校　high school　会 L1
こうこうせい　高校生　high school student　会 L1
こうせいぶっしつ　抗生物質　antibiotic　会 L12(s)
こうたくあり　光沢あり　glossy finish　会 L5(s)
こうたくなし　光沢なし　mat finish　会 L5(s)
こえ　声　voice　読 L10-II
コーヒー　coffee　会 L3
ゴールド　gold　会 L9(s)
ごがつ　五月　May　会 L4(s)
こくさいかんけい　国際関係　international rela-
　　　　　　　　　　　　　　　　tions　会 L1
こくばん　黒板　black board　会 L2(s)
ここ　here　会 L4
ごご　午後　P.M.　会 L1
ここのか　九日　the ninth day of a month　会 L4(s)
ここのつ　九つ　nine　会 L9
ごさい　五歳　five years old　会 L1(s)
ごじ　五時　five o'clock　会 L1(s)
ごしゅじん　ご主人　husband　会 L7(s)
ごぜん　午前　A.M.　会 L1
ごぜんちゅう　午前中　in the morning　読 L9-II
こたえ　答　answer　会 L11(s)
こたえる　答える　to answer　読 L8-II
ごちそう　excellent food　読 L9-II
ごちそうさま　Thank you for the meal. (after eating)　会 G
こちら　this person (polite)　会 L11
こづつみ　小包　parcel　会 L5(s)
ことし　今年　this year　会 L4(s), 会 L10
こども　子供　child　会 L4
この　this . . .　会 L2
このごろ　these days　会 L10
ごはん　御飯　rice; meal　会 L4
ごふん　五分　five minutes　会 L1(s)
ごめんなさい　I'm sorry.　会 L4
〜ごろ　at about　会 L3
これ　this one　会 L2

こわい　怖い　frightening　会 L5
こんがっき　今学期　this semester　会 L11
こんげつ　今月　this month　会 L4(s), 会 L8
コンサート　concert　会 L9
こんしゅう　今週　this week　会 L4(s), 会 L6
こんど　今度　near future　会 L9
こんにちは　Good afternoon.　会 G
こんばん　今晩　tonight　会 L3
こんばんは　Good evening.　会 G
コンビニ　convenience store　会 L7
コンピューター　computer　会 L1, 会 L2

サーフィン　surfing　会 L5
〜さい　〜歳　. . . years old　会 L1, 会 L1(s)
さいごに　最後に　lastly　読 L8-II
さいふ　財布　wallet　会 L2
さかな　魚　fish　会 L2
さくぶん　作文　essay; composition　会 L9
さけ　酒　sake; alcohol　会 L3
サッカー　soccer　会 L10
さっき　a little while ago　会 L4
ざっし　雑誌　magazine　会 L3
さびしい　寂しい　lonely　会 L9
サボる　to cut classes　会 L11
〜さま　〜様　Mr./Ms. . . .　読 L5-II
さむい　寒い　cold (weather)　会 L5
さようなら　Good-bye.　会 G
さらいげつ　再来月　the month after next　会 L4(s)
さらいしゅう　再来週　the week after next　会 L4(s)
さらいねん　再来年　the year after next　会 L4(s)
〜さん　Mr./Ms. . . .　会 L1
さんがつ　三月　March　会 L4(s)
ざんぎょう　残業　overtime work　読 L8-II
さんさい　三歳　three years old　会 L1(s)
さんじ　三時　three o'clock　会 L1(s)
さんじゅっぷん　三十分　thirty minutes　会 L1(s)
ざんねんですね　残念ですね　That's too bad.　会 L8
さんふじんか　産婦人科　obstetrician and gynecol-
　　　　　　　　　　　　　　　ogist　会 L12(s)
さんぷん　三分　three minutes　会 L1(s)
さんぽする　散歩する　to take a walk　会 L9

し

〜じ　〜時　o'clock　会 L1
しあい　試合　match; game　会 L12

あいうえお　かきくけこ　さしすせそ　たちつてと　なにぬねの　はひふへほ　まみむめも　やゆよ　らりるれろ　わをん

しあがり　仕上がり　date/time something is ready　会L5(s)

しあわせな　幸せな　happy　読L10-Ⅱ

ジーンズ　jeans　会L2

しか　歯科　dentist　会L12(s)

しがつ　四月　April　会L4(s)

〜じかん　〜時間　hour　会L4

しけん　試験　exam　会L9

しごと　仕事　job; work; occupation　会L1, 会L8

じしょ　辞書　dictionary　会L2, 会L2(s)

しずか(な)　静か　quiet　会L5

じぞう　guardian deity of children　読L10-Ⅱ

した　下　under　会L4

しちがつ　七月　July　会L4(s)

しちじ　七時　seven o'clock　会L1(s)

しっています　知っています　I know　会L7

しつもん　質問　question　会L11(s)

していせき　指定席　reserved seat　会L10(s)

じてんしゃ　自転車　bicycle　会L2

しぬ　死ぬ　to die　会L6

じはつ　次発　departing second　会L10(s)

じびか　耳鼻科　otorhinolaryngologist; ENT doctor　会L12(s)

じぶん　自分　oneself　読L10-Ⅱ

しみんびょういん　市民病院　Municipal Hospital　会L6

しめきり　deadline　会L11(s)

しめる　閉める　to close (something)　会L6

じゃあ　then . . . ; if that is the case, . . .　会L2

しゃしん　写真　picture; photograph　会L4

しゃちょう　社長　president of a company　会L11

シャツ　shirt　会L10

じゅういちがつ　十一月　November　会L4(s)

じゅういちじ　十一時　eleven o'clock　会L1(s)

じゅういちにち　十一日　the eleventh day of a month　会L4(s)

じゅういっさい　十一歳　eleven years old　会L1(s)

じゅういっぷん　十一分　eleven minutes　会L1(s)

じゅうがつ　十月　October　会L4(s)

〜しゅうかん　〜週間　for . . . weeks　会L10

じゅうきゅうふん　十九分　nineteen minutes　会L1(s)

じゅうごふん　十五分　fifteen minutes　会L1(s)

じゅうさんぷん　十三分　thirteen minutes　会L1(s)

じゅうじ　十時　ten o'clock　会L1(s)

ジュース　juice　会L12

じゆうせき　自由席　general admission seat　会L10(s)

しゅうでん　終電　last train　会L10(s)

じゅうななふん　十七分　seventeen minutes　会L1(s)

じゅうにがつ　十二月　December　会L4(s)

じゅうにじ　十二時　twelve o'clock　会L1(s)

じゅうにふん　十二分　twelve minutes　会L1(s)

じゅうはちふん/じゅうはっぷん　十八分　eighteen minutes　会L1(s)

しゅうまつ　週末　weekend　会L3

じゅうよっか　十四日　the fourteenth day of a month　会L4(s)

じゅうよんぷん　十四分　fourteen minutes　会L1(s)

じゅうろっぷん　十六分　sixteen minutes　会L1(s)

じゅぎょう　授業　class　会L11

じゅく　塾　cram school　読L7-Ⅱ

しゅくだい　宿題　homework　会L5, 会L11(s)

しゅじゅつ　手術　operation　会L12(s)

しゅじん　主人　husband　会L7(s)

じゅっさい　十歳　ten years old　会L1(s)

しゅっしん　出身　coming from　会L11

じゅっぷん　十分　ten minutes　会L1(s)

しゅふ　主婦　housewife　会L1

しゅみ　趣味　hobby　読L11-Ⅱ

しょうかいする　紹介する　to introduce　会L11

しょうがつ　正月　New Year's　会L11, 読L10-Ⅱ

じょうしゃけん　乗車券　(boarding) ticket　会L10(s)

じょうず(な)　上手　skillful; good at . . .　会L8

しょうらい　将来　future　会L11

しょくどう　食堂　cafeteria; dining commons　会L7

しり　buttocks　会L7(s)

しりません　知りません　I do not know　会L7

しる　知る　to get to know　会L7

シルバー　silver　会L9(s)

しろ　城　castle　読L5-Ⅱ

しろい　白い　white　会L9, 会L9(s)

しろくろ　白黒　black and white　会L9(s)

じろじろみる　じろじろ見る　to stare (at)　会L8

〜じん　〜人　people　会L1

しんかんせん　新幹線　Shinkansen; "Bullet Train"　会L9

しんごう　信号　traffic light　会L6(s)

じんじゃ　神社　shrine　読L11-Ⅱ

しんせつ(な)　親切　kind　会L7

しんぱいする　心配する　to worry　会L12

しんぶん　新聞　newspaper　会L2

じんるいがく　人類学　anthropology　会L1

す

すいようび　水曜日　Wednesday　会L4, 会L4(s)
スウェーデン　Sweden　会L1
スーパー　supermarket　会L4
すき(な)　好き　fond of; to like　会L5
スキー　ski　会L9
すぐ　right away　会L6
すごく　very　会L11
すこし　少し　a little　読L7-Ⅱ
すずしい　涼しい　cool (weather)　会L10
すてき(な)　素敵　fantastic　会L12
ストレス　stress　読L8-Ⅱ
スポーツ　sports　会L3
すみません　Excuse me.; I am sorry.　会G
すむ　住む　to live　会L7
スライド　slide　会L5(s)
する　to do　会L3
すわる　座る　to sit down　会L6

せ

せいかつ　生活　life; living　会L10
せいけいげか　整形外科　orthopedic surgeon
　　　　　　　　　　　　　　　会L12(s)
せいじ　政治　politics　会L1, 会L12
せいせき　成績　grade (on a test, etc.)　会L12
せいりけん　整理券　vouchers; zone tickets
　　　　　　　　　　　　　　　会L10(s)
せかい　世界　world　会L10
せがたかい　背が高い　tall　会L7
せがひくい　背が低い　short (stature)　会L7
せき　cough　会L12
せきがでる　せきが出る　to cough　会L12
せなか　背中　back　会L7(s)
ぜひ　是非　by all means　会L9
せまい　狭い　narrow; not spacious　会L12
せんげつ　先月　last month　会L4(s), 会L9
せんじつ　先日　the other day　読L9-Ⅱ
せんしゅう　先週　last week　会L4, 会L4(s)
せんせい　先生　teacher; Professor . . .　会L1
ぜんぜん＋negative　全然　not at all　会L3
せんせんしゅう　先々週　the week before last
　　　　　　　　　　　　　　　会L4(s)
せんたくする　洗濯する　to do laundry　会L8
せんぱつ　先発　departing first　会L10(s)
せんもん　専門　major　会L1

そ

そうじする　掃除する　to clean　会L8
そうです　That's right.　会L1
そうですね　That's right.; Let me see.　会L3
そくたつ　速達　special delivery　会L5(s)
そこ　there　会L4
そして　and then　会L11, 読L9-Ⅱ
その　that . . .　会L2
そば　near　会L4
そふ　祖父　(my) grandfather　会L7(s)
そぼ　祖母　(my) grandmother　会L7(s)
それ　that one　会L2
それから　and then　会L5

た

ダイエットする　to go on a diet　会L11
たいおんけい　体温計　thermometer　会L12(s)
だいがく　大学　college; university　会L1
だいがくいんせい　大学院生　graduate student　会L1
だいがくせい　大学生　college student　会L1, 会L8
だいきらい(な)　大嫌い　to hate　会L5
だいじょうぶ　大丈夫　It is okay.; Not to worry.;
　　　　　　　　Everything is under control.　会L5
だいすき(な)　大好き　very fond of; to love　会L5
たいてい　大抵　usually　会L3
たいへん(な)　大変　tough (situation)　会L6, 読L5-Ⅱ
たかい　高い　expensive　会L2
だから　so; therefore　会L4
たくさん　many; a lot　会L4
～だけ　just . . . ; only . . .　会L11
ただいま　I'm home.　会G
たつ　立つ　to stand up　会L6
たとえば　for example　会L11(s)
たのしい　楽しい　fun　会L5
たのしみにする(～を)　楽しみにする
　　to look forward (to)　読L7-Ⅱ
たばこをすう　たばこを吸う　to smoke　会L6
たぶん　多分　probably; maybe　会L12
たべもの　食べ物　food　会L5
たべる　食べる　to eat　会L3
だれ　who　会L2
たんご　単語　word; vocabulary　会L9
たんざく　strip of fancy paper　読L12-Ⅱ
たんじょうび　誕生日　birthday　会L5
だんな　husband　会L7(s)

ち

ちいさい　小さい　small　会L5
ちかく　近く　near place　読L11-Ⅱ
ちかてつ　地下鉄　subway　会L10
ちこくする　遅刻する　to be late (for an appointment)　会L11
ちち　父　(my) father　会L7, 会L7(s)
ちゃ　茶　green tea　会L3
ちゃいろい　茶色い　brown　会L9(s)
ちゅうごく　中国　China　会L1, 会L2
ちゅうしゃ　注射　injection　会L12(s)
ちょっと　a little　会L3

つ

ついたち　一日　the first day of a month　会L4(s)
つかいすてカメラ　使い捨てカメラ　disposable camera　会L5(s)
つかう　使う　to use　会L6
つかれている　疲れている　to be tired　読L8-Ⅱ
つかれる　疲れる　to get tired　会L11
つぎ　次　next　会L6
つぎに　次に　secondly　読L8-Ⅱ
つぎは〜　次は〜　next (stop), . . .　会L10(s)
つくえ　机　desk　会L2(s), 会L4
つくる　作る　to make　会L8
つける　to turn on　会L6
つごうがわるい　都合が悪い　inconvenient; to have a scheduling conflict　会L12
つとめる　勤める　to work for　会L7
つま　妻　wife　会L7(s)
つまらない　boring　会L5
つめたい　冷たい　cold (thing/people)　会L10
つり　fishing　読L11-Ⅱ
つれてかえる　連れて帰る　to take back　読L12-Ⅱ
つれてくる　連れてくる　to bring (a person)　会L6

て

て　手　hand　会L7(s)
〜で　by (means of transportation); with (a tool)　会L10
ていきけん　定期券　commuter's pass　会L10(s)
Tシャツ　T-shirt　会L7
ディスコ　disco　会L8
ていねいないいかた　ていねいな言い方　polite expression　会L11(s)

デート　date (romantic, not calendar)　会L3
テープ　tape　会L2
でかける　出かける　to go out　会L5
てがみ　手紙　letter　会L4
できるだけ　as much as possible　会L12
でぐち　出口　exit　会L10(s)
〜でしょう　probably; . . ., right?　会L12
テスト　test　会L5
てつだう　手伝う　to help　会L6
テニス　tennis　会L3
では、おげんきで　では、お元気で　Take care.　読L5-Ⅱ
デパート　department store　会L4
てぶくろ　手袋　gloves　会L10
でも　but　会L3
てら　寺　temple　会L4
でる　出る　to appear; to attend; to exit　会L9, 読L6-Ⅰ
テレビ　TV　会L2(s), 会L3
テレビゲーム　video game　会L6
てん　天　the heavens; the sky　読L12-Ⅱ
〜てん　〜点　. . . points　会L11
てんき　天気　weather　会L5
でんき　電気　electricity　会L2(s), 会L6
てんきよほう　天気予報　weather forecast　会L8
でんしゃ　電車　train　会L6
でんち　電池　battery　会L5(s)
でんわ　電話　telephone　会L1
でんわをかける　電話をかける　to make a phone call　会L6

と

と　戸　door　読L10-Ⅱ
〜と　together with (a person)　会L4
〜ど　〜度　. . . degrees (temperature)　会L12
ドア　door　会L2(s)
どうして　why　会L4
どうぞ(〜を)　Here it is.　会L2
どうぞよろしく　Nice to meet you.　会G
どうですか　How about . . .?; How is . . .?　会L3
どうも　Thank you.　会L2
どうやって　how; by what means　会L10
とお　十　ten　会L9
とおか　十日　the tenth day of a month　会L4(s)
とき　時　when . . .; at the time of . . .　会L4
ときどき　時々　sometimes　会L3

とけい　時計　watch; clock　会L2

どこ　where　会L2

とこや　床屋　barber's　会L10

ところ　所　place　会L8

ところで　by the way　会L9

とし　年　year　読L10-Ⅱ

としょかん　図書館　library　会L2

どちら　which　会L10

とっきゅう　特急　super express　会L10(s)

どっち　which　会L10

とても　very　会L5

となり　隣　next　会L4

どの　which . . .　会L2

どのぐらい　how much; how long　会L10

トマト　tomato　会L8

とまる　泊まる　to stay (at a hotel, etc.)　会L10

ともだち　友だち　friend　会L1

どようび　土曜日　Saturday　会L3, 会L4(s)

ドライブ　drive　会L11

とる　撮る　to take (pictures)　会L4

とる　取る　to take (a class); to get (a grade)
　　　　　　　　　　　　　会L11, 読L7-Ⅱ

とる　取る　to take off　読L10-Ⅱ

どれ　which one　会L2

トレーナー　sweat shirt　会L2

とんかつ　pork cutlet　会L2

どんな　what kind of . . .　会L5

ないか　内科　physician　会L12(s)

なか　中　inside　会L4

ながい　長い　long　会L7

なく　泣く　to cry　読L12-Ⅱ

なくす　to lose　会L12

なつ　夏　summer　会L8

～など　and so forth　読L12-Ⅱ

ななさい　七歳　seven years old　会L1(s)

ななつ　七つ　seven　会L9

ななふん　七分　seven minutes　会L1(s)

なにか　何か　something　会L8

なにも＋negative　何も　not . . . anything　会L7

なのか　七日　the seventh day of a month　会L4(s)

なまえ　名前　name　会L1

ならう　習う　to learn　会L11

なる　to become　会L10

なん/なに　何　what　会L1

にかげつまえ　二か月前　two months ago　会L4(s)

にがつ　二月　February　会L4(s)

にぎやか(な)　lively　会L5

にく　肉　meat　会L2

にさい　二歳　two years old　会L1(s)

にさんにち　二三日　for two to three days　会L12

にし　西　west　会L6(s)

にじ　二時　two o'clock　会L1(s)

にじはん　二時半　half past two　会L1

にじゅうよっか　二十四日　the twenty-fourth day
　　　　　　　　　　　　　of a month　会L4(s)

にじゅうよんまいどり　24枚撮り　24-print roll
　　　　　　　　　　　　　　　　会L5(s)

にじゅっぷん　二十分　twenty minutes　会L1(s)

にちようび　日曜日　Sunday　会L3, 会L4(s)

～について　about; regarding to　読L8-Ⅱ

にっき　日記　diary　読L9-Ⅱ

にふん　二分　two minutes　会L1(s)

にほん　日本　Japan　会L1

にほんご　日本語　Japanese language　会L1

にほんじん　日本人　Japanese people　会L1

にもつ　荷物　baggage　会L6

にょうぼう　女房　wife　会L7(s)

～に～をかぶせる　to put (a hat) on a person's head
　　　　　　　　　　　　　読L10-Ⅱ

～にん　～人　[counter for people]　会L7

にんきがある　人気がある　to be popular　会L9

ネガ　negative　会L5(s)

ねがい　願い　wish　読L12-Ⅱ

ねこ　猫　cat　会L4

ねつがある　熱がある　to have a fever　会L12

ねむい　眠い　sleepy　会L10

ねる　寝る　to sleep; to go to sleep　会L3

～ねん　～年　. . . years　会L10

～ねんせい　～年生　. . . year student　会L1

ノート　notebook　会L2

～ので　because . . .　会L12

のど　throat　会L12

のどがかわく　のどが渇く　to become thirsty　会L12

のぼる　登る　to climb　会L11

あいうえお　かきくけこ　さしすせそ　たちつてと　なにぬねの　はひふへほ　**まみむめも**　やゆよ　らりるれろ　わをん

あいうえお　かきくけこ　さしすせそ　たちつてと　なにぬねの　はひふへほ　**ま**みむめも　やゆよ　らりるれろ　わをん

みつける　見つける　to find　読 L12-Ⅱ
みっつ　三つ　three　会 L9
みどり　緑　green　会 L9(s)
みなさん　皆さん　everyone　読 L6-Ⅲ
みなみ　南　south　会 L6(s)
みみ　耳　ear　会 L7(s)
みやげ　土産　souvenir　会 L4
みる　見る　to see; to look at; to watch　会 L3
みんな　all　会 L9, 読 L7-Ⅱ
みんなで　all (of the people) together　会 L8

むいか　六日　the sixth day of a month　会 L4(s)
むかしむかし　昔々　once upon a time　読 L10-Ⅱ
むこう　向こう　the other side; over there
　　　　　　読 L12-Ⅱ
むずかしい　難しい　difficult　会 L5
むすめ　娘　daughter　読 L12-Ⅱ
むっつ　六つ　six　会 L9
むね　胸　breast　会 L7(s)
むらさき　紫　purple　会 L9(s)

め　目　eye　会 L7, 会 L7(s)
めがね　眼鏡　glasses　会 L7
メニュー　menu　会 L2

もう　already　会 L9
もうすぐ　very soon; in a few moments/days
　　　　　会 L12
もくようび　木曜日　Thursday　会 L4, 会 L4(s)
もしもし　Hello? (used on the phone)　会 L4
もち　rice cake　読 L10-Ⅱ
もちろん　of course　会 L7
もつ　持つ　to carry; to hold　会 L6
もっていく　持っていく　to take (something)　会 L8
もってくる　持ってくる　to bring (a thing)　会 L6
もっと　more　会 L11
もの　物　thing (concrete object)　会 L12
もらう　to get (from somebody)　会 L9

やきまし　焼き増し　reprint　会 L5(s)
やきゅう　野球　baseball　会 L10
やさい　野菜　vegetable　会 L2

やさしい　easy (problem); kind (person)　会 L5
やすい　安い　inexpensive; cheap (thing)　会 L5
やすみ　休み　holiday; day off; absence　会 L5
やすむ　休む　to be absent (from); to rest　会 L6
やせています　to be thin　会 L7
やせる　to lose weight　会 L7
やっつ　八つ　eight　会 L9
やま　山　mountain　会 L11, 読 L5-Ⅱ
やまみち　山道　mountain road　読 L10-Ⅱ
やめる　to quit　会 L11
やる　to do; to perform　会 L5

ゆうびんきょく　郵便局　post office　会 L2
ゆうめい(な)　有名　famous　会 L8
ゆうめいじん　有名人　celebrity　会 L10
ゆき　雪　snow　会 L12, 読 L10-Ⅱ
ゆっくり　slowly; leisurely; unhurriedly　会 L6
ゆび　指　finger　会 L7(s)
ゆめ　夢　dream　会 L11

ようか　八日　the eighth day of a month　会 L4(s)
ようじ　用事　business to take care of　会 L12
よかったら　if you like　会 L7
よく　often; much　会 L3
よじ　四時　four o'clock　会 L1(s)
よっか　四日　the fourth day of a month　会 L4(s)
よっつ　四つ　four　会 L9
よむ　読む　to read　会 L3
よやく　予約　reservation　会 L10
よる　夜　night　会 L6, 読 L5-Ⅱ
よんさい　四歳　four years old　会 L1(s)
よんぷん　四分　four minutes　会 L1(s)

らいがっき　来学期　next semester　会 L10
らいげつ　来月　next month　会 L4(s), 会 L8
らいしゅう　来週　next week　会 L4(s), 会 L6
らいねん　来年　next year　会 L4(s), 会 L6

りゅうがくする　留学する　to study abroad　会 L11
りゅうがくせい　留学生　international student　会 L1
りょう　寮　dormitory　読 L9-Ⅱ
りょうり　料理　cooking　読 L6-Ⅲ

あいうえお　かきくけこ　さしすせそ　たちつてと　なにぬねの　はひふへほ　まみむめも　やゆよ　ら**りるれろ**　**わ**をん

A B C D E F G H I J K L M N O P Q R S T U V W X Y Z

さくいん2 English-Japanese

各項目の表示は以下の内容を示す。
Items at the end of each entry indicate the following:
会…… 会話・文法編
　　　(Conversation and Grammar section)
読…… 読み書き編
　　　(Reading and Writing section)
G…… あいさつ (Greetings)
(s)…… 課末コラム (Supplement)
Ⅰ・Ⅱ・Ⅲ……問題番号(読み書き編)
　　　(number of excercise in the Reading and Writing section)

A

about　〜について　読 L8-Ⅱ
about (approximate measurement)　〜ぐらい　会 L4
absence　やすみ　休み　会 L5
absent (from)　やすむ　休む　会 L6
adult　おとな　大人　読 L12-Ⅱ
aerogramme　エアログラム　会 L5(s)
after . . .　〜ご　〜後　会 L10
after (an event)　(〜の)あと　(〜の)後　会 L11, 読 L8-Ⅱ
again　また　読 L5-Ⅱ
air　くうき　空気　会 L8
airmail　こうくうびん　航空便　会 L5(s)
airplane　ひこうき　飛行機　会 L5
alcohol　(お)さけ　(お)酒　会 L3
all　みんな　会 L9, 読 L7-Ⅱ
all (of the people) together　みんなで　会 L8
alone　ひとりで　一人で　会 L4
already　もう　会 L9
always　いつも　会 L12, 読 L6-Ⅲ
A.M.　ごぜん　午前　会 L1
and so forth　〜など　読 L12-Ⅱ
and then　それから　会 L5
and then　そして　会 L11, 読 L9-Ⅱ
(get) angry　おこる　怒る　読 L12-Ⅱ
answer　こたえ　答　会 L11(s)
answer　こたえる　答える　読 L8-Ⅱ
anthropology　じんるいがく　人類学　会 L1
antibiotic　こうせいぶっしつ　抗生物質　会L12(s)
anything else　ほかに　会 L11(s)
apartment　アパート　会 L7
appear　でる　出る　会 L9

apple　りんご　会 L10
April　しがつ　四月　会 L4(s)
art museum　びじゅつかん　美術館　会 L11
as far as (a place)　〜まで　会 L5
as much as possible　できるだけ　会 L12
Asian studies　アジアけんきゅう　アジア研究　会 L1
ask　きく　聞く　会 L5
at about　〜ごろ　会 L3
at the time of . . .　とき　時　会 L4
attend　でる　出る　会 L9
August　はちがつ　八月　会 L4(s)
Australia　オーストラリア　会 L1, 会 L11

B

back　うしろ　後ろ　会 L4
back　せなか　背中　会 L7(s)
bad　わるい　悪い　会 L12
baggage　にもつ　荷物　会 L6
bag　かばん　会 L2, 会 L2(s)
bamboo hat　かさ　読 L10-Ⅱ
band　バンド　読 L11-Ⅱ
bank　ぎんこう　銀行　会 L2
barbecue　バーベキュー　会 L8
barber's　とこや　床屋　会 L10
baseball　やきゅう　野球　会 L10
bath　(お)ふろ　(お)風呂　会 L6
battery　でんち　電池　会 L5(s)
be on the heavy side　ふとっています　太っています　会 L7
beautiful　きれい(な)　会 L5
beauty parlor　びよういん　美容院　会 L10
because . . .　〜から　会 L6
because . . .　〜ので　会 L12
become　なる　会 L10
beer　ビール　会 L11
begin　はじめる　始める　会 L8
(something) begins　はじまる　始まる　会 L9
best　いちばん　一番　会 L10
between　あいだ　間　会 L4
bicycle　じてんしゃ　自転車　会 L2
birthday　たんじょうび　誕生日　会 L5
black　くろい　黒い　会 L9, 会 L9(s)
black and white　しろくろ　白黒　会 L9(s)
black board　こくばん　黒板　会 L2(s)
blonde hair　きんぱつ　金髪　会 L9(s)
blue　あおい　青い　会 L9, 会 L9(s)
board　のる　乗る　会 L5

boarding ticket　じょうしゃけん　乗車券　会L10(s)
boat　ふね　船　会L10
book　ほん　本　会L2, 会L2(s)
bookish expression　かたいいいかた　かたい言い方　会L11(s)
bookstore　ほんや　本屋　会L4
boring　つまらない　会L5
borrow　かりる　借りる　会L6
bound for . . .　～いき　～行き　会L10(s)
boxed lunch　(お)べんとう　(お)弁当　会L9
boy　おとこのこ　男の子　会L11
boyfriend　かれ　彼　会L12
bread　パン　会L4
break up　わかれる　別れる　会L12
breakfast　あさごはん　朝御飯　会L3
breast　むね　胸　会L7(s)
bright　あたまがいい　頭がいい　会L7
bring (a person)　つれてくる　連れてくる　会L6
bring (a thing)　もってくる　持ってくる　会L6
Britain　イギリス　会L1, 会L2
brothers and sisters　きょうだい　兄弟　会L7
brown　ちゃいろい　茶色い　会L9(s)
Bullet Train　しんかんせん　新幹線　会L9
business　ビジネス　会L1, 会L2
business to take care of　ようじ　用事　会L12
bus　バス　会L5
bus stop　バスてい　バス停　会L4
busy (people/days)　いそがしい　忙しい　会L5
but　でも　会L3
but　が　会L7, 読L5-II
buttocks　(お)しり　会L7(s)
buy　かう　買う　会L4
by . . .　～までに　読L12-II
by (means of transportation)　～で　会L10
by all means　ぜひ　是非　会L9
by the way　ところで　会L9
by what means　どうやって　会L10

C

cafe　きっさてん　喫茶店　会L2
cafeteria　しょくどう　食堂　会L7
camera　カメラ　会L8
camp　キャンプ　会L11
cap　ぼうし　帽子　会L2
car　くるま　車　会L7
carry　もつ　持つ　会L6
castle　(お)しろ　(お)城　読L5-II
cat　ねこ　猫　会L4
catch a cold　かぜをひく　風邪をひく　会L12

celebrity　ゆうめいじん　有名人　会L10
chair　いす　会L2(s)
cheap (thing)　やすい　安い　会L5
cheerful　あかるい　明るい　読L11-II
Cheers! (a toast)　かんぱい　乾杯　会L8
child　こども　子供　会L4
child　おこさん　お子さん　会L7(s)
(my) child　うちのこ　うちの子　会L7(s)
China　ちゅうごく　中国　会L1, 会L2
Chinese character　かんじ　漢字　会L6
chopsticks　はし　会L8
city　まち　町　会L4
class　クラス　会L4
class　じゅぎょう　授業　会L11
clean-　きれい(な)　会L5
clean　そうじする　掃除する　会L8
clever　あたまがいい　頭がいい　会L7
climb　のぼる　登る　会L11
clock　とけい　時計　会L2
close (something)　しめる　閉める　会L6
clothes　ふく　服　会L12
cloudy weather　くもり　曇り　会L12
clumsy　へた(な)　下手　会L8
coffee　コーヒー　会L3
cold　かぜ　風邪　会L12
cold (thing/people)　つめたい　冷たい　会L10
cold (weather)　さむい　寒い　会L5
college　だいがく　大学　会L1
college student　だいがくせい　大学生　会L1, 会L8
colloquial expression　くだけたいいかた　くだけた言い方　会L11(s)
color　いろ　色　会L9
come　くる　来る　会L3
coming from　しゅっしん　出身　会L11
commuter's pass　ていきけん　定期券　会L10(s)
company　かいしゃ　会社　会L7
composition　さくぶん　作文　会L9
computer　コンピューター　会L1, 会L2
concert　コンサート　会L9
convenience store　コンビニ　会L7
convenient　べんり(な)　便利　会L7
cook　りょうりする　料理する　会L8
cooking　りょうり　料理　読L6-III
cool (weather)　すずしい　涼しい　会L10
corner　かど　角　会L6(s)
correct (○)　まる　会L11(s)
cough　せき　会L12
cough　せきがでる　せきが出る　会L12
counter　まどぐち　窓口　会L5(s)

A B C D E F G H I J K L M N O P Q R S T U V W X Y Z

A B C D E F G H I J K L M N O P Q R S T U V W X Y Z

A B C D E F **G H** I J K L M N O P Q R S T U V W X Y Z

gloves　てぶくろ　手袋　会L10

go　いく　行く　会L3

go back　かえる　帰る　会L3

go on a diet　ダイエットする　会L11

go out　でかける　出かける　会L5

go to sleep　ねる　寝る　会L3

God　かみさま　神さま　読L12-II

gold　きんいろ　金色　会L9(s)

gold　ゴールド　会L9(s)

good　いい　会L3

Good afternoon.　こんにちは　会G

good at . . .　じょうず(な)　上手　会L8

good child　いいこ　いい子　会L9

good deed　いいこと　読L10-II

Good evening.　こんばんは　会G

Good morning.　おはよう/おはようございます　会G

Good night.　おやすみなさい　会G

Good-bye.　さようなら　会G

grade (on a test, etc.)　せいせき　成績　会L12

graduate student　だいがくいんせい　大学院生　会L1

grammar　ぶんぽう　文法　会L11(s)

grandfather　おじいさん　会L7(s)

(my) grandfather　そふ　祖父　会L7(s)

grandmother　おばあさん　会L6, 会L7(s)

(my) grandmother　そぼ　祖母　会L7(s)

gray　グレー　会L9(s)

gray　はいいろ　灰色　会L9(s)

great-looking　かっこいい　会L7

green　グリーン　会L9(s)

green　みどり　緑　会L9(s)

green tea　(お)ちゃ　(お)茶　会L3

guardian deity of children　じぞう　読L10-II

guitar　ギター　会L9

H

hair　かみ　髪　会L7, 会L7(s)

half　はん　半　会L1

half past two　にじはん　二時半　会L1

hamburger　ハンバーガー　会L3

hand　て　手　会L7(s)

handsome　ハンサム(な)　会L5

hangover　ふつかよい　二日酔い　会L12

happy　しあわせな　幸せな　読L10-II

hat　ぼうし　帽子　会L2

hate　だいきらい(な)　大嫌い　会L5

have a fever　ねつがある　熱がある　会L12

have a fight　けんかする　会L11

have a lot of free time　ひま(な)　暇　会L5

have a scheduling conflict　つごうがわるい　都合が悪い　会L12

have a talk　はなしをする　話をする　読L9-II

head　あたま　頭　会L7(s)

healthy　げんき(な)　元気　会L5

hear　きく　聞く　会L3

heavens, the　てん　天　読L12-II

Hello? (used on the phone)　もしもし　会L4

help　てつだう　手伝う　会L6

here　ここ　会L4

Here it is.　(〜を)どうぞ　会L2

high school　こうこう　高校　会L1

high school student　こうこうせい　高校生　会L1

history　れきし　歴史　会L1, 会L2

hobby　しゅみ　趣味　読L11-II

hold　もつ　持つ　会L6

holiday　やすみ　休み　会L5

home　いえ　家　会L3

home　うち　会L3

homesickness　ホームシック　会L12

homestay　ホームステイ　会L8

homework　しゅくだい　宿題　会L5, 会L11(s)

hospital　びょういん　病院　会L4

host family　ホストファミリー　会L11, 読L9-II

hot (objects)　あつい　熱い　会L5

hot (weather)　あつい　暑い　会L5

hot spring　おんせん　温泉　会L9

hotel　ホテル　会L4

hour　〜じかん　〜時間　会L4

house　いえ　家　会L3

house　うち　会L3

housewife　しゅふ　主婦　会L1

how　どうやって　会L10

How about . . . ?　どうですか　会L3

How do you do?　はじめまして　会G

How is . . . ?　どうですか　会L3

how long　どのぐらい　会L10

how much　いくら　会L2

how much　どのぐらい　会L10

(become) hungry　おなかがすく　会L11

hurry　いそぐ　急ぐ　会L6

hurt　いたい　痛い　会L12

husband　うちのひと　うちの人　会L7(s)

husband　おっと　夫　会L7(s)

husband　(ご)しゅじん　(ご)主人　会L7(s)

husband　だんな　会L7(s)

A B C D E F G H **I J K** L M N O P Q R S T U V W X Y Z

A B C D E F G H I J K L M N O P Q R S T U V W X Y Z

O

P

A B C D E F G H I J K L M N O **P Q R S** T U V W X Y Z

S

A B C D E F G H I J K L M N O P Q R **S** T U V W X Y Z

A B C D E F G H I J K L M N O P Q R S T U V W X Y Z

A B C D E F G H I J K L M N O P Q R S **T U V W** X Y Z

TV テレビ 会L2(s), 会L3

twelve minutes じゅうにふん 十二分 会L1(s)

twelve o'clock じゅうにじ 十二時 会L1(s)

twentieth day of a month, the はつか 二十日 会L4(s)

twenty minutes にじゅっぷん 二十分 会L1(s)

twenty years old はたち 二十歳 会L1(s)

twenty-four-print にじゅうよんまいどり 24枚撮り 会L5(s)

twenty-fourth day of a month, the にじゅうよっか 二十四日 会L4(s)

two ふたつ 二つ 会L9

two minutes にふん 二分 会L1(s)

two months ago にかげつまえ 二か月前 会L4(s)

two o'clock にじ 二時 会L1(s)

two people ふたり 二人 会L7

two people each ふたりずつ 二人ずつ 会L11(s)

two years old にさい 二歳 会L1(s)

uh-huh うん 会L8

uh-uh ううん 会L8

um . . . あの 会L1

umbrella かさ 傘 会L2

under した 下 会L4

understand わかる 会L4

unhurriedly ゆっくり 会L6

university だいがく 大学 会L1

U.S.A. アメリカ 会L1, 会L2

use つかう 使う 会L6

usually たいてい 大抵 会L3

various いろいろな 読L9-II

VCR ビデオ 会L2(s), 会L3

vegetable やさい 野菜 会L2

very とても 会L5

very すごく 会L11

very fond of だいすき(な) 大好き 会L5

very soon もうすぐ 会L12

video game テレビゲーム 会L6

video tape ビデオ 会L2(s), 会L3

vocabulary たんご 単語 会L9

voice こえ 声 読L10-II

vouchers せいりけん 整理券 会L10(s)

W

wait まつ 待つ 会L4

wallet さいふ 財布 会L2

warm あたたかい 暖かい 会L10

wash あらう 洗う 会L8

watch とけい 時計 会L2

watch みる 見る 会L3

water みず 水 会L3

we わたしたち 私たち 読L12-II

weather てんき 天気 会L5

weather forecast てんきよほう 天気予報 会L8

weave はたをおる はたを織る 読L12-II

Wednesday すいようび 水曜日 会L4, 会L4(s)

week after next, the さらいしゅう 再来週 会L4(s)

week before last, the せんせんしゅう 先々週 会L4(s)

weekend しゅうまつ 週末 会L3

Welcome (to our store) いらっしゃいませ 会L2

Welcome home. おかえりなさい 会G

west にし 西 会L6(s)

what なん/なに 何 会L1

what kind of . . . どんな 会L5

when いつ 会L3

when . . . とき 時 会L4

where どこ 会L2

which どちら/どっち 会L10

which . . . どの 会L2

which one どれ 会L2

white しろい 白い 会L9, 会L9(s)

who だれ 会L2

why どうして 会L4

wife おくさん 奥さん 会L7(s)

wife かない 家内 会L7(s)

wife かみさん 会L7(s)

wife つま 妻 会L7(s)

wife にょうぼう 女房 会L7(s)

wife ワイフ 会L7(s)

window まど 窓 会L2(s), 会L6

winter ふゆ 冬 会L8

wish ねがい 願い 読L12-II

with (a tool) 〜で 会L10

woman おんな 女 読L11-II

woman おんなのひと 女の人 会L7

word たんご 単語 会L9

work しごと 仕事 会L1, 会L8

work はたらく 働く 会L11

A B C D E F G H I J K L M N O P Q R S T U V W X Y Z

work for　つとめる　勤める　会L7
world　せかい　世界　会L10
worry　しんぱいする　心配する　会L12
write　かく　書く　会L4
wrong (✕)　ばつ　会L11(s)

X-ray　レントゲン　会L12(s)

year　とし　年　読L10-Ⅱ
year after next, the　さらいねん　再来年
　　　　　会L4(s)
year before last, the　おととし　会L4(s)
. . . year student　〜ねんせい　〜年生　会L1
. . . years　〜ねん　〜年　会L10

. . . years old　〜さい　〜歳　会L1, 会L1(s)
yellow　きいろい　黄色い　会L9(s)
. . . yen　〜えん　〜円　会L2
yesterday　きのう　昨日　会L4, 会L4(s)
yes　ええ　会L1
yes　はい　会L1
yes　うん　会L8
you　あなた　会L4
young　わかい　若い　会L9
younger brother　おとうと(さん)　弟(　さん)
　　　　　会L1, 会L7, 会L7(s)
younger sister　いもうと(さん)　妹(さん)
　　　　　会L1, 会L7, 会L7(s)

zone tickets　せいりけん　整理券　会L10(s)

数 Numbers
かず

	regular				h → p	h → p/b	p	k
1	いち				いっp	いっp	（いっ）	いっ
2	に							
3	さん				p	b		
4	よん	し	よ	よ	p			
5	ご							
6	ろく				ろっp	ろっp	（ろっ）	ろっ
7	なな	しち	しち					
8	はち				（はっp）	はっp	（はっ）	はっ
9	きゅう	く	く					
10	じゅう				じゅっp	じゅっp	じゅっ	じゅっ
how many	なん				p	b		
	〜ドル *dollars* 〜円 えん *yen* 〜枚 まい *sheets* 〜度 ど *degrees* 〜十 じゅう *ten* 〜万 まん *ten thousand*	〜月 がつ *month*	〜時 じ *o'clock* 〜時間 じかん *hours*	〜年 ねん *year* 〜年間 ねんかん *years* 〜人 にん *people*	〜分 ふん *minute* 〜分間 ふんかん, *minutes*	〜本 ほん *sticks* 〜杯 はい *cups* 〜匹 ひき *animals* 〜百 ひゃく *hundred*	〜ページ *page* 〜ポンド *pounds*	〜か月 げつ *months* 〜課 か *lesson* 〜回 かい *times* 〜個 こ *small items*

This chart shows how sounds in numbers (1-10) and counters change according to their combination.

1. *Hiragana* indicate the sound changes in numbers, and alphabets show the changes in the initial consonant of counters.
2. ( ) means that the change is optional.
3. An empty box means no sound change occurs.

k → g	s	s → z	t	special vacabulary for numbers			
いっ	いっ	いっ	いっ	ひとつ	ついたち	ひとり	1
				ふたつ	ふつか	ふたり	2
g		z		みっつ	みっか		3
				よっつ	よっか		4
				いつつ	いつか		5
ろっ				むっつ	むいか		6
				ななつ	なのか		7
はっ	はっ	はっ	はっ	やっつ	ようか		8
				ここのつ	ここのか		9
じゅっ	じゅっ	じゅっ	じゅっ	とお	とおか		10
g		z		いくつ			how many
～階 floor ～軒 houses	～セント cents ～週間 weeks ～冊 books ～歳 years of age	～足 shoes ～千 thousand	～通 letters ～丁目 street address	*small items* *years of age* cf. はたち (20 years old)	*date* cf. じゅうよっか (14) はつか(20) にじゅう よっか(24) なんにち (how many)	*people* cf. ～人 (three or more people)	

Furigana: ～階 (かい), ～軒 (けん), ～週間 (しゅうかん), ～冊 (さつ), ～歳 (さい), ～足 (そく), ～千 (せん), ～通 (つう), ～丁目 (ちょうめ), ～人 (にん)

活用表 Conjugation Chart
かつ よう ひょう

verb types	dictionary forms	long forms (*masu*) (L. 3)	*te*-forms (L. 6)	short past (L. 9)	short present neg. (L. 8)	short past neg. (L. 9)
irr.	<u>する</u>	します	して	した	しない	しなかった
irr.	<u>く</u>る	きます	きて	きた	こない	こなかった
ru	たべ<u>る</u>	〜ます	〜て	〜た	〜ない	〜なかった
u	か<u>う</u>	〜います	〜って	〜った	〜わない	〜わなかった
u	ま<u>つ</u>	〜ちます	〜って	〜った	〜たない	〜たなかった
u	と<u>る</u>	〜ります	〜って	〜った	〜らない	〜らなかった
u	あ<u>る</u>	〜ります	〜って	〜った	*ない	*なかった
u	よ<u>む</u>	〜みます	〜んで	〜んだ	〜まない	〜まなかった
u	あそ<u>ぶ</u>	〜びます	〜んで	〜んだ	〜ばない	〜ばなかった
u	し<u>ぬ</u>	〜にます	〜んで	〜んだ	〜なない	〜ななかった
u	か<u>く</u>	〜きます	〜いて	〜いた	〜かない	〜かなかった
u	い<u>く</u>	〜きます	*〜って	*〜った	〜かない	〜かなかった
u	いそ<u>ぐ</u>	〜ぎます	〜いで	〜いだ	〜がない	〜がなかった
u	はな<u>す</u>	〜します	〜して	〜した	〜さない	〜さなかった

The forms with * are exceptions.